"What can I say? Quite simply, this is the book that I wish had been available to me two decades ago. It is brilliant. Practical, instantly accessible and (as you would expect given the authors) infused with real-world experience. Whether you are a secondary school student interested in pursuing law at university, or a criminal barrister in the early years of practice, the lessons in these chapters are invaluable. It has even caused me to reflect on some of my own ingrained (bad) habits. Life as an advocate is (or should be) a continuous search for self-improvement. This book will be an indispensable companion in that endeavour".

The Secret Barrister, *A Leading Barrister specialising in Criminal Law, 2026*

"This humble and brilliant book gently takes the hand of the aspiring lawyer and calmly walks them along the road of how evidence is obtained in court, signposted with the essential skills and dangers. It is a book that goes back to basics and in doing so reveals how the criminal justice system has evolved over the centuries to create a fair trial. Whether you are starting your law journey or are established as a silk or a Judge, this book is your companion to being a better lawyer in court."

Kirsty Brimelow KC, *Chair of the Bar, 2026*

"This book is a 'must have' for every aspiring and established advocate. Written by two real experts, it tells you exactly what you need to do and why in every courtroom situation, with clear and simple instructions, explanations and examples. Buy one and keep it close. It will not let you down".

Sarah Clarke KC, *Serjeants' Inn Chambers, 2026*

"Excellent".

HHJ Pearce, *Manchester Business and Property Courts, 2026*

The Skills of Modern Advocacy

The Skills of Modern Advocacy provides a comprehensive practical guide to modern advocacy, explaining its core components and demonstrating how you can develop and apply the necessary skillsets in practice.

Presented as an engaging mix of explanation and practical examples, each aspect of modern-day advocacy is considered in three stages to suit all readers: the essential rules, practical how-to demonstrations and advanced technique. The book begins with an introduction to the language and etiquette of advocacy before moving to the important witness handling skills involved in examination-in-chief, cross-examination, re-examination and dealing with expert witnesses. The different skills involved in submission advocacy are then addressed in three main areas before the book gives guidance on the separate topics of questioning vulnerable witnesses, remote advocacy and written advocacy. The final chapter deals with the special court environment of the Inquest, an area where new barristers can often expect to receive instructions. The chapters draw repeatedly on a substantial set of mock case documents to give the skills demonstrations a consistent sense of context and realism.

The authors have been practising barristers since the mid-1990s, and the book is packed with their combined experience and skills.

This book will appeal to interested school and college students with little or no experience, to undergraduate law students and students of advocacy on Bar or solicitor training courses, or the SQE, and to newly qualified advocates who wish to deepen their knowledge and expand their skills.

The book is supported by further online resources.

Jaime Hamilton K.C. is a practising barrister. He was Leader of the Northern Circuit of the Bar of England and Wales between 2023 and 2026 and is a Bencher of Gray's Inn. He is an advocacy trainer for the Northern Circuit and sits on the International Committee of the Inns of Court College of Advocacy.

Nigel Booth is Programme and Student Lead for the Bar Practice Course at the University of Law, Manchester and Liverpool campuses. Called to the Bar in 1994 by Gray's Inn, he was in practice between 1995 and 2020 before taking up his teaching post. In addition to teaching on the Bar Practice Course, Nigel contributes to updating of the materials for the criminal skills course and he designs oral skills assessments.

The Skills of Modern Advocacy

Jaime Hamilton K.C. and Nigel Booth

Routledge
Taylor & Francis Group
LONDON AND NEW YORK

Designed cover image: Shutterstock

First edition published 2027
by Routledge
4 Park Square, Milton Park, Abingdon, Oxon, OX14 4RN

and by Routledge
605 Third Avenue, New York, NY 10158

Routledge is an imprint of the Taylor & Francis Group, an informa business

British Library Cataloguing-in-Publication Data
A catalogue record for this book is available from the British Library

Library of Congress Cataloging-in-Publication Data
Names: Hamilton K.C., Jaime author | Booth, Nigel author
Title: The skills of modern advocacy / Jaime Hamilton K.C., Nigel Booth.
Description: 1. | New York : Routledge, 2026. | Includes bibliographical references and index. |
Identifiers: LCCN 2026024074 | ISBN 9781032990491 hardback |
ISBN 9781032990477 paperback | ISBN 9781003602019 ebook
Subjects: LCSH: Trial practice–Great Britain | Activism–Great Britain |
Examination of witnesses–Great Britain | Evidence, Expert–Great Britain
Classification: LCC KD7483 .H36 2027
LC record available at https://lccn.loc.gov/2026024074

ISBN: 9781032990491 (hbk)
ISBN: 9781032990477 (pbk)
ISBN: 9781003602019 (ebk)

DOI: 10.4324/9781003602019

Typeset in Times New Roman
by Deanta Global Publishing Services, Chennai, India

Access the Support Material: www.routledge.com/9781032990477

Contents

	Foreword by the Common Serjeant of London	*ix*
	Foreword by Eleanor Saunders	*xi*
1	Introduction	1
2	The Language and Etiquette of the Advocate	5
3	Examination-in-Chief	12
4	Cross-Examination	37
5	Re-Examination	69
6	Expert Evidence	74
7	Submission Advocacy 1: Submissions to a Judge	88
8	Submission Advocacy 2: Opening and Closing Speeches	97
9	Submission Advocacy 3: The Plea in Mitigation	117
10	Questioning Vulnerable Witnesses	128
11	Remote Advocacy	134
12	Written Advocacy	140
13	Advocacy in the Coroner's Court	149
14	Advocacy Assessment Criteria	160
15.1	*Rex v Tegan Plant*, Case Documents	165
15.2	*Rex v Tegan Plant*, Defence Statement	198
15.3	*Rex v Tegan Plant*, Case Theories	200
15.4	*Rex v Tegan Plant*, Prosecution Opening Speech	209

16 *Rex v Gordon Heyworth* 213

17 Afterword, Reflections on Advocacy from the Authors 229

Index *233*

Foreword by the Common Serjeant of London

Advocacy is a real skill which takes years of practice to hone. Indeed, the best advocates, however able, will always be seeking to improve and to ask themselves, could I have done that better?

It is hugely rewarding, not least when you can discern that your advocacy is succeeding in winning over a jury in a criminal case or a judge in a civil case.

An up-to-date book on advocacy has been very long overdue. I commend this excellent exposition to the reader, whether they are just embarking on a career as an advocate or are already experienced. Indeed, as I was reading it, my thoughts were that if only it had been available to me years ago, I would have been a much better advocate than I was!

Using an imaginary case, the book comprehensively takes you through the approach that you might take at each case in your conduct of the case and particularly helpfully highlights the pitfalls to be avoided.

The considerable skill and experience of both the authors have enabled them to share invaluable and insightful information and advice, and I say with confidence that reading and absorbing all of this will make you a better advocate.

I have been very kindly invited by the authors to add a few brief words as to my perspective as to headline advocacy tips, which I venture with some diffidence. I do so from a criminal advocacy point of view as that is the area in which I have always operated.

My headline observations are as follows.

1. Obviously, preparation and knowing your case is critical and, of course, the devil or a gem can be in the detail.
2. Succinctness, in examination of witnesses, and in submissions to a judge (whether in relation to a point of law or in a plea in mitigation) as well as to a jury, is a great virtue. By way of example, a one-hour pithy closing speech to a jury will invariably work so much better than addressing them for a whole day. Likewise, in a plea in mitigation, addressing a judge by starting with your objective and then stating that you have, say, four points you wish to make, making them and then sitting down can be extremely effective.
3. Thinking very carefully about your first question(s) in cross-examination can pay huge dividends. If you are able to begin by undermining the witness, you

will have engaged the attention of the jury from the outset and set the tone so far as they are concerned.

4. Do not underestimate how much skill is involved in examination-in-chief and how important it is to prepare what you want to ask and in what order.
5. Particularly with a jury, keep it simple and have in mind the importance of using language which readily enables the jury to relate to the content of what you are saying and the way in which you are saying it.
6. You may have prepared the questions that you want to ask a witness, but rather than concentrating on the next question, always remember how important it is to listen to the answer, which may necessitate taking a very different course with the witness to that which you had envisaged.

HHJ Richard Marks KC
The Common Serjeant of London
Central Criminal Court
London

Foreword by Eleanor Saunders

It is my pleasure to write this foreword.

In July 2025 I was called to the Bar by the Honourable Society of Gray's Inn, and in October that year, I commenced pupillage at Cobden House Chambers in Manchester. During pupillage, I began to specialise in business, property and housing law. Having then made the transition from student to practitioner, I know the value of clear, practical guidance on advocacy. It is one of the most important skills a barrister can develop, yet one of the most difficult to learn. For that reason, I am particularly pleased that this book has been written by Jaime Hamilton KC and Nigel Booth.

I came to know of Jaime Hamilton KC through his role as Leader of the Northern Circuit. He presided over my election to the Northern Circuit in December 2025. I met Nigel Booth when assisting with a Business and Property moot at the University of Law, where I saw the influence of his advocacy skills through the students he teaches.

When I was reviewing this book at the outset of practice, I felt particularly well placed to say how useful it would be to those preparing for pupillage, the Bar Course, or simply exploring a career at the Bar. It offers the kind of practical advice I would have welcomed as a student, and I strongly encourage any aspiring barrister to read it. What sets this book apart is its use of a fictitious yet realistic case as the framework for its guidance. This immersive structure is not only engaging but genuinely instructive, allowing the reader to understand how advocacy operates in practice rather than in theory. It is unlike any material I encountered in my preparation for my Bar course. Although the case itself is criminal, the authors draw out equivalent civil considerations where relevant and address broader points of courtroom conduct that often go unexplained.

As a civil practitioner, elements such as examination-in-chief or opening speeches are uncommon in my day-to-day practice, yet I found the guidance both useful and compelling. The discussions of expert evidence and vulnerable witnesses, in particular, are especially strong, offering a level of clarity and detail rarely encountered even at Bar Course level. It is this practical depth that makes the book stand out.

This is a work of real value not only to aspiring barristers but also to those already in practice. I have found considerable benefit in revisiting the foundational principles of advocacy and have gained insight into areas not covered during my training. I am certain that I will return to its pages as my career progresses, and I have little doubt that it will become a frequent point of reference in university applications, pupillage interviews and beyond.

For anyone serious about advocacy, this book deserves to be read.

Eleanor Saunders
Cobden House Chambers
Manchester

1 Introduction

Advocacy is a skill, and like all skills it can only be learned by doing. You cannot learn to play football just by reading any more than you can learn to perform card tricks just by reading. The same goes for advocacy: success lies in practice, practice and more practice. This book is designed to give you a strong head start along that path by equipping you with the essential knowledge and skills you need. As you begin to study advocacy formally, you will do so on a solid and confident foundation. Indeed, by focusing our advocacy chapters in three parts covering the fundamentals, some how-to demonstrations and then a discussion of advanced techniques, we hope that this book will remain of great value to you as you progress from study into practice.

As with any skill, some people starting out will find that it comes more naturally to them than it might to others, but we are both firmly of the view that the skills of advocacy can be learned by everyone. You can begin at any time to learn the rules of advocacy. You can start learning at any time to think like an advocate, to understand a case like an advocate and to plan and strategise like an advocate. You can start to build your understanding and your confidence right now so that when you do advocacy, you already feel comfortable with it. That is how this book will help you.

For advocates who have completed initial training – whether on professional courses or vocational programmes – this book serves to reinforce your foundations whilst introducing perspectives that can deepen your understanding of advocacy.

For more experienced beginners, in the early stages of practice, it will help you extend your existing skills and continue your professional growth. We have written our advocacy chapters with three guiding principles in mind to help you learn and develop your skills.

First, we have organised our chapters so that each one deals with an important topic for advocacy training. Cast your eyes down our chapter list. We have mapped out the key skill sets required for advocates to excel in their role. You will notice as you read the book that there is sometimes overlap between various skill sets, and we show this. In particular, we have created three separate chapters dealing with two different aspects of "submission advocacy", followed by a chapter devoted to the plea in mitigation. This is advocacy that often involves you making a legal application or delivering a speech. Of course, you should read those three chapters together.

DOI: 10.4324/9781003602019-1

Second, our skillset chapters are divided into three parts:

a. The fundamentals of that skillset to give you a thorough understanding of the rules that apply;
b. Demonstrations of how to deploy that skillset;
c. Advanced techniques designed to help you elevate your performance while you develop the skillset.

The exception to this formula is the chapter on advocacy in the coroners' courts. Inquests are such a different judicial system that your approach as an advocate requires a complete change of mindset. Our focus with that chapter has been to set out how inquests are different and what is the appropriate way for you to approach your task in that court environment, and so we have departed from our Fundamentals/How-To/Advanced Technique approach.

Third, we have created a fictional case scenario that we return to in our chapters to demonstrate the skills that we are teaching you. This is our case of *Rex v Tegan Plant*. We know that it is impossible to develop skills if you are only reading about them in the abstract, so in this book we have set out to be intensely practical. We have written a complete set of fictional case documents for a fictional defendant called Tegan Plant. Our aim with the design is to make the documents resemble as closely as possible what a set of case documents actually looks like. You get an authentic experience. There is a smaller fictional case, *Rex v Gordon Heyworth*, that we use in the plea in mitigation chapter.

You will find that we refer to the case documents time and again in our chapters to demonstrate how you might put the different skillsets into practice. Our unfortunate Mr Plant faces a charge of attempted robbery of a bank. It is a criminal case, but the principles and thought processes of the advocate are the same whatever the case may be – civil, criminal, family or anything else.

As well as the case documents, you will see that we have drafted examples of a case theory for one side of the *Plant* case (the prosecution) and a case theory for the other side of the *Plant* case (the defence). Developing a case theory is a fundamental part of the way that advocates prepare our approach to a case. As an advocate, you are only as good as your material. You need to know what to look for, how to read a case and how to use case documents when you are preparing for advocacy. You will find that 90 per cent of your success as an advocate lies in your preparation, thinking and case theory. The other 10 per cent is down to your performance, but that 10 per cent will mean little if your preparation has been weak. The best way to ensure that your preparation is strong is to learn how to formulate a case theory. We show you how to think about a case and how to develop a case theory by using our scenario of *Rex v Tegan Plant.*

In fact, we feel so strongly about the importance of an advocate understanding how to create a case theory that we recommend you begin your reading of this book by going straight to the chapter that contains the *Plant* case documents, particularly if you are relatively new to the skills of advocacy.

Read them with the thought in mind that you have been instructed to prosecute Mr Plant. Identify your strong points and your weak points. Think about how you might try and counter the weak points, about how you might organise and structure your questioning of the witnesses. Commit your thoughts to writing and organise them coherently. Then walk away and do something else completely; have a cup of tea, go for a walk. A little later return to the case documents and read them again, this time with the thought in mind that you have been instructed to defend Mr Plant. Carry out the same analysis exercise. And we stress again: do all of this *before you read* any of the skillset chapters.

The more experienced advocate can read the chapters as stand-alone studies of the skillsets.

Both sets of fictional case papers are sufficient for you to get together with your peers or friends and put into practice the skills that are discussed. Divide the roles up in the case. Play the witness when your colleague examines you in chief. Swap and try to cross-examine the witness. Write and deliver a closing speech.

When you undertake formal training with the aim of being Called to the Bar or admitted as a solicitor, you will need a sound understanding of the rules of litigation and evidence to underpin your advocacy. Litigation and evidence are too extensive to cover in this book where the focus is on advocacy. What we can do, however, is focus on the key rules of advocacy and explain how they apply across the different advocacy contexts explored in this book.

We discuss the different aspects of advocacy as they apply to the jurisdiction in England and Wales. But we know that students from many jurisdictions across the globe come to the UK to study for the Bar. Our goal has been to produce material that students from around the world can turn to as they develop their advocacy skills.

May we record our thanks to the following:

- Fiona Wise, barrister at Nine Chambers in Manchester, is an expert in inquest law and has expertly put together our chapter on advocacy in the coroners' courts;
- James Booth, Senior Lecturer at the University of Law's Manchester and Liverpool Campuses. James is Head of the Bar Practice Course Civil Team on campus and has made invaluable contributions to our chapters on the application of advocacy skills in civil law cases. James and Nigel were briefly once in Chambers together and happily met again when they joined the campus BPC lecturer team on the same day in September 2020;
- John Potter, retired Cicuit Judge who sat at the Crown Court at Manchester. John has been generous with his time looking over early versions of some chapters and giving expert feedback and suggestions for additional content. John and Nigel have known each other since Nigel's very first days in the courts back in 1995 when Nigel was a new lawyer with the Crown Prosecution Service and John was President of the Manchester Law Society and a partner in a criminal defence firm. John became one of the fairest and most courteous crown court judges on the Northern Circuit;

- HHJ Richard Pearce at the Manchester Business and Property Courts. HHJ Pearce kindly offered some comments and ideas on some earlier chapter drafts, for which we are very grateful;
- Pui Ying Chan and Lucy Moran, former Bar Practice Course students who were taught by Nigel. Pui Ying is now in legal practice in Kuala Lumpur, and Lucy is at the Bar in Liverpool. Pui Ying and Lucy offered great insight and second opinions on some early drafts – and helped prevent some errors;
- Jenny Boyden, former lecturer on the Bar Practice Course at the University of Law's London Moorgate campus, has now returned to practice with Blackfords LLP in London. Jenny has the keenest eye for detail and made valuable recommendations for our *Tegan Plant* case scenario;
- Alex Frodsham, barrister at Hundred Court Chambers and Assistant Coroner in Cheshire and Manchester West;
- We both thank our partners and family for their support. They have had to hear the words "*Can you just hang on a sec, I need to look at this chapter again...*" far too many times.

We hope there are no errors in the case scenario documentation, but it remains our fault if there are. (In any case, we will simply assert that they are deliberate errors designed to test you.)

Jaime Hamilton KC
Nine Chambers, Manchester

Nigel Booth
University of Law, Manchester and Liverpool campuses
Nine Chambers, Manchester

2 The Language and Etiquette of the Advocate

Before we turn to the specific skills required of an advocate, it is important to pause and consider a more fundamental point. Other chapters in this book focus on two key areas of your development as an advocate: understanding the rules that govern the type of advocacy you are undertaking and learning the techniques that will help you perform effectively. This chapter, however, introduces something equally essential: your attitude as an advocate – how you conduct yourself on behalf of a client, and what is appropriate, respectful and expected of you in that role.

We would like you to think about how you will conduct yourself and the way you will speak. We call these things the language and etiquette of the advocate, and they are so important that we are devoting this whole chapter to them. These things can be very subtle. They have developed over time as matters of convention and are most pertinent to practice in the courts of the United Kingdom. Sometimes they can feel as though they are more difficult to get used to than they ought to be.

How Will You Address the Client and How Will the Client Address You?

We are talking here about the point before you begin conducting any advocacy. Meeting the client often comes first and, when it does, you will need to introduce yourselves to each other. You should consider how you would like the client to address you. Although there is no rule about this, we recommend against encouraging the client to call you by your first name. The reason is less to do with whether you prefer your relationship to be formal or informal; that would increasingly be an old-fashioned way to think of it. You will need to work together in a productive way, sometimes over a long period of time. You do not want to be stumbling over excessive formality all the time, but that does not mean that you need to be on first-name terms.

We invite you to consider that you and the client are in a professional relationship with each other. You are not friends. In that relationship, you are the professional, and in your working environment of courts and tribunals, you will be referred to as "Mr Booth" or "Miss Addo" or similar. You will choose the appropriate form of address. The client will likely think nothing of how they should refer to you beyond perhaps having briefly wondered whether there is a correct way to address you. They will appreciate that you have clarified this in your introduction:

DOI: 10.4324/9781003602019-2

Hello, it's nice to meet you. I'm Mr Booth, and I'm your barrister.

We recommend that you address the client in a similar way. It is important to get this right and, in advance of the conference, you may wish to ask your instructing solicitor whether the client has a preferred style of address. If this is not possible, introduce yourself in the style in which you want to be addressed and ask the client how you should address them. It's fine to clarify tactfully, if you need to, that you prefer to avoid first names.

Entering and Leaving the Courtroom

We begin by looking at how you conduct yourself in a courtroom before you even start speaking. We bow in the direction of the judge. If that seems very old-fashioned, that is because it is!

Think of bowing as a sign of respect to the authority of the court. It is nothing exaggerated, just a slight tip of the head forward and a slight bend of the waist, then up again. Keep your feet together and make sure that your only movement is the bow. It does not matter if the judge is not looking at you; bow anyway. Bowing takes a second, but it conveys respect to the court.

Not bowing may be taken as a sign of disrespect or ignorance, which are not the impressions you want a judge to form about you. Never lose the respect of the court.

If you are in court already when the judge comes in, you should expect to stand and (yes, you guessed it) bow before taking your seat again. When you enter court and the judge is there already, the first thing to do is to bow in the direction of the judge – but then what do you do? You may be making your way to counsel's benches ready for your case to be called on, in which case slide in quietly and unobtrusively, and make sure not to move in front of another barrister if they are addressing the judge. If there is no space, your best option may simply be to stand still and wait for a few moments.

Leaving court can be tricky – when should you leave, and when should you *not* leave? Usually, if your case is concluded and you have no further business in that courtroom, you may leave. Bow as you leave the advocates' row and bow again before you exit through the door. There is no need to walk backwards out of court; the judge is not royalty. But if you are the only barrister in court and the judge is remaining in court themselves, you should not simply get up and leave without the judge's permission. You should wait until another barrister enters court before you leave. There is a longstanding convention that a judge should not be left alone in their court. It is difficult to explain the reason for this beyond saying that it is an old-fashioned courtesy that has stuck around for centuries.

The modern reality is that judges will appreciate you have places to go and people to see. Collect your files and books together and sit patiently. The judge will likely notice and will excuse you by saying something like "Thank you, Miss X, there's no need to wait", which is your cue for the exit procedure.

There is another time when it would not be appropriate for you to leave court. This is where there is something going on that involves one of the litigants personally (as opposed to their advocate on their behalf). Examples in a criminal case are situations where the judge is addressing the defendant directly, where the defendant is entering their pleas to the charges on the indictment, or where someone (a witness or the jury) is taking an oath. Again, this is a courtesy, this time to the non-legally trained participant whose attention the court is actively engaging in that moment. Remaining still and silent will mean that you are not providing a distraction. If you happen to enter the courtroom to find that a procedure like this is happening, then simply remain still and silent until it is at an end.

Modes of Address

The absolute first thing to get right when you start to speak is how you address the tribunal before whom you are appearing. The Judiciary website gives you a straightforward table showing the different modes of address: just search for "What do I call a judge". A good rule of thumb is that during court advocacy:

a. High Court judges and higher are "My Lord" or "My Lady";
b. Circuit judges in the crown and civil courts are "Your Honour";
c. District judges in the magistrates' courts, civil courts and employment courts, and tribunal judges are "Judge";
d. Lay magistrates are "Sir", "Madam" or, collectively, "Your Worships";
e. Coroners are "Sir" or "Madam".

There are complications to watch out for. If your judge is sitting, perhaps temporarily, in a higher court than they usually do, then refer to them by the title of that higher court. A circuit judge sitting in the Court of Appeal is "My Lord" or "My Lady", and a district judge sitting in the crown court is "Your Honour". (The titles used for lay magistrates are always the same.) A second complication is that in some court centres the circuit judge in charge, often called the resident judge, is called "My Lord" or "My Lady" – as are all judges who sit at the Central Criminal Court (the Old Bailey). If you are addressing a coroner, use "Sir" or "Madam" as appropriate.

The use of these titles means that you will have to get used to the rhythm of the language. Do not be tempted, after beginning with "Your Honour", to revert to "you": keep with "Your Honour". It may sound repetitive, but it's the correct way.

> In light of that, may I next deal with Your Honour's third point?
>
> Your Honour is saying ...

The expression "Your Honour" conveys the "you" or "your" part of what we are saying. Do the same for "My Lord" or "My Lady" ("In light of My Lady's observation, may I next deal with My Lady's third point?") Do you see the rhythm of the language?

Where the judge is referred to as "Judge", however, it is quite normal to say "you":

> Judge, in light of your observation, may I next deal with your third point?

Notice that here we began with the preface "Judge", which shows respect, but we continue with "you". The expression "Your Honour" already conveys the *you* part of what we want to say, whereas "Judge" does not. (Can you see that if we were to say instead, "may I next deal with *Judge's* third point", the rhythm would not be right?)

Language and courtroom etiquette in the civil courts tend to be more flexible and pragmatic than in the criminal courts, reflecting differences in both function and tone. While formal judicial forms of address remain correct, particularly in the High Court and appellate courts, there is often greater latitude in civil proceedings to refer to the tribunal orally as "the Court" or, in appropriate contexts, "you".

Advocates may choose this formulation to promote clarity and directness, especially during submissions on case management, procedural matters, or points of law where the exchange can resemble a structured discussion rather than an adversarial contest. This approach can assist efficiency and aligns with the civil courts' emphasis on dialogue between judge and advocates as part of active case management.

That informality is generally more acceptable in the civil courts because the judge's role is explicitly interventionist and managerial under the Civil Procedure Rules, rather than primarily that of an impartial arbiter between prosecution and defence. Civil judges routinely engage with advocates during submissions, ask questions, and test arguments in real time, which can make less rigid modes of address feel natural and proportionate.

By contrast, in the criminal courts, particularly before a jury, strict formality serves to reinforce the authority and neutrality of the tribunal and to preserve the solemnity of proceedings involving personal liberty. Civil litigation, being generally focused on the resolution of private disputes, can therefore accommodate a more conversational mode of address without undermining respect for the court or the seriousness of the process.

> "May it please the court" and "my learned friend".

It is both traditional and polite that the first time you address a judge you should say "May it please the court". This is an expression that has lingered in the courts for centuries. It conveys your understanding that this is the judge's court and that you will speak when it is convenient to the judge for you to speak. It is of course a very old-fashioned thing (yet another very old-fashioned thing) but it is here to stay, and you will be out of place if you do not say it. It may have become less widely used in civil courts in recent times.

The other expression that is used all the time, this time when referring to another barrister in your case, often your opponent, is "my learned friend". If there is more than one other advocate involved in the case, for clarity, tag their name on the end, e.g.

my learned friend Mr Hamilton, King's Counsel.

With Counsel, there is a long-standing tradition of not shaking hands. Its origins lie in those distant days when offering your hand was a way to show that you were not carrying a weapon, usually a sword, and that you came with honourable intentions. It was also a time when the Bar was exclusively male. Barristers were regarded as "gentlemen", and by virtue of that status were presumed to be trustworthy. A handshake, therefore, was unnecessary; you did not need to prove your honour.

Among the newer generations at the Bar, the tradition of not shaking hands may be dying away. This means that it is all the more difficult for you to know what to do. Until you get settled in at the Bar, perhaps the best advice is to avoid shaking hands unless a hand is offered to you.

Advocacy Is Not the Same Thing as Having a Conversation

Whether you are examining a witness or making an application for an injunction, or indeed if you are engaged in any other kind of court advocacy, it is very far from being a conversation in style and language. What you are doing is adopting a structured and focused approach to dealing with the important issues that are demanding the attention of the court. It is not a chat.

Work to eliminate conversational fillers such as these typical ones:

OK
you guys
right so ...
sort of
yeah
no worries

You should avoid using conversational English or slang. Slang is often used to express ideas in a way that requires the listener to interpret what you mean in order fully to understand what you are saying. You do not want the judge to have to interpret your meaning because the judge might come to the wrong interpretation and misunderstand your point completely.

It is the same with a witness: the evidence they give in answer to your questions can be crucial, and you cannot afford any misunderstandings. Your aim is to speak clearly. Mean what you say and say what you mean. Leave no doubt and be direct. Make it as easy as possible for everyone to understand your points first time. Avoiding slang is one element that will help you achieve those aims.

Similarly, do not use expressions with hidden meaning, such as "barking up the wrong tree", "kicking the can down the road", "straight from the horse's mouth". In ways that you cannot always foresee, expressions such as these may be misunderstood by a witness, and sometimes by your tribunal.

Do not interrupt the judge. A feature of ordinary conversations is that often different people talk at once. Overlapping the end of someone else's sentence is quite normal. Given that court hearings are not conversations, you must always wait until the judge has finished speaking before you start. Making submissions to a judge always follows this structured process.

There is an aspect of courtesy to this. First, the judge is in charge of her court; you are not. Second, until someone finishes the point they are making, you do not know what the point is yet; all the more reason not to interrupt.

Similarly, it would be a discourtesy to interrupt another advocate's submissions. Even if they have got something wrong, let them finish; then, at an opportune time, you might wish "respectfully" to make the correction.

Do not ever guess. We do this in ordinary conversations all the time, but when you are acting in a professional capacity, your words matter and can bring consequences. It will happen that sometimes you are asked a question, and you do not know the answer. Acknowledge that you do not know, even if that causes you some embarrassment. If the judge asks you a question, it is best to answer it directly, following with an explanation or qualification if necessary. Do not give the explanation first.

Get Along with People

It costs nothing to be polite. It will never be part of your job to behave otherwise. Human beings respond well to being treated courteously. This may be the judge and other barristers, the witnesses, the court clerks and the ushers (*especially* the court clerks and the ushers), the security staff on duty at the main court doors or anyone else at all. You will be remembered – just make sure it is for making a good impression, not a bad one.

You will also be tested. There will be times when other people are difficult with you – sometimes that will be professionals who have not had proper regard to the advice we are giving here. Keep your composure intact. Do not let the other person interfere with the clinical, thoughtful and measured response you will want to give to the points they raise against you. If you find that another professional is intent on bringing conflict to you by way of rudeness, abuse or other conduct that you consider inappropriate, your best response may be simply to walk away. Give the other space and time to cool down, then consider returning to try and deal with the merits of the hearing or trial.

Always remember that you are never alone in the professions. Speak to supportive colleagues, your head of team or head of Chambers, or your senior partner. It is important to consider reporting bullying or other inappropriate behaviour to the appropriate regulatory body (e.g. the Bar Standards Board).

There is an increasing emphasis on wellbeing in the professions in recent times. This is important. Wellbeing was never mentioned when we were at Bar School in the mid-1990s. It is quite usual now to find that Chambers and solicitors' firms have wellbeing officers and discussions on wellbeing are now a regular part of professional life. Wellbeing is a good thing. Look after yourself.

Instructions

There are particular ways of speaking about how barristers are engaged to conduct cases. Notice, for instance, how we use the word "engaged" in that last sentence, and not "employed". This choice of word was deliberate. If you are not familiar with the range of language used, it may sometimes be difficult to understand what is going on.

We say "engaged" because a lot of barristers are self-employed and work from Chambers. The nature of being self-employed makes it sound odd to say that barristers are "employed" to conduct cases.

We use the terms "instruct" or "instructions", instead. You might be *instructed* to prosecute or defend the case of Tegan Plant, or it might be said that you have received *instructions* to prosecute or defend the case. Sometimes this is referred to as "Counsel getting the brief" or "being briefed". These terms are used also where barristers work outside the world of Chambers, for example if they are employed within a solicitors' firm to work exclusively for that firm.

Instructions will usually come from a solicitors' firm which has been engaged first by the client. If you are self-employed in Chambers, the brief will come to your clerks in Chambers who will pass it on to you, or if you are working for a firm directly it will be passed to you from one of your clerks there.

Incidentally, when we say "brief", that word is used these days more in memory of the traditional way in which counsel were once instructed (it still happens occasionally). Counsel used to receive a paper bundle of instructions and case documents, called the brief, folded gently lengthways and tied with pink ribbon. With the onset of electronic working, briefs now tend to exist as documents in secure online storage systems and Counsel are permitted access by their clerks. In some jurisdictions, notably in the criminal courts, there is an online platform, shared between the judges and the lawyers in the case, where case documents are uploaded.

When you receive a brief, you will mostly find that there is a section at the start containing Instructions to Counsel. These are often written in the third person. The Instructions to Counsel part is always confidential to you from your Instructing Solicitor. Look at the typical case documents for our case of *Rex v Tegan Plant* which begin like this:

> Counsel is instructed to prosecute in the case of *Rex v Tegan Plant*. The defendant is charged with allowing himself to be carried in a Renault Clio motor vehicle without consent and attempted robbery.

Instructions can be given or taken away, so you will always be keen to provide a high standard of service. It is professional, and it is also smart for your career.

In time, the language and etiquette of the courtroom and advocates will become entirely familiar to you. What may feel formal or unfamiliar at first will, through practice and observation, become second nature, enabling you to engage with confidence and professionalism.

3 Examination-in-Chief

Examination-in-chief is the name given to the part of a trial or other hearing where you, the advocate, are asking questions of your own witness. Typically, this is so that the witness can explain to the court or tribunal what they saw, heard, or did on a particular occasion.

Fundamentals

You have already decided that what the witness can say will help you win the case, which is why the witness is being called in the first place. You know what you expect the witness to say in their evidence because you already have a written record of what the witness saw, heard or did. That written record is usually in the form of a witness statement or proof of evidence. Your job is to ask questions of the witness in court in order to elicit their account.

Evidence-in-chief is a main part of criminal trials which in England and Wales take place before a judge and jury or before magistrates. In the future, it may be that some crown court trials will be heard by judges sitting without juries. Evidence-in-chief also features in proceedings before other tribunals. It is something very different from cross-examination, which is the name given to your task when you are asking questions of a witness who is called not by you but by another party to the case.

Two introductory points for you about examination-in-chief in a criminal context:

First: you can only really begin to understand what examination-in-chief is once you have realised that criminal trials have an obsession with oral evidence that has developed over centuries. Generally speaking, and unless in rare situations all parties to the case agree, or the judge makes a ruling on it, what is in someone's witness statement is not evidence in the case. This has the stark result that if the witness does not tell the court in their own voice what they saw, heard or did, then as far as the jury or magistrates are concerned, it never happened.

Second: you are the lawyer, and the witness is the witness. You know the rules of evidence; the witness does not. You are presenting the witness's evidence. It is your job to make sure that the witness's evidence in court complies with the rules of evidence.

DOI: 10.4324/9781003602019-3

Examination-in-chief is one of the most difficult skills for any student of advocacy to master. It is so difficult that everything ever written about examination-in-chief will probably start with a similarly doom-laden introduction about its level of difficulty. But do not be afraid. We would encourage you to think that examination-in-chief is an exercise in disciplined simplicity. Once the underlying method becomes clear – once you appreciate that its power lies in you keeping things simple and straightforward – you establish the foundation on which all effective questioning is built. From that point on, you can develop the skills that you need to guide a witness through giving their account.

The best examination-in-chief will leave you, the advocate, almost invisible in the courtroom. Your objective is to control the narrative whilst allowing the witness to tell their story in the best way for the listener and to avoid any inadmissible material. All whilst not being part of the story yourself.

But let us start with the basics.

Relevance

You do not simply say to your witness something like this:

> About the events of 19th November 2026 at the New Dilhorne Bank in Marple, please tell the court what happened.

You do not then leave it to the witness to give their full account in a kind of monologue. The witness does not know the rules of evidence; but you do. You must ensure that your witness's account to the court includes facts that are *relevant* to the issues that the court is being asked to consider. Facts are relevant if they tend to prove or disprove the thing that the court is being asked to consider. You should take care that you do not allow your witness to introduce irrelevant material when you are examining them in chief.

Admissibility

Even evidence that is relevant is not always permitted in court. Lawyers often say that evidence must not only be relevant; it must be relevant *and* admissible.

It is your job to make sure that your witness only gives admissible evidence. In this sense the word "admissible" means that the particular evidence is legally permitted or (to put the same thing another way) that there is no legal rule excluding it. Some facts may not be admissible unless, for instance, the court has given permission. An example of this can be evidence of a defendant's or a witness's previous convictions in a criminal case.

All of this requires substantial knowledge of procedure and evidence. It is why the most difficult assessments that you will take in your journey to become a skilful and expert advocate will be the assessments testing your knowledge of criminal and civil litigation and evidence.

Memory-Refreshing

Sometimes the best of us can forget things. It happens because we are human, and it does not mean we are being dishonest. The criminal process permits you, the advocate, to allow your witness to refresh their memory from a written account they gave before the case began (usually a witness statement).

> *The springboard for this is section 139 of the Criminal Justice Act 2003:*
> *A person giving oral evidence in criminal proceedings about any matter may, at any stage in the course of doing so, refresh his memory of it from a document made or verified by him at an earlier time if–*
>
> (a) *he states in his oral evidence that the document records his recollection of the matter at that earlier time; and*
> (b) *his recollection of the matter is likely to have been significantly better at that time than it is at the time of his oral evidence.*

It is usually for you to decide whether to ask permission of the judge for your witness to refresh their memory, although it will not surprise you that the prompt often comes from the witness who responds to one of your questions by saying something like "I cannot remember".

You must be ready at all times to deal with section 139 and help witnesses who need to refresh their memory. The test in the statute is very exact. The witness must say that they made a document (usually a witness statement) at an earlier time; that the document recorded their recollection of the events at the time they made the document; that their recollection of the events was likely to have been significantly better at the time they made their document than today. It is important for you to establish all of these with the witness if you want the judge to allow the witness to refresh their memory. The most important criterion is the expression "significantly better". It is not "better", not "slightly better", but "significantly better".

Hostile Witnesses

Rarely might you find that you are in a situation where the witness you have called simply has no desire to tell the truth to the court. A witness in this situation is described as "hostile". We are perhaps imagining a scenario where you are prosecuting in our case of *Rex v Tegan Plant*, and you call William Hawkins to give evidence. Imagine that Hawkins immediately says he did not see anything on the street. He stands in the witness box and fixes you with a hard stare. You look at his witness statement in front of you, and you cannot quite believe what you are hearing.

In this sort of situation, you are likely to make an application to the judge for you to be permitted to treat the witness as hostile. If successful, you may then confront him with his own witness statement in the witness box and, if necessary, ask him leading questions to elicit from him the account that he outlined in his witness statement.

> *The law dealing with hostile witnesses is mostly in section 3 of the Criminal Procedure Act 1865 which is headed – How far witness may be discredited by the party producing:*
> *A party producing a witness shall not be allowed to impeach his credit by general evidence of bad character; but he may, in case the witness shall in the opinion of the judge prove adverse, contradict him by other evidence, or, by leave of the judge, prove that he has made at other times a statement inconsistent with his present testimony; but before such last-mentioned proof can be given the circumstances of the supposed statement, sufficient to designate the particular occasion, must be mentioned to the witness, and he must be asked whether or not he has made such statement.*

First, you will have to give the witness a fair chance to change his mind by asking him to confirm that he made the statement, give him the date of it and show it to him.

It is important to note that witnesses often say things in evidence that are different from what they put in their witness statements. These witnesses are not hostile. You should consider engaging the memory-refreshing procedure first with such witnesses. Describing a witness as a "hostile" witness refers to a specific situation in which it becomes evident that the witness is deliberately choosing not to tell the truth.

Do Not Ask Leading Questions to Elicit Evidence That Is Disputed by the Other Side

Now we are getting to the part that often causes most difficulty for the student of advocacy. It is that during examination-in-chief you have to be careful not to ask leading questions of your witness to elicit from them evidence about topics that the other parties do not agree with. The ability to avoid asking leading questions on matters that criminal lawyers would say are "in issue" is essential. It is the principal rule that governs examination-in-chief. A main aim of this chapter is to help you learn to develop this skill.

In its most basic form, a leading question is one that essentially gives the witness the answer and just invites the witness to agree. The opposite of a leading question is, unsurprisingly, a non-leading question, and that is a question that does not contain the answer.

An immediate example from our case of *Rex v Tegan Plant* will demonstrate the point. You will appreciate from your reading of the case documents that a major issue in the case will be whether the witness Ullger has correctly identified Tegan Plant as the man who came into the bank. Because identification is a main issue in the case, you will not want to lead the witness on the quality of the view that she had of the man. Imagine that you ask the witness Isobel Ullger this question:

Q: "Would you say that you had a good quality view of the man?"

Here you would be leading on the description "good". It is you who are describing the quality of the witness's view as good, and the witness only has to agree with you.

A way of asking this with a non-leading question would be:

Q: "How would you describe the quality of your view of the man?"

Here you are making clear that you want the witness to speak about the quality of her view of the man. Your question does not suggest what you want the witness to say about this. It is not a leading question.

Be prepared sometimes to take a series of two or three non-leading questions to get the answers you need. This is often necessary in order to avoid asking a single leading question. Do not be tempted by the leading question shortcut!

Identifying what is or is not a leading question is only the beginning. You have to learn how to formulate non-leading questions in the moment in order to help develop the witness's account in evidence.

How-To

Avoid Asking Leading Questions on Matters in Issue

How to avoid leading your witness on matters in issue can be a difficult concept to grasp and to apply. Let us therefore begin by looking at this in more detail.

Imagine that you are prosecuting our case of *Rex v Tegan Plant*. You will appreciate that although the defendant can give no evidence or instructions of his own about what happened at the bank, for the reason that he was not there, the defence will nonetheless want the witness's assertions about the man's description to be tested. You are therefore very conscious when you examine your witnesses in chief that they should give evidence about description to the court that will help your case. You need to have a sound case analysis. Remembering that the questioning rule prohibits leading the witness on matters that are in dispute, it follows that you may not lead your witnesses on the topic of the quality of the view that they had and (for Ullger) the identification of the man at the line-up as being the man she had seen in the bank.

Case theory:
Consider our anticipated examination-in-chief of Isobel Ullger in our case of Rex v Tegan Plant, *focusing on the quality of the witness's view of the man. Our main task here is to be clear about what evidence we want the witness to give to the jury on this issue. Our only tools are the witness statements that the witness has given. We are looking for evidence about how close the man gets to the witness, how long the witness had him under investigation*

for, and what she noticed about him. (NB: Identification is always dealt with very carefully in criminal cases when it is in issue. There is a special need for caution that judges must warn juries about, and special directions that they must give juries arising from the famous case of Regina v Turnbull *in 1977.)*

1. *"The main spotlights inside the bank were still on and the public areas were brightly illuminated";*
2. *"I looked up to see a man running from the entrance door into the main atrium where I was working. The door where the man came in was about 6 metres to my left";*
3. *"He was just drawing level with my counter";*
4. *"He got up slowly then staggered over to my counter. He looked a bit shaken and was walking with a limp. I could see now that he was wearing a mask, but the fall must have dislodged it because it was now mostly up across his forehead. His eyes and lower face from the nose down were plainly visible to me";*
5. *"He then winced and slipped a little as his leg appeared to give way for a moment";*
6. *"I believe that I would recognise the man's face again because of the good view I had across the counter when he stood in front of me demanding the money. I had the man's face under observation for a good few seconds and in good light. He was about 5 feet 5 tall and had a long nose, small eyes and a small chin";*
7. *"At 1.30 pm I watched the sequence of images twice through in silence. After that, Police Inspector Canter said to me, "I am now going to ask you whether you are able to identify the man you saw enter the New Dilhorne Bank in Marple on 19th November 2026 and who came up to you and asked you to hand over money. Are you able to make any identification?" I answered, "Yes". Police Inspector Canter said, "Can you tell me the image number relating to the man you identify?" I replied, "Yes, number 6";*
8. *Police Inspector Canter then said, "I will now run through the images again and pause the sequence at the man shown in image number six". She did this. When the man in image number 6 was displayed on the screen, she asked me, "Is this the person you mean?" I said, "Yes". Police Inspector Canter said, "To be clear, is this the person you saw enter the New Dilhorne Bank on 19 November 2026 and who threatened you?" I replied, "Yes, one hundred percent. He has the same eyes and nose and face shape. I recognised him straightaway".*

These are perhaps the most important areas to elicit that serve you and your case in relation to the witness's view of the man. But you will notice other parts of the witness's statement where her evidence may not help us so much, including perhaps the part where her description of the man's clothing differs from the description of the same man offered by the other witness William Hawkins. (Or maybe Ullger's description is correct, and the description offered by Hawkins is wrong?) You will likely want to elicit the facts from Ullger in evidence-in-chief that do not help us as well as the ones that do. If you can do this, you will take away some of the impact that defence counsel's questioning may otherwise have if they were to establish the unhelpful facts for the first time in cross-examination.

A piece of information, a part of the narrative, that we can foresee defence counsel in the *Plant* case will not agree with, is that the public area inside the bank was brightly lit. Of course, you want the witness to give evidence to exactly this effect because it increases the credibility and reliability of her evidence. The rule against leading questions forbids you from using the disputed expression "brightly lit", or similar, in connection with the public area inside the bank.

Q: "Was the inside of the bank brightly illuminated?" (leading)
A: "Yes".

You could think your way around how to ask about this issue in this way, perhaps by using two questions as follows:

Q1: "How was the public area inside the bank lit?" (non-leading)
A1: "There are spotlights on the ceiling".
Q2: "How much light did those spotlights give?" (non-leading)
A2: "Lots; they were very bright".

You will have picked up by now that a test which can sometimes help identify a leading question is to ask yourself, what would the answer be? If the answer would likely be "yes" or "no", then that is an indicator that the question may be a leading question. Applying that to our Q2 above, you are not going to get a yes/no answer:

Q2: "How much light did those spotlights give?"

The yes/no test tends to indicate that Q2 is unlikely to be leading. The test is not definitive, though it is a helpful guide.

Look again at Q2 above and imagine that you are asking a version of it on its own *without asking Q1 first:*

Q2 revised: "How much light did the spotlights give in the public area of the bank?"

That question might now be a leading question because now the question assumes that there were spotlights in the bank. If defence counsel does not accept that the public area in the bank was lit by spotlights, you cannot lead on that.

You will probably think that the concept of leading questions is simple both to explain and to understand, and it is; nonetheless, there is a very good reason why students and even new advocates can struggle with it. The reason is that asking questions this way is against the way that we generally communicate in everyday life.

Imagine that you are in ordinary conversation with a friend about the attempted robbery at the New Dilhorne Bank. You may know this piece of information about the spotlights, and so might your friend. The quickest and most effective way of moving the conversation forward is simply to get your friend to confirm what you already know – that the public area inside the bank was brightly illuminated by spotlights. You will feel a *conversational urge* to give this information yourself. In ordinary conversation, this would be perfectly normal:

Q: "and the public area was well lit by bright spotlights, wasn't it?" (leading)
A: "Yes, of course it was!"

The rules mean that you must approach the topic very differently when you are conducting an examination-in-chief. It is counterintuitive. It is difficult because you are going against everything you have always done in ordinary conversation during your life so far. To counter your intuition, you need to adopt a certain mind-set: you know how the story goes, but you have to get the witness to tell it in response to questions that contain *no spoilers*. The fact that you know the story in advance gives you some of the control.

You might think of it this way, that you are the pen and the paper by which the witness will tell their story; but you are not the storyteller.

Your focus should be on asking questions designed to get to the answer, without including the answer.

As a student of advocacy you will know what you should be doing, but sometimes you may feel that you are struggling nonetheless to do it. A good tip is that if you frame your question so that it begins with "what", "where", "when", "who" and "how", then you are making a better start to asking a non-leading question. If you begin with the words "did" or "was", for example, then you are at increased risk of asking a leading question.

Think about the purpose of what you are doing when you ask the question. Usually, you will have thoughts in your head such as:

- what happened next;
- how the story developed;
- how someone reacted;
- what the next event was;
- what are the details of what was happening.

All of these thoughts can easily produce a variety of questions that do not suggest the answer that you want. They are all inquisitive.

The "What Happened Next?" Question

In examination-in-chief you are going to want to move the witness through their story of what they witnessed. Often this involves describing a sequence of events in chronological order. Each question that you ask should be designed to progress through the story little by little. Let us consider next how to do that effectively.

The question "what happened next?" is your friend, but do not get too cosy. A vast proportion of what you need to achieve in examination-in-chief can in principle be achieved by this question; however, just because you *could* does not mean that you *should.*

Returning to our examination-in-chief of Isobel Ullger, take a moment again to remind yourself of the account she gives in her witness statements, both of the incident in the bank and of the identification procedure at the police station. Let us consider how we might get that account from the witness in court by a series of non-leading questions, mainly by asking the non-leading question "what happened next".

Imagine that the witness has told the court that she was working in the bank, and it was towards the end of the day. She has described that she was behind the counter using the note-counting machine.

Q1: "What time was it?"
A1: "About a quarter to five in the evening".
Q2: "What happened?"
A2: "A man burst in".
Q3: "How did you know?"
A3: "I heard him come in. The door swung open suddenly and banged against the wall behind".
Q4: "What happened next?"
A4: "He slipped on the highly polished floor and slid right past me to the wall at the other side".
Q5: "What happened next?"
A5: "He crashed into the wall, then got up".
Q6: "What happened next?"
A6: "He came over to my counter position".
Q7: "What happened next?"
A7: "He said, 'Give me the money or I'll shoot you'".
Q8: "What happened next?"
A8: "I ducked underneath my counter and pressed the alarm button".
Q9: "What happened next?"
A9: "The man then said to me, 'I said, hand over the money'".

This is an example of an examination-in-chief that is achieved without a single leading question; nonetheless, it is a problematic examination-in-chief for three reasons.

The first problem is that the advocate has become an irritant because they have become the *what-happened-next* advocate. They are drawing attention to themselves and away from the witness's evidence, which is the very opposite of what they should be doing. Sooner or later someone in court will start keeping count of how many times the advocate uses this phrase. There may even be a sweepstake bet on it. But one thing is for sure: everyone in court will be focusing so much on the question that no one will really be paying much notice to the witness's evidence.

The second problem is that the *what-happened-next* advocate is not exercising sufficient control over the evidence. The question "what happened next" is an impossibly wide question. The witness could take their evidence in any number of directions, and the questioner will become a mere passenger. The questioner may as well engage autopilot. There is no skill here. There is no style.

The third problem for the *what-happened-next* advocate is that they will be tempted into a default position whereby they are focusing too hard on things that happened. They may overlook other evidence that the witness can give that is helpful to the case. As far as the witness Isobel Ullger is concerned, those things would include the quality of the view she had and any special reason she had for remembering the man.

Do Not Be the **What-Happened-Next** *Advocate*

Let us look at the first of those problems: repetition. There is a simple change that can be made: vary the way that you ask the question "what happened next". You can arm yourself with a variety of versions of the same question asked in different ways. This can be as simple as having some variations on the theme of "what happened next?"

Considering Miss Ullger's evidence above, we can begin at Q2 – the moment when the man bursts in – and then vary the format of the basic question, "What happened next?"

Q2: "What happened?"
A2: "A man burst in".
Q3: "How did you know?"
A3: "I heard him come in. The door swung open suddenly and banged against the wall behind".
Q4: "What was the next thing that happened?"
A4: "He slipped on the highly polished floor and slid right past me to the wall at the other side".
Q5: "After that, what happened?"
A5: "He crashed into the wall, then got up".
Q6: "What happened after that?"
A6: "He came over to where I was sitting at my counter position".
Q7: "And then?"
A7: "He said, 'Give me the money or I'll shoot you'".
Q8: "Then what happened after that?"

A8: "I ducked underneath my counter and pressed the alarm button".
Q9: "What happened after this?"
A9: "The man then said, 'I said, hand over the money'".

All of these questions are a means of moving the narrative on, of getting to the next event in the story, and they are not *exactly* the same. Yet the whole thing still does not quite work, you may think, although it is getting better. The next evolution is to have some control over the direction of the narrative.

The problem with the "what happened next" question, and its variants, is your loss of control. You are, in effect, delegating to the witness the task of selecting which specific information to give in response to each very general question. The witness could give any answer. When asked "what happened next", the witness may start to tell you all the irrelevant things – their stomach rumbled, they remembered that they had forgotten to turn the oven off, a bus drove by, a bird tweeted.

Worse than that, the witness may choose to give you an answer containing some highly prejudicial evidence. Not the witness's fault. They are trying their best to help you. The fault in this situation would lie with the *what-happened-next* advocate who is not being precise enough to help the witness understand what sort of evidence they want the witness to give.

Knowing, as you do, what the witness has put in their witness statement, you should tailor your "what happened next" question to direct the attention of the witness in the right area, without leading. This is how you control the evidence.

This is where a powerful tool of the advocate comes to the fore: your imagination. Picture the scene in your head and, by your questions, try to recreate it in your witness's mind. This is the way that the witness will recall events when they are giving evidence about them. Get the witness to describe things along the way.

Add to that, the vital attribute of the successful and effective advocate – the ability to listen. Listen to the last answer, picture the scene, then move the story on. If you need to pause your flow to get more detail on a piece of evidence given by the witness, take that detour, then return to where you were and carry on. Above all, think of the questions and answers not as separate things, but together as a flow that develops the story being told by the witness.

You can only shape your question clearly once you have fully grasped the answer that you are aiming for. Ask the question about what happened next in the form of how the witness would have experienced it:

- "What did you see?";
- "What did you hear then?";
- "What did you do?",
- "What did they do?",

Looking again at our examination-in-chief of Isobel Ullger, we might consider approaching our task in the following way, and you will see straight away how this change of approach changes the flow of the exchanges between advocate and witness:

Q1: "What happened?"
A1: "A man burst in".
Q2: "Why do you say, 'burst in'?"
[using the witness's expression to help the witness give her account in her own words from her own recollection]
A2: "Because the door swung open suddenly and banged against the wall behind. It was a really loud sound. The man was suddenly there in the doorway".
Q3: "Where were you looking?"
[getting to the reliability of the witness – she cannot be reliable if she wasn't looking at the events that she is describing]
A3: "I looked up as I heard the bang and I looked right at him".
Q4: "At this point, what could you see of him?"
A4: "Only really his clothes".
Q5: "How would you describe his clothes?"
A5: "It was pretty much all dark clothing".
Q6: "What was the distance between you and the door where the man came in?"
[distance is relevant to the witness's ability to identify]
A6: "About six metres".
Q7: "And whereabouts was the door in relation to where you were?"
[building the picture]
A7: "It was to my left".
Q8: "What was the man doing at that moment when you first saw him at the door?"
[moving now from the quality of the witness's view to what she saw the man do]
A8: "He was running at quite some speed".
Q9: "How far did he run?"
[advancing the account using the witness's last answer as a springboard, the advocate knowing that the witness says in her statement that the man ran until he slipped and fell over]
A9: "Well, he only got as far as being level with my counter before he slipped on the polished floor and slid right past me and collided with the wall at the other side".
Q10: "The wall at the other side of -" ?
[leaves question hanging with an inquisitive tone that shows the witness we need some clarification]
A10: "The wall at the other end of the bank opposite the door".
Q11: "Was the wall the only thing he collided into?"
[not leading because the question does not presuppose that there was something else that the man collided with]
A11: "No. He knocked over a potted plant before he hit the wall".
Q12: "What would you say is the closest he got to you when he was level with your counter?"
[advancing the account using the witness's answer from a few seconds ago; getting to the quality of the witness's view]
A12: "About a metre away, that's all".

Q13: "What happened to the man after he hit the wall?"
A13: "He groaned a bit, then got up and came over to where I was sitting at my counter position".
Q14: "What was the distance you saw him cover from the wall that he collided into and your counter position?"
A14: "About seven metres".
Q15: "Can you describe for the jury the way in which he came from the wall to your counter position?"
A15: "He was more staggering than walking".
Q16: "Is 'staggering' the only thing that you noticed at that time about the way he was moving?"
[as with the "potted plant" question earlier, this is not leading because the question does not presuppose that there was something else that the witness noticed in addition to the staggering]
A16: "He was limping as well".
Q17: "When the man came to your counter position, how far from you was he?".
A17: "About half a metre away".
Q18: "How steady was he on his feet when he was at your counter position?"
A18: "Not very. At one point he winced and his leg gave way for just a second or so".
Q19: "And what happened when he got there?"
A19: "He said, 'Give me the money or I'll shoot you'".
Q20: "Could you see what he might have used to shoot you?"
A20: "No, I could not see anything".
Q21: "How did you feel about what was happening?"
A21: "It was terrifying".
Q22: "What happened after the man said, 'Give me the money or I'll shoot you'?"
A22: "I ducked underneath my counter and pressed the alarm button".

We will briefly discuss Q11 and Q16 from this section of the examination-in-chief:

Q11: "Was the wall the only thing he collided into?"
and
Q16: "Is 'staggering' the only thing that you noticed at that time about the way he was moving?"

These two questions are follow-up questions from the advocate in response to answers already given by the witness. Look again at the sequence of questions overall. Before the "wall" question at Q11, the witness had already given evidence that the man collided with the wall. Before the "staggering" question at Q16, the witness had already said the man was staggering. The reason why we are focusing for a moment on these two questions is that they demonstrate the danger of what we have called the *conversational urge* to ask a leading question instead. It is so easy to slip into asking those questions in a different way like this:

Q11 alternative: "What else did he collide with?" (leading)
Q16 alternative: "What else was he doing apart from staggering?" (leading)

In these questions, the advocate would be leading on the fact that the witness saw the man do something else. On our facts, the "something else" is (for Q11) colliding with the potted plant as well as the wall, and (for Q16) limping as well as staggering. These questions are stating that there was something else and asking what it was. Even variations are leading:

Q11 variation: "Was there anything else he collided with?" (still leading)
Q16 variation: "What else, if anything, did he collide with?" (still leading)

Look again at the two questions Q11 and Q16 in the model examination. They do not ask whether anything else was done. Instead, each one looks back at the witness's answer and asks, "is that all?" It looks back, not forward. Each one is not leading.

Hopefully by now you will have noticed that simplicity is at the heart of the way the questions are formulated. You need short, concise questions that use simple language. The foundations of examination-in-chief are achieved by having a stock of short, concise questions that you can always fall back on, if the moment needs it, so that you can move the story along in a way that does not involve leading:

- "What happened next?";
- "Where did you go?";
- "What was the next thing you saw?";
- "What did you hear/say/do?";
- "How did it progress from there?";
- "Who could you see?"; or
- "What did they do?".

You can practise your skills with a friend or family member. You are going to need a few helpful friends and family. Sit them down and ask them to help you by telling you about their day, but only in response to your questions. Start with this question, perhaps: "What did you do at lunchtime today?"Then get the narrative moving on with a series of questions as above. Record the session and listen back. Check that you are not leading. Make sure you are keeping it simple. (Get used to being recorded . It is standard workshop procedure at Bar School to record advocacy sessions and share the recordings with you.)

The next thing you need to practise is asking about a paragraph or two of a story. Your friend can write out something they have experienced, or you can get them to read some paragraphs from an autobiography. Get them to tell that exact story, but only in response to you asking the questions. You know what the story is, the direction it needs to go in. Now is the time to deploy the technique of adapting the base question to the facts that you hope to develop. Given thought and practice, a lot of practice, you will soon be able to grasp the basics of asking a question that does not include the answer. You will have a collection of questions that you can fall back on when the mind goes blank.

Being able to ask a series of non-leading questions and getting an account via them is only the beginning. You may be able to ask a non-leading question, and that is a very important skill; however, by itself that will not give you a successful examination-in-chief. You need more than just that.

Control and Pace

We mention control many times in this book. It is for the advocate to control the examination-in-chief. In every way. Be the driver, not the passenger. Closely linked to your control in the minds of your tribunal will be the pace of your witness handling.

The pace is your responsibility, not the witness's. The majority of witnesses will want to get it all out there. In most circumstances, they will be very nervous. A garbled, rushed account from a nervous witness is not going to be easy for your tribunal to follow. An advantage of asking a directed question is that the witness's answer will be limited to a specific topic. For example.

Q: "Please tell the jury what you could see of the man's head area?"

It is worth giving a great deal of thought to your tribunal's perspective of the witness's evidence. Your own pace should be measured with your voice speaking at a volume that is appropriate for the room that you are in. Do not be afraid of pauses. Pauses allow everyone to digest what has been said. It is not enough for the witness to give the information that you require. Your tribunal needs to process the information, understand it, and appreciate its importance to the whole case.

Proceeding at a sensible pace is key. Remember also that your tribunal is likely to be making notes. If your tribunal includes a judge, they will certainly be making notes. Several judges fed back to us when we were writing this book that most advocates (not many; but most), even those of great experience, tend to take witnesses through their evidence too quickly. This can be highly counterproductive for you, the advocate. You will have planned your examination carefully with all our guidance in mind. You will be particular about eliciting evidence that you hope will have an impact on the tribunal and that will present your case in the best way. Do not fall at the final hurdle by making it difficult for your tribunal to keep up with you.

Occasionally, witnesses will start to speed up when giving their account despite you asking directed non-leading questions. You must exercise control by stopping the witness with a polite but firm "pause there". You do not need to say anything more than that. You do not need a long explanation about the judge taking a note and how important it is for the witness to slow down. That is putting the onus on the witness to moderate the pace. Again: it is your responsibility, not theirs. The vast majority of even the most nervous witnesses will get the message after a few "pause there" interruptions.

If you are having to pause the witness frequently, and if the witness is giving too much information in their answers, extend your "pause there" into a recap and an additional question about the detail:

> Pause there. [Wait for two seconds] You have said that the man got out of a white car and ran into the bank. How far from you was the car?

This allows a repeated "pause there" to be less of an irritant to the listener. It provides a moment for everyone to catch up whilst you repeat the evidence just given and allows you to maintain control with a focused question. The focused question in the example above is a further refinement that is sometimes needed, a context to the question.

The simple question "Where was the bank?" might get an answer like "Marple" or "on the corner of Market Street" or "next to the chemists" from a nervous or neurodiverse witness, or any witness at all. After all, any of those answers might be a perfectly proper answer to what is in fact quite a wide question. A context preamble can greatly assist in further directing the answer to the issue that you want the answer to deal with. If you want to know where the bank is relative to the witness, introduce that by a short preamble that sets the parameters:

Q: "How far from where you were standing was the bank?"

The golden rule for this is that the preamble must be short and must not contain the answer to the question! It would be cheating if you asked a question like this:

Q: "Cars can be all sorts of colours, including white – what colour was the car?" (leading)

Another form of cheating (that is to say, a leading question used in examination-in-chief) is one which gives alternatives. It is still a leading question if you ask:

Q: "Was the car blue, green or white?" (leading)

The answer that you want is there, embedded in your question, even if other answers are too.

If your question contains some context, make sure that the context does not sneak in the answer you want. Alternatively, use as your context some part of the witness's evidence that they have already said.

The Closed Question

It is not just the pace of the witness evidence that you have to control in examination-in-chief; occasionally, you have to adduce evidence in a very careful way in order to avoid something that is inadmissible. This is where a closed question has to be part of your weaponry. Earlier in this chapter, we said that whether the answer to the question is a yes or a no could indicate whether the question was a leading question. We said that it was not definitive. The closed non-leading question is the exception to that loose rule.

"What happened next?" is a very open question. The witness may say anything at all, and we have been discussing how you can begin to control that by narrowing the focus of the question, for instance by specifying "What did the man do next?" or by adding context "After getting out of the car, how long did the man remain on the pavement?" These are all still open questions, and there are a variety of answers that you might expect to receive. Instead, you could choose to ask closed questions, which are questions where the answer is one from a certain and limited range of options. There are two types of closed non-leading questions that you will deploy in examination-in-chief.

The first type of closed question is where the known answer is really only one option. Saying to a witness "Can you introduce yourself to the court please?" may produce a whole raft of biographical detail; whereas the closed question "What is your name?" is only going to elicit one known actual response. The importance of this approach is that if the witness gives extraneous detail, that is not because you allowed them to. You have carefully framed the question in a way which limits the potential answers. In other words (you know by now what we are saying), you are in control.

The second form of closed question is the exception to the "yes/no" answer rule. Whilst most leading questions can be answered "yes/no", it is possible to have a closed, non-leading question. The most common way in which these are deployed in examination-in-chief is to ascertain a primary fact before examining some detail. Often this will break the "avoid starting the question with did" rule. An example of deploying the closed question in these circumstances is where a primary fact is required before the next piece of evidence is admissible, for example, that someone witnessed the event (as opposed to, for example, being told about it):

Q1: "Did you see what colour the car was?" (not leading)
A1: "Yes".
Q2: "What colour was the car?" (closed)
A2: "White".

There are only two possible answers to the question of whether the witness saw the colour: yes or no. If the answer is yes, then you can go on to ask the next question that enquires as to the colour. If the answer is no, then stop there. There is nothing the witness can say to help the court with the colour of the car.

If you do it the other way round, asking open questions, you may find yourself in trouble:

Q1: "What colour was the car?"
A1: "White".
Q2: "How are you able to say it was white?"
[perhaps expecting the answer "because I saw it"]

A1: "I saw it, but also Joe from the chemist's shop later told me it was white".

[What Joe from the chemist's shop said to the witness is hearsay evidence and inadmissible – you have inadvertently introduced inadmissible evidence from the witness]

Only use the closed question technique where there is an element of doubt as to the witness's source of knowledge which you wish to clarify first, or where you wish to narrow the scope of the answer with precision. You do not need to ask "Did you see" or "Can you recall" before every question.

A closed question can be asked once you have established a primary fact. For example, once the witness has said that they have seen the car (the primary fact), you can ask a question about it which is a closed question but neutral as to the answer required.

Q1: "How did the man arrive?"
A1: "In a car".
Q2: "Did you see what colour the car was?"
A2: "Yes".
Q3: "What colour was the car?"
A3: "White".
Q4: "Have you ever seen that car before?" (closed)
A4: "No".

The fourth question is neutral as to what the answer should be but is closed as to the options. The leading form of that question might be:

Q4: "You had not seen that car before, had you?" (leading)
A4: "No".

We have deliberately left the topic of closed questions to the end of this section for a reason: we recommend that you learn the very basic foundations of how to ask open, non-leading questions first. Mastering the ability to ask closed questions is the final basic skill that you need.

Civil Cases

In civil cases, examination-in-chief plays a far more restrained role than in criminal proceedings. Under the Civil Procedure Rules, a witness's statement serves as their evidence-in-chief. This means that the witness does not need to answer questions from their advocate and (effectively) repeat to the tribunal what is in their witness statement. Instead, the judge will simply read the witness statement. Consequently, the oral component of examination-in-chief is typically confined to a brief confirmation: first, that the document before the witness is indeed their statement; second, that the signature on the statement of truth is theirs; and third, that the witness believes that the facts stated in the witness statement are true.

Judges retain a discretion to permit a witness to expand upon their statement, but this discretion is exercised sparingly. Permission is usually limited to two situations. The first is the correction of minor errors – such as typographical mistakes – that require clarification. The second arises where the witness needs to update the court on developments occurring after the statement was signed. For instance, in a personal injury claim, a witness may be allowed to describe the current state of their symptoms. In such circumstances, the advocate must apply the same principles of structured, non-leading questioning that govern examination-in-chief more broadly and which are described above.

Although rare, there are notable exceptions to these general rules. A civil trial conducted before a jury – such as those historically seen in defamation, false imprisonment, or malicious prosecution – requires a full examination-in-chief. However, jury trials in civil matters have become increasingly uncommon. Examination-in-chief may also be required in committal proceedings for contempt, given their quasi-criminal character. Even then, the judge may choose to rely solely on the evidence contained within the written statements and dispense with oral examination altogether.

Advanced Technique

In the "How-To" section, we discussed the basic skills that you will need in order to conduct an examination-in-chief that conforms to the rules and displays your skills. As with everything in advocacy, it is those basic skills that you will fall back on, time and time again. They will become second nature. They will sustain you through any temporary periods of uncertainty in court.

What you are aiming for as you develop your career is excellence through advanced technique. Not basic. Advanced technique is required at two ends of the spectrum. At one end, you want to improve your advocacy in order to turn your examination-in-chief from something which is competent to something which is compelling advocacy. At the other end of the spectrum, you will need advanced technique when things are beginning to go wrong.

Always remember what the purpose of calling a witness is. It is not an exercise in simply getting certain bits of information "out there"; it is about presenting the evidence in an attractive and digestible way. Your preparation for examination-in-chief cannot involve you having written out every question that you are going to ask. That is why it is so important to have mastered the basics described earlier. Brilliance always begins with the basics.

It Is (Almost) All in Your Preparation

The preparation of a skilled advocate for each examination-in-chief has four distinct components:

(i) You know the contents of the witness statement thoroughly;
(ii) You know your whole case and how the witness's evidence fits into it;

(iii) You have thought about how you will structure and present the witness's evidence;
(iv) You have mastered the basics.

Structure

The competent advocate will be able to conduct an examination-in-chief by taking the witness through their witness statement from start to finish without leading once. The advocate possessing advanced skills will have worked out how the witness's account can *best* be given, and they will ask questions to elicit that evidence in the *best* way. The skilled advocate will not simply ask the witness to regurgitate the contents of their witness statement.

See yourself as the editor of the witness's evidence. When you are a new advocate, consider marking up your paper copy of the witness's statement, breaking it down into bite-sized chunks, or keywords. Draw lines on the statement so that the sentences are divided into the different answers that you are looking to get from the witness, almost like musical bars. Or draw boxes round the parts you need the witness to say and number the boxes down the margin so that you get the evidence out in a structured order that you think is appropriate.

Sometimes an order that makes sense *on the page* may not be the best order for your tribunal to assimilate and understand when they are *listening* to it. What you may need to do is effectively rewrite the statement, either in full by changing the order of the words or by writing yourself a narrative plan as to how you want the chronology of the evidence to take shape.

Bear in mind that when we are reading something in a document, our eyes instinctively flick about the document, backwards and forwards, up and down, as our brain makes sense of what we are reading. Your tribunal cannot do that when they are listening to someone speak their evidence. Your tribunal has one chance, and one chance only, to listen to the witness's evidence. It is your job to make that task easy for your tribunal.

Often you cannot do better in examination–in-chief than to elicit the evidence in chronological order. Witnesses are more likely to remember events if they are explaining them in the order in which the events happened. Tribunals listening to an account are more likely to understand and remember it if they hear the account chronologically.

We can take an example from our case of *Rex v Tegan Plant*. Did you notice in our example evidence-in-chief, above, the timing of this question and answer:

Q6: "What was the distance between you and the door where the man came in?"
[distance is relevant to the witness's ability to identify]
A6: "About six metres".

Read that section of our evidence-in-chief again. You will see in our structure that Q6 comes at the point when the witness is giving evidence about seeing the man at the door. The evidence of distance that Q6 asks about is directly relevant at exactly that point of the witness's account.

Did you also notice the timing of this question and answer:

Q14: "What was the distance you saw him cover from the wall that he collided into and your counter position?"
A14: "About seven metres".

Again, our structure is that Q14 comes at the point when the witness is giving evidence about seeing the man at the wall. The evidence of distance that Q14 asks about is directly relevant at exactly that point.

But if you go to the written witness statements of Isobel Ullger, you will see that it is not until the final two sentences of the very last paragraph of her first witness statement that the witness describes both these distances:

> The door where the man came in was about six metres to my left. The wall that he collided with was about seven metres to my right.

When planning the structure of our evidence-in-chief, we have actively considered when we are going to deal with these two facts, and we have adjusted our approach so that the witness will give evidence about these at the most appropriate time.

Sometimes you will form the view that a certain part of the statement does not bear on the issues of the case. Do not just ask about it because it is there. Ask about it because you have considered the whole case, and you see that that part will help the jury, judge or tribunal with the issues they will need to decide.

Always remember that in the conduct of your examination-in-chief you are the medium by which the evidence of the witness is being conveyed. This is why you need to have thought in advance about not just what the witness can say that will help your case but also how the witness's evidence sits with the rest of the narrative. Each witness you call is a building block in the case that you are presenting, and you are the one putting the blocks together.

You Are Always Listening

The reason why you cannot just write out each question that you are going to ask is that you have to listen to the answer to your preceding question, and it is that answer which will dictate the next question. In that moment between questions, you need to listen and decide. Use your knowledge of the case and that vital secret tool of the advocate, *your imagination*, to evaluate the information that the judge/jury/tribunal need to assist them.

Listen. Evaluate. Adapt. Do not merely try to adduce in oral evidence the sentence that comes next in the witness statement. Instead, be the advocate who gets the witness to tell the story of what happened. This is how to take your skills to a higher level. Does the last answer that the witness gave the court need further clarification? Does it need added context? Does it need extra detail? Does it paint the picture properly about what was happening, or do you need to amplify it with the witness?

Adapt Your Questioning Style to the Needs of the Witness

The art of handling witnesses lies in its unpredictability. Some witnesses just do not give you an easy ride for reasons that you cannot know. They may be feeling nervous. They may have suffered a significant life event in the recent past that is affecting them. They may just be a difficult personality. All the more reason to keep your questions short and concise. Even though you are now proficient at keeping it simple, you always need to be alive to the capabilities of the witness so that you can adapt your approach at any moment.

As a skilled advocate, you will also need to tailor your questioning to the needs of each witness that you *do* know about. For example, the witness may be young, have a particular vulnerability, or require specific communication support. The examination of witnesses with particular needs is considered in more detail in the chapter of this book that deals with the questioning of vulnerable witnesses, where you will be focusing your learning on the advocates' toolkits.

React Practically When Things Go Wrong

A common error occurs when you notice that the witness you have called is not "coming up to proof". This means that whilst giving evidence in court in answer to your questions, the witness does not state a detail or a portion of their witness statement when you are expecting them to say it in answer to your question. You are expecting the witness to be able to answer you because the information that your question seeks is in the witness's statement or proof of evidence. It can leave the competent advocate stumped.

Returning to our example evidence-in-chief, let us imagine that the witness misses out one of the details, which we will indicate by an underline at Q4:

Q1: "What happened?"
A1: "A man burst in".
Q2: "Why do you say 'burst in'?"
A2: "Because the door swung open suddenly and banged against the wall behind. It was a really loud sound. The man was suddenly there in the doorway".
Q3: "Where were you looking?"
A3: "I looked up as I heard the bang and I looked right at him".
Q4: "At this point, what could you see of him?"
A4: "Don't know, really".

[PAUSE. THINK. As a skilled advocate, you do not just take the answer "Don't know really" as the end of it. The witness does know; she just is not bringing it to mind right now. You immediately come to the issue in a different way.]

Q5 NEW: "What was the distance between you and the door where the man came in?"
A5 NEW: "About six metres".
Q6 NEW: "And whereabouts was the door in relation to where you were?"
A6 NEW: "It was to my left".
Q7 NEW: "So, how were you able to see the door?"
A7 NEW: "Oh very easily. There's a clear plastic sheet in front of my desk, but it's very big and you just have to turn your head and you can see the door right there".
Q8 NEW: "And when you were looking over towards the door, what could you see of the man?"
A8 NEW: "Only really his clothes".
Q9 NEW: "How would you describe his clothes?"
A9 NEW: "It was pretty much all dark clothing".

You will see that what we are doing here is taking a little detour in order to explore what the witness could see of the scene at that exact point and then we are circling back to the clothing – which is the point where the witness seemed to get lost a little. That is the first way to work round the problem, but what if it does not work? You may find that your first few additional questions may not work in the moment. It may be best to park the topic and come back to it later.

The second way you can try and get the witness to say the part that they missed is to find some other part of the evidence that may give you a way back in. Imagine that you leave the clothing point for the moment. You intend to work your way back to it, but for now you will restructure. You were always going to ask about the man wearing a mask, but you will bring forward that section of your evidence-in-chief and deal with it now. Your strategy is to keep the witness in the "description" frame of mind before then circling back to the missed evidence relating to clothing:

Q4: "At this point, what could you see of him?"
A4: "Don't know, really".
Q5 BRINGING FORWARD THE MASK EVIDENCE: "When the man was standing half a metre from you, how much of him were you able to see?"
A5: "Everything from his waist up".
Q6: "Please tell the jury what you could see of his head area?"
A6: "He was wearing a mask, but it had pushed up so that it was on his forehead, and covering his hair".
Q7: "What about the part of his head below the forehead?"
A7: "I could see that plainly".
Q8: "What could you see?"
A8: "I could see his eyes, his nose. Everything on his face from his eyes down".
Q9: "Could you see the colour of his eyes?"
A9: "I couldn't see that".
Q10: "The colour of his skin?"
A10: "White".

Q11: "How long did you have the man in your view for?"
A11: "It was a good few seconds".
Q12 RETURNING TO THE CLOTHING ISSUE: "Were you able also to notice his clothing?"
A12: "Oh, yes, I remember now. It was all dark clothing".
Q13: "When did you first notice that?"
A13: "Actually, it was when he first came in, and I saw him at the door".

The third way you can try and get the witness to say the part that they missed is to find a suitable moment, either at the end of that phase of the witness's account, or towards the end of their evidence, so that you can take the witness back to the moment. We mean, *really take them back.* Put them back at the scene or back in the moment. Look around the scene with them. Recreate the movie of what happened in their minds. Get them to describe what is happening.

Q4: "At this point, what could you see of him?"
A4: "Don't know, really".
Q5 NEW: "Earlier in your evidence you described the moment when the man first entered the bank; do you remember?"
A5 NEW: "Yes".
Q6 NEW: "Describe the scene for us. First of all, what were you doing when you heard the door bang open?"
A6 NEW: "I was putting notes through the automatic counting machine".
Q7 NEW: "Where was the machine?".
A7 NEW: "Just on my desk in front of me".
Q8 NEW: "What else was going on in that part of the bank at that time?".
A8 NEW: "Nothing".
Q9 NEW: "Before the man came in, could you hear any sounds?".
A9 NEW: "No, it was quiet".
Q10 NEW: "How noticeable was it that the man had come through the doors?"
A10 NEW: "Oh, it drew my attention straight away".
Q11 NEW: "Picture it in your mind now, at that point when you were looking at the man, what could you see of him?"
A11 NEW: "I remember that he was dressed in dark clothing".

Remember that questions such as these two are not leading:

Q1: "Was there anything else you noticed at that time?"
Q2: "Picture it in your mind now, was there anything else that caught your attention?"

The repeated use of "anything else" is not leading the witness because it is not leading on what the "anything else" was; but it is nudging the witness. The witness will pick up on the fact that there may be something else there. Help them look for it. You may not always get every detail out, but that should not be for want of trying.

If, on the other hand, you were to ask Q2 like this, it would be leading:

Q2: "Picture it in your mind now, what else caught your attention?"

This is very much in the advanced advocacy section of this chapter because the rules about leading questions are open to interpretation. There are some who may argue that you are leading by suggesting there was something else that caught the attention of the witness. If you were to ask these questions you would have to be prepared to defend asking them on the basis that they do not contain the ultimate answer which you are seeking and therefore do not offend the rule against a leading question. We would be confident that asking these questions is not against the rules, but you would have to understand why that is.

Remember, however, that if you are studying advocacy on a professional course, you should always follow the teaching that you are given about leading questions, as about everything else. If you are taught to avoid the two questions above ("Was there anything else you noticed at that time?"/"Was there anything else that caught your attention?") for the reason that they are leading, then avoid those formulations for your assessments. The reason for this approach will likely be the desire to test by way of assessment your overall ability to progress the witness through their evidence comprehensively without leading questions. In other words, follow the assessment rules.

And Finally

This has been left to the last. It is vital that you are able to conduct every examination-in-chief from start to finish by deploying non-leading questions. And you have to do so artfully. But the skilled advocate does not do that. The skilled advocate knows the areas in which they can lead the witness. This is generally on the areas of the witness's evidence that are not in dispute. Sometimes that will be dates and times, sometimes it will be most of the witness's evidence and sometimes it will only be just one small part of it.

There are two important aspects to this. First, if in doubt as to what is in dispute and what is not, check with your opponent. And probably check with your opponent, even if you are not in any doubt. The second aspect is this: even if you *can* achieve the majority of the examination by leading the evidence, do not do so. Why do we say not to do that? It is because practice makes perfect. Hone your skills over dozens and hundreds of examinations. And never, ever make it seem like it is your evidence. It is not your evidence. Let the witness give the evidence; you are just conducting the orchestra.

4 Cross-Examination

Cross-examination is the name given to that stage of a hearing where you are questioning a witness called by another party to the case. Often it will be a witness who has told the court something that your client does not accept, and it is your job to deal with that on behalf of your client. Imagine that you are defending in our case *Rex v Tegan Plant*. When you ask Miss Ullger questions, this is cross-examination. Similarly, at his trial, Tegan Plant may choose to give evidence. If he does, the prosecutor would expect to cross-examine him.

Fundamentals

A fundamental rule governs cross-examination, just as it does examination-in-chief: questions must be directed towards establishing facts. Cross-examination is not the place for commentary, argument, or name-calling.

Your Main Aims When Cross-Examining

Your main aims when you are cross-examining will depend very much on the extent to which your client disagrees with the evidence being given by the other side's witness. Let us take an example so that we can explore this concept.

You will recall that the witness Isobel Ullger is saying that the person she picked out at the identification procedure conducted at Stockport Police Station was the man who came into the New Dilhorne Bank and tried to rob it. Let us look at this on the basis that you are defence counsel. Unless you spot something has gone very wrong with the way the identification procedure was conducted, you are likely to accept that it is factually accurate that Ullger picked your client out at the procedure, and so you would *not* expect to be cross-examining on that point. On the other hand, knowing that your client is saying he was not the man who went into the bank, your case is that the witness is wrong to identify the defendant as that man, and you *would* expect to be cross-examining on that point.

Logically, people get things wrong either when they have made a mistake or when they are malicious and have invented an account which they know full well is wrong. But what is your client saying to you? He may be giving you instructions that he and Ullger know each other well, and they have a bad history together – so bad that he believes she would not think twice before maliciously identifying him

DOI: 10.4324/9781003602019-4

as the man. Or is he saying, "I do not know this person, I do not know why she would pick me out at an identification procedure". The instructions that your client gives you will shape how you cross-examine.

Often, your aim in cross-examination is to explore the witness's evidence and to expose the reasons why the witness's evidence may be inaccurate and/or unreliable: you are seeking to cast doubt on their evidence so that the tribunal of fact will hesitate to accept it.

Sometimes, and actually far more frequently than you might think, you are looking for ways in which the witness can help you. They may have observed things that up to now they have not talked about. Your cross-examination may therefore uncover evidence that helps your case succeed.

Finally, there may be a way in which you can directly attack the credibility of the witness. Credibility is the lawyer's way of expressing reasons why a court may choose not to believe the witness. Here we mean questions that are less about the alleged crime itself, and more about the credibility, or believability, of the witness.

Imagine, for instance, that Miss Ullger has a conviction for perjury for telling lies to a court in retribution against someone she did not like. That may be an extreme example, but you see how it may be a foundation for directly attacking her credibility. Even this is not as simple as you may think, though. Your knowledge of the rules of criminal litigation will be critical to your decision-making in a situation like this. First, you would need the permission of all other parties to the case, or of the judge, before you could adduce evidence of Miss Ullger's conviction.

Second, this approach may come at a cost. It would likely result in the court being told about your client's previous convictions so that the court can assess the credibility of the person (your client) who is attacking the credibility of another witness. Now in the case of *Tegan Plant*, it may be that the court is already going to hear evidence of the bad character of your client; but you can imagine other, different scenarios where you might decide not to attack the credibility of another witness for the reason that you do not want your client's previous convictions revealed in the trial.

Attack, Attack, Attack?

Cross-examination is all about destroying the other side's witness and destroying your opponent's case. It is the time when, if the case were a boxing match, you deliver the knockout blow. Right?

Wrong. Cross-examination is, at its heart, a defensive skill. The true foundations of a good cross-examination lie in control and anticipation. You will need to learn an unlikely combination of skills: rigorous preparation and spontaneous improvisation. This is advocacy at its most organic. More than ever, you will have to listen to the answers that you get to your questions and react to them.

Tread Carefully

If your approach is too bold or too aggressive, you risk losing, not winning. If this is your only style of cross-examination, then you risk losing more cases than you win.

The winning moments hardly ever come in some concession from the witness, exhausted after a cross-examination onslaught from you, that they have been lying all along. That sort of thing only really happens in movies, not in real life. Only one of us has ever experienced a defendant admit the crime under cross-examination. It did not come as the result of bold and determined questions; and the defendant did not even appreciate that what he was saying amounted to an admission. It came quite by chance, which illustrates our point: setting out to destroy is a high-risk strategy in cross-examination, and it rarely succeeds.

It is far more likely that the winning moments in a case will be around some contexts that are barely perceptible to the witness themselves; it will be some piece of evidence that you have teased from the witness or some doubt that you have planted about their credibility which the witness did not dispel. Why is that? It is because you have learned to tread carefully and because you respect the fact that cases can easily be lost in cross-examination rather than won.

Put Your Case

It is a central requirement that you "put your case" to an opposing witness in cross-examination. If the witness has given evidence about certain facts and on behalf of your client you disagree with what the witness has said, then you must challenge the witness on what they have said.

You also need to put the general nature of your case if they are a witness who could reasonably be expected to deal with it. If you were defending our case of *Rex v Tegan Plant*, for example, your case is that the witness Ullger was wrong to identify your client at the police station identification procedure as being that man who came into the bank. You would expect to cross-examine Miss Ullger and put to her your case that she was mistaken. To do this, you would first want to cross-examine her about the circumstances of her observation with a view to exploring whether she had a good view of what happened, and of the man in particular; and whether her evidence matches other available evidence or not.

On the other hand, William Hawkins does not purport to identify the man who robbed the bank, and so you would not expect to cross-examine that witness on the specific point whether your client was that man. It is not something that he can help with.

There are two reasons why it is important to put your case. First, you must challenge the witness on the points which, on behalf of your client, you disagree with. By putting your case you are being fair to the witness. If your case is that the witness is wrong about something that they have given evidence about (e.g. "the man I identified at the identification procedure was the man who came into the bank"), then you must give the witness a fair opportunity to deal with the defence case on that exact point (e.g. by asking her, "you are mistaken to say that the man you identified was the man who came into the bank, aren't you?").

Second, there are great risks if you do not put your case properly. It creates a measure by which the tribunal can compare what you put to a witness on your client's behalf with the evidence that your client will give later in the trial. If your client gives evidence about something that you did not ask the witness about, the court may draw the conclusion that your client has recently fabricated their account – otherwise you, the advocate, doing your job properly, would have put it to the witness. That is the reasoning.

Not putting your case can directly disadvantage your client: strictly, if you do not put your case on a certain point, you are (on behalf of your client) taken to have positively accepted what the witness has said. That can be very damaging to you and your client and your client's case. You can see instantly why it is so very important to put your case and to do so accurately.

There is a proviso here, and that applies sometimes in cases where there are vulnerable witnesses – as we consider in our chapter dealing with this type of evidence. There can be occasions in such trials where the court will expressly expect that you will *not* put your case to a vulnerable witness.

How Do You Go About Putting Your Case?

We begin with how you do *not* go about it. You do not immediately say:

Q: "I put it to you that you were mistaken when you identified the man at position six as the man who came into the bank?"

Strictly, there is nothing improper about that question. The problem, rather, is that the above question uses the imagined language of the courtroom drama, probably a black and white movie made in the 1940s. A judge may ask you, "Have you put your case, Mr Booth?" and as criminal lawyers together, you and your opponent and the judge will all know what the judge means. But a witness – will they know? They may not, at least not fully. The witness is not a criminal lawyer. The witness may be completely confused by you asking a series of "I put it to you" type questions. In a sense, "I put it to you" is more of a statement than a question anyway, and it may not be instantly clear to every witness that they are being asked to agree or disagree or respond by giving detail.

There are several ways in which you can put your case. You can, for example, highlight the evidence that has been given by the witness, then challenge it directly:

Q: "You said that the man at position 6 was the man who came into the bank, but in fact you were mistaken, weren't you?"

or

Q: "Your evidence was that the man at position 6 was the man who came into the bank, but that's not right, is it?"

If you wish, you can highlight the positive case that your client will advance on the point:

Q: "The defendant says that he was not the man who went into the bank; you were mistaken, weren't you?"

But be careful with the "positive case" approach. It can be clumsy. You are effectively advertising in advance what evidence your client will give on that topic, if he does indeed give evidence. That has the risk of backfiring on you if in fact your client does not go on to say it. The court may think there is something suspicious about your client not saying what you advertised so loudly he would say!

Now on our facts here in *Rex v Tegan Plant*, it is likely very safe for you to consider that when your client gives evidence he will deny being the man who went into the bank. But you will encounter other situations in other cases where you are putting your case on a specific and more limited point. All we are saying is, be wary before you pointedly and directly connect what the witness is saying on that limited point with what you expect your client to say. You may think that phrasing such as "The defendant will say ..." is best avoided.

How-To

Always Ask Leading Questions

The basic building block of cross-examination is the leading question. We have seen in the chapter on examination-in-chief that asking good non-leading questions can be difficult. Asking good leading questions in cross-examination is difficult too. A leading question is one which contains the answer. It leads the witness to the exact response that you, the questioner, want:

Q: "You can't be sure that the registration number of the car you saw included the letters 'XCM'?"
A (desired): "No, I can't be sure".

Here you are working on the basis that the witness cannot be sure that the registration number or the car included the letters XCM, and you want to lead the witness to agree with that. Notice that the question and answer are focussed on that single point and nothing else. That is typical of all questions in court advocacy: always one point, one question – more about that later in this chapter.

Incidentally, have you noticed that we did not phrase the question like this:

Q: "The registration number did not include the letters 'XCM', did it?"

The reason why we do not ask this question is very subtle. It is because our client Tegan Plant is instructing us that he was not there at the New Dilhorne Bank on the occasion when someone tried to rob it. He knows nothing about any car pulling up. He knows nothing about any man running from a car to the bank. You therefore have no instructions from him that the witness Hawkins is wrong about anything he is telling the court he saw. In other words, you cannot positively suggest to Hawkins that, contrary to what he is saying, the registration number did not include the letters "XCM".

But you may explore whether he is a reliable witness about what he says he saw, and so this question would be perfectly acceptable:

Q: "You can't be sure that the registration number of the car you saw included the letters 'XCM'?"

Asking "Tag" Questions

There are other ways to ask the same question:

Q: "You can't be sure that the registration number of the car you saw included the letters 'XCM', can you?"

This format is known as a "tag" question. It is a statement ("You can't be sure that the registration number of the car you saw included the letters 'XCM'") followed by a question known as the tag ("can you"). Just as we discussed earlier, the question is directed to result in the witness agreeing with the statement. In different contexts, the tag question may be "couldn't you", "didn't they", "wasn't he", etc. The tag question is the easiest way to ask a leading question that affords you, the questioner, control. Think of it this way, like a simple mathematical equation:

statement + affirming question = control

Here is an example of how your cross-examination questions may develop, and we will see how it gives you, the questioner, control. Take a moment before you read on to look again at Mr Hawkins's witness statement, and we will imagine that what Mr Hawkins tells the jury in his examination-in-chief at the trial mirrors what he says in that statement. You are now cross-examining on behalf of your client, Tegan Plant. See how the following questions, by virtue of their leading nature, make it easy for the witness to agree with you:

Q1: "You saw the car from 30 metres away, didn't you?"
Q2: "It was snowing heavily when you were trying to observe the car, wasn't it?"
Q3: "It was late afternoon, wasn't it?"
Q4: "In the middle of winter?"
Q5: "So, it was getting dark, too, wasn't it?"
Q6: "The streetlamp nearest the car wasn't lit, was it?"
Q7: "You used the word 'dramatic' when you described the incident to the police, didn't you?"
Q8: "That's because you found what you were seeing was dramatic?"
Q9: "Whilst the car was there, you were searching in your clothing for your mobile phone, weren't you?"
Q10: "And then you dropped the phone and had to scrabble round in the snow to pick it up, didn't you?"
Q11: "Didn't all these things distract you from your task of observing the car?"
Q12: "You can't be sure that the registration number of the car you saw included the letters 'XCM', can you?"

> *Case theory:*
>
> *Your case theory matters greatly, and you must think through everything. It is fine to suggest in cross-examination of Hawkins all the reasons why the witness may not be reliable about the registration number but remember also that the witness says that the car he saw was white. If he is accurate about the car being white, then that is more difficult for the prosecution because Amy Barber's car was green – and the prosecution say the car was Amy Barber's car, the one with your client's fingerprints on it.*
>
> *In a sense, you want the witness to be wrong about the registration number and it would not bother you if he were right about the colour – but it's difficult to have both! For these reasons, perhaps, you are very likely to be asking no questions in cross-examination of the witness Hawkins that cast doubt on his assertion that the colour of the car was white (and perhaps also the fact that he observed it to have two doors when Amy Barber's car had four – did you spot this difference when reading the case documents?)*

But back to our leading questions that we have formulated. Can you see how they leave the witness very little room to volunteer information? The response is highly likely to be either "yes" or "no". You, the questioner, are exercising control in two important ways, often by deploying the "tag" question:

- You are asking questions that target the areas that you choose;
- You are limiting the witness's responses to those areas that you assess will be of value to your case.

Beware that the tag question can easily become quicksand and swallow you up. Keep the language precise, simple and clear. Edit your language. Do not, for instance, ask a question like this:

Q: "I am going to suggest to you that what you saw was this motor vehicle stopped, that is to say stationary, 30 metres away from you, at the bank, and that's right isn't it? That's how far away it was, wasn't it?"

Long questions with excessive words are bad enough, but when they contain tags as well, they are worse. They will only act to hide the point you are wanting to make. Short questions, each one expressing a simple concept, can be very eloquent. Use an economy of words so that what you are getting at will be understood immediately by both the witness and the tribunal. Consider these short, simple questions that you as defence counsel could ask the witness Hawkins:

Q1: "You saw the clothing that the man was wearing, didn't you?"
Q2: "You saw that his top was of two colours, didn't you?"

Q3: "It was black and white, wasn't it?"
Q4: "Black and white stripes?"
Q5: "The stripes were horizontal, weren't they?"
Q6: "His top was quite distinctive to you because of its colour pattern, wasn't it?"

> *Case Theory:*
>
> *Why are you asking these questions?*
>
> *You are asking these questions in order to build the image of how striking the man's clothing was to Hawkins. You intend to say to the jury in your closing speech that there is some doubt about the overall quality of Ullger's ability to describe and identify the man because she has described the man's top very differently: "dark trousers and a dark top ... pretty much all in black". If the jury form the opinion that Ullger may have got the basic description of his clothing wrong, then they might doubt the remainder of her evidence, including her later identification of your client as the man who went into the bank.*

In the formulation of these questions, can you see how the simple device of the tag question gives you control? Most tag questions will only allow for a controlled answer that is logically either yes or no. This is part of the defensive nature of cross-examination. The more you can control the flow of information, the more likely it is that you will gain evidence that is useful to you whilst exposing yourself to minimal risk of getting an answer that damages your client's case.

One Question, One Topic

When using tag questions, clear and simple language is important, and keeping the question to a single topic is absolutely paramount. Remember our equation:

statement + affirming question = control

The "statement" part of your equation must contain only one factual proposition so that when the witness gives their answer, there is no doubt at all about what the witness is saying. A new advocate (who has not had the benefit of reading this book) may ask a question such as this:

Q: "The car was <u>stopped</u> <u>outside the bank</u> <u>30 metres away</u> with <u>no physical obstruction to your view</u>, wasn't it?"

This is potentially four questions in one. Each of those four questions is shown above by underlining. When a question consists of several questions, we call it a compound question. If the witness were to answer, for instance, "yes" to the compound question, how would the court know which part they were agreeing with? The compound question is not a fair question:

a. Not fair to the witness: how should they answer if they agree with one part of the question but not another?
b. Not fair to your tribunal who have to try and draw a conclusion about what the witness meant by that single answer "yes";
c. Not fair to your client or your case: what if the tribunal understands the answer to mean something different than you and your client understand it to mean?

Consider what your tribunal, the jury, are being asked to do in the trial. They were not there in Marple outside the New Dilhorne Bank when the incident took place; yet they are being asked to consider the accounts from witnesses who were there and then decide whether those witnesses are reliable. Building the picture in stages makes it easier for the jury to follow you. Compound questions are the classic way in which the learner advocate tries to achieve too much too quickly. They are too long, too confusing and too difficult. You risk your jury losing focus and concentration. You will lose control.

Be clear about what the separate facts are that you wish to establish with the witness:

First fact: *the car stopped;*
Second fact: *outside the bank;*
Third fact: *30 metres away from the witness;*
Fourth fact: *no physical obstruction to the witness's view.*

You can see how the answer "yes" to each of those questions would give the court gradually more detail until, as a whole, the witness's full evidence provides a complete picture. This way, there will be no doubt at all about what the witness is saying.

The real value in building the picture like this comes if the witness disagrees with part of your compound question. The witness might simply answer "no" because they are rejecting everything you have said to them in the compound question or because they are rejecting one element of it. If, however, the four parts of the question are broken down and put one by one, you will at least get to know exactly what the witness agrees with and what they do not. And you, the questioner, can go on to explore the disputed facts if you wish to.

Tag Questions Are Good, but Be Careful Not to Overuse Them

In our examination-in-chief chapter, we explored how the question "what happened next?" is a useful tool. We have seen just now how in cross-examination, the tag question is also a useful tool. It is a basic building block. It is an effective way of leading the witness. It offers control. It is a "go-to" safe way of asking a leading question.

But a cross-examination that consists wholly of "tag" questions can begin to sound repetitive and clumsy, just as the question "what happened next?" can in evidence-in-chief. This is especially so if the cross-examination has to deal with many different topics and necessarily has to last a long time. Tag questions are a necessary tool, but they can be cumbersome.

This means that you are going to need to develop different ways of asking questions. You must vary your style to make it easier and more interesting for your tribunal or jury to follow you. You must always keep their attention!

It is not just for style purposes that you need to be able to lead effectively without asking tag questions. There are circumstances where you are absolutely prohibited from asking them. In cases involving young witnesses, the neurodiverse or witnesses with some form of cognitive impairment, the asking of tag questions can be banned by a judge in criminal proceedings.

This is because of the risk that a witness with particular vulnerabilities may simply agree with an advocate asking a tag question. This may be because the witness is influenced by their view that the advocate is in a position of power. It may be because the witness finds the structure of the tag question confusing on account of its two-clause nature, *statement + question.* We have devoted a chapter of this book to how advocates treat witnesses with these vulnerabilities.

The "tag" question, being the form of leading question that gives you ultimate control, can in some circumstances almost become "too" leading. You must be able to ask a leading question without relying on "tags". The ability to do this is one of the foundations of the skills of the advocate. It is essential for reasons of both style and procedure.

Now, let us imagine that we are the prosecutor and that we are cross-examining Tegan Plant about his previous convictions.

Q: "Do you have a conviction for an offence of blackmail?"

This is a closed, leading question. We say it is "closed" because it strictly limits the witness's answer to a single point. In this example, it is the fact that the conviction you are asking about was for blackmail. It is slightly less powerful than the *statement + question* formula ("You have a conviction for an offence of blackmail, don't you"). It does do the same job. Perhaps it is more natural and less cumbersome.

There are other ways to ask the question in a closed and leading way that you can probably think of, but our closed, leading question about the blackmail conviction may well be asked as two questions:

Q1: "Were you convicted of a criminal offence at Manchester Crown Court on 15 March 2023?"
Q2: "Was it a conviction for an offence of blackmail?"

There is another way of asking what would be a tag question but without the tag. This is where the inflection in your voice turns a statement into an inquisition. This tone or inflection is often referred to as the "inquisitive tone". This happens all the time in ordinary life, especially if someone tells you a remarkable detail. You will often check it by simply repeating it back to them but with your voice rising on the final word. Imagine, for instance, that your friend says to you:

> I have been working really hard recently, and the company has made a load of money, so the boss came in today and gave me the keys to a brand-new Rolls Royce.

Your natural reaction may be to say, incredulously:

> She gave you a <u>Rolls Royce</u>?

And you can imagine the way you would say it, with the emphasis on the words *Rolls Royce* and your tone really rising at that point. Demonstrating your raised tone is difficult with words on a page. We showed it just now with an underline, but we could use up-arrows to indicate the rise in tone, as follows:

> What! She gave you a ↑ Rolls Royce ↑?"

If you get the tone right, everyone can virtually hear the question mark at the end of the sentence. The non-tag, inquisitive-tone question would be:

Q: "The conviction was for ↑ blackmail ↑?"

The context tells us that our tone on the word ↑ blackmail ↑ is not likely to be incredulous or amazed, as it may be in our Rolls Royce example; instead, it is more likely to be firm and enquiring.

This technique is probably best deployed when you want to crystallise specific points for the jury by asking the witness to confirm things they have already said in answers they have given, perhaps over the course of a lengthy evidence-in-chief.

If we put that all together in a series of questions, we can see how it works. We can return to our role as defence counsel in the case of Tegan Plant, and your cross-examination of Hawkins about his description of the car.

> *Case Theory:*
> *Why are we asking these questions at all?*
> *Remember that because our client denies being there at the scene, we have no positive case to put to the witness about what happened, so our main aim instead is to explore the reliability of the whole of the prosecution evidence, seeking to undermine evidence where appropriate. We know that Hawkins describes the getaway car as being a Renault Clio – this supports the prosecution case that the getaway car was Amy Barber's car, on which scientific evidence was found that incriminates our client. But Hawkins says that the car he saw was white (Barber's car is green) and he says that the car had two doors (Barber's has four). Hawkins makes no mention of any door being a different colour, namely blue (the rear doors on Barber's car were blue).*

Imagine that the witness has already said in evidence-in-chief that the car was white. You want to establish more about his account:

(1) That he is saying the car was a two-door car; and
(2) That he is saying all of the car was white.

Your task is fraught with danger. You do not want the witness to give an answer that is anything like this: "oh yes, I remember now, there were rear doors and they were blue!" This is why you want to control the witness tightly.

Q1: "You were outside Martin's Mart Corner Supermarket, weren't you?"
Q2: "You saw the car pull up, didn't you?"
Q3: "You observed that the car had two doors, isn't that right?"
Q4: "Your evidence is that this car was white, isn't it?"

This pattern of questions is very safe. You, the questioner, are completely in control. But perhaps the pattern of the tags is getting a little annoying to everyone listening and they are getting distracted. You want your tribunal to be focusing on your cross-examination and how useful to your case the answers are. Try varying your questioning style:

Q1: "You were outside the ↑ bank ↑?"
Q2: "You saw the car pull up?"
Q3: "Your evidence is that the car was ↑ white ↑?"
Q4: "And that it had ↑ two doors ↑?"

Here in just a few short moments you are crystallising for your tribunal what you say are the important points about the witness's observation of the car. Strategically, you are setting things up for your closing speech so that you can draw the contrast with Barber's car, leading you to cast doubt in the prosecution case that it was your client in Barber's car who tried to rob the bank.

Notice that every single one of those questions is a leading question. The majority of them only really permit one of a limited range of answers: "yes" or "no" (or "I don't know"), though your aim in our example here is for the witness to agree with what you are saying to him. You are getting confirmation from the witness about information that you are supplying in your questions. You are controlling the flow of the information. You are doing so in a way that the tribunal is likely to find engaging as opposed to monotonous.

Undermining the Witness

We have seen how a good cross-examination uses the foundation skill of the leading question to elicit "yes" or "no" answers to all or nearly all the questions asked. So far, we have looked at the style of questioning in cross-examination and how best to do it in order to maintain your control. You will often have other aims, too, and most notably you may want to undermine a witness's credibility and/or to challenge their account.

Sometimes criminal lawyers use the expression "undermining a witness" very widely to mean both situations where you might be suggesting (a) the witness is lying or (b) the witness has, without being dishonest, got it wrong. As we look at this, remember that the first rule of attack is defence. Do not go all in. Do not become gung-ho. Every attack, every challenge, must be weighed against the risk to your case. Cross-examination is not the plaything of the gambler. It is not roulette where you pick a number and hope. It is planned and precise.

Remember also that not all witnesses are lying. An honest witness can be a mistaken witness. In conference with you, your client might label every witness against them as a liar. But that does not mean that *you* have to. Be calm, be dispassionate.

Your overall task is to show by your questioning of the witness why their evidence should not be accepted by the tribunal. You do not undermine the credibility of a witness by calling them a liar; you undermine their credibility by demonstrating that they *are* a liar. Start with the set of questions that the tribunal will be asking themselves about the witness:

1. Are they accurate?
2. Are they honest?
3. Are they reliable?

Undermining the Credibility of the Witness

A common error for advocates starting out is to operate on the basis that a witness who gives evidence contrary to your case must be lying. There are occasions when your instructions are that it is a lie or where the circumstances are that something could only be a lie; but you should always keep an open mind. Do not exclude the possibility of error rather than falsehood.

You will need to consider your case theory very carefully. Is the tribunal going to accept that a witness with no allegiance to either side and no reason to dislike the client is lying? Or are they more likely to think they are mistaken? Are you trying to establish a motive to lie? In which case deal with the reason why the witness is lying (showing the motive) before you allege the witness has lied. Before you suggest to the witness that they are lying, you should be sure that your grounds justify that accusation. You must demonstrate by your questions the reasons why the witness is lying. This way, when you come to make the suggestion "You are lying, aren't you?" everyone in court understands where you are coming from.

If your aim is to show that the witness is or may be mistaken, then equally you should deal with the reasons first so that when you allege the witness is wrong, your tribunal already has appreciated why you say that.

The Lying Witness

Maybe your case is that the witness has fallen out with the defendant or has a reason to lie to protect themselves, whatever it may be. But you do it by degrees, by one piece of evidence followed by another piece of evidence, then another, then another, until you have built the picture of a lying witness. Imagine this question:

Q: "You did not like the defendant, did you?"

This may well be an appropriate question to ask of a witness; however, it is not the place to start. There has been no build-up, no focus. No one will understand why you are making the allegation. Suppose the witness answers "Yes, I did", you are at an immediate disadvantage, and your task now becomes all about whether you can recover the advantage. Let us imagine that your suggestions are in fact true:

1. The witness did not like the defendant; and
2. The witness is dishonest and will try to hide the fact that he never liked the defendant.

By launching straight into your central allegation in this way ("You did not like the defendant, did you?"), you have potentially given away your strategy to a dishonest witness who will now change the way they answer your questions to try and defeat you. You have lost control, and it will be more difficult for you to recover the advantage.

Instead, build the picture. Let us take an example. It is not our case of *Rex v Tegan Plant*, because the facts of that case do not really lend themselves to an allegation that a witness is lying. Imagine this instead: you are defending and your case is that the main witness has invented the allegation against your client. Why? Because the witness is bitter – the defendant got a promotion, and the witness thinks he should have been the one to get it.

Q1: "During the year leading up to the defendant's arrest, you worked in the shop Jones the Butchers, didn't you?"
Q2: "And so did the defendant?"
Q3: "You wanted to be head butcher, didn't you?"
Q4: "You had been at Jones the Butchers for longer than the defendant, hadn't you?"
Q5: "You once said to the defendant that you were a better butcher, didn't you?"
Q6: "When the job of Head Butcher became available, was the defendant promoted to Head Butcher?"
Q7: "Did you tell the defendant he had stolen your job?"
Q8: "Did you hold a grudge against the defendant?"
Q9: "You disliked the defendant, didn't you?"
Q10: "Because you didn't like the defendant, you made up this whole allegation against him out of malice, didn't you?"

If it is your case that the witness is telling lies and has made up their account for a malicious motive, you must make this clear to the witness, and this is what our last two questions deal with very directly. We cover this obligation in the section of this chapter to do with "putting your case".

Strategically, you want to build up to that point. You would want to be as sure as you can of your facts such that you anticipate the witness will answer "Yes" to these questions, though perhaps with the exception of that very last question, maybe the last two. If the witness answers the last question or two "Yes", you can see that you will be some way towards establishing a motive to lie.

If, on the other hand, they answer "No", you have nonetheless had some success. Your aim of the build-up is that when you finally get that "No" answer, the tribunal are already thinking that they do not believe it. Run through those questions with a friend and have them answer "Yes" to everything except the last one or two – to which they answer "No" – you will see what we mean.

You have the advantage in this situation because you have built the picture and established first the *reasons why* the witness may hold a grudge. In many ways, it does not matter what the final answer is; you have established the facts upon which the tribunal of fact can make their own assessment.

Mistaken Witnesses

You may seek to undermine the witness not on the basis that they have reason to lie but that they are mistaken. How you do it is, in essence, the same as for a witness you allege is mistaken. Lay the groundwork for the causes of the witness's mistake. It was dark; it was a long distance away; it was a fast-moving incident; there was not a clear line of sight; whatever the facts may be that you can deploy. The important thing is that you build the picture gradually and clearly before the word "mistaken" or "wrong" ever leaves your mouth.

Remember what we considered previously, that the tribunal will be asking itself three questions about every witness they hear from:

1. Are they accurate?
2. Are they honest?
3. Are they reliable?

Each part of your cross-examination which seeks to undermine the account of the witness should be structured to assist the tribunal in determining in your favour at least one of those three questions.

The Best Cross-Examinations Are More About Build-Up and Less About Confrontation

By now you are getting the idea that cross-examinations are not angry, bad-tempered or argumentative. Your tribunal will never be assisted by an exchange that is little better than "yes you did/no I didn't". Ideally, you should aim to establish from the witness those facts of the case and of relevant background that the witness will agree with you about. Sometimes there will be a lot of areas of agreement;

sometimes there will not. Aim to start with areas of agreement as you build up to your conclusion, exactly as we suggest in the section above to do with lying witnesses. It is a good template, whatever the issue.

We suggest a structure a little like this:

Cross-examination topic [X]:

"Here is a fact; you agree with this fact, don't you?" – "Yes";
"And here is another fact that you will agree with?" – "Yes";
"And here is another fact that you will agree with?" – "Yes";
"And here is another fact that you will agree with?" – "Yes";
"And here is another fact that you will agree with?" – "Yes";
"You are mistaken in your conclusion when you say [X]?" – "No, I'm not!".

Cross-examination topic [Y]:

"Here is a fact; you agree with this fact, don't you?" – "Yes".
[and follow the same pattern as above]

You can see how this process, if repeated topic by topic, theme by theme, can have a great impact on your tribunal. All we are doing in this cross-examination template is identifying the topics [X] and [Y], or as many as you like, where our case disagrees with what the witness is saying, and we are dealing with them one after the other. We are ending each section with the challenge. We do not necessarily expect the witness to agree that our challenge is correct, obviously. We have to put the challenge as part of our duty to put the case. By building up to the challenge, we give the challenge more credibility when it comes.

If we look at an example to demonstrate the point from our case scenario *Rex v Tegan Plant*. Your client instructs you that he was not the man who went into the bank, that Miss Ullger who identified him has made a mistake. You could choose to put your case to the witness simply, like this:

Q: "When you identified the man at the identification procedure as being the man who came in the bank, you were mistaken, weren't you?"

But simply doing this would not really advance your case. The only realistic answer that you can expect from the witness is an indignant reply along the lines of "No, I wasn't!" Your question would stand lonely without any support. You are right to ask this question: your case is that the witness is mistaken, and you are obliged to put your case. But if you adopt the simplistic approach of just asking that single question, what will be the outcome? You will likely leave the court with the *only thing they hear on the issue of the greatest importance* to you being the witness's answer that your client was the man in the bank. That would be counterproductive to your case. You will have not in any way advanced your case that the witness is mistaken; nor will you have demonstrated why the witness's account that she has picked out the man correctly can be undermined. Advancing your case and undermining the witness are two central aims of cross-examination.

Your best way forward is to view the question about the witness being mistaken as a conclusion that comes at the end, not at the beginning. You build up to that conclusion by asking several questions first that set the scene. You fully expect the witness to deny that she has made a mistaken identification. Rather, your aim is to get to a position where the witness's answer to that, when the question comes, is already not credible.

Our advice, then, is that this question comes at the end:

Q: "When you identified the man at the identification procedure as being the man who came in the bank, you were mistaken, weren't you?"

Do not do it the other way round. Do not start with that challenge, then ask all your build-up questions afterwards. That is not effective. With that in mind, we are able to plan a cross-examination of the witness Isobel Ullger.

> *Case Theory:*
> *It suits the defence case that the witness gives evidence about the man's clothes being all dark because this is very different from the description offered by the eyewitness William Hawkins. Might this difference undermine the reliability of both witnesses? We intend not to challenge the witness Ullger on clothing description. But how can we maintain that she is reliable on clothing, but unreliable on her identification – is this a credible position for us to take? Bearing in mind that our client's case is he was not there, we cannot advance a positive case to the witness that any of her evidence is wrong, save that we say that her identification of our client as the offender was mistaken. The witness says the man had a limp and our client has a limp. This is unhelpful to our case; however, we have no basis for suggesting that the witness is deliberately inventing any of the details she has given in her evidence. We cannot suggest positively that she is wrong about any of her evidence. What we can do, however, is test it.*

Cross-examination showing that the witness's view of the man at the door was good enough for her to describe his clothes:

Q1: "You could see the man's clothing clearly as he entered the bank".
A1: "Yes".
Q2: "When the man came through the door, you looked up at him".
A2: "Yes".
Q3: "The whole length of his body was in your view at that point?"
A3: "Yes".
Q4: "You had a chance to take in his clothing?"

A4: "Yes".
Q5: "That is why you describe his clothing as being 'dark trousers', 'dark top', 'pretty much all black'?"
A5: "Yes".
Q6: "At this point, though, you did not identify that the man was wearing a mask?"
A6: "No, I didn't notice that until later".

Cross-examination testing the witness's assertion that the man walked with a limp:

Q7: "After the man came through the door, you saw him fall to the floor".
A7: "Yes".
Q8: "You saw him skid then crash into a potted plant?"
A8: "Yes".
Q9: "Then into a wall?"
A9: "Yes".
Q10: "After he had crashed into the potted plant and the wall, the man lay still for a time?"
A10: "Yes".
Q11: "Though you could hear him groan?"
A11: "Yes".
Q12: "When he got up, you noticed that he was unsteady on his feet?"
A12: "Yes".
Q13: "And when he was at your counter he winced?"
A13: "Yes".
Q14: "Did it look like he was in pain?"
A14: "Yes".
Q15: "He was still unsteady on his feet?"
A15: "Yes".
Q16: "You interpreted this unsteadiness as a limp?"
A16: "Yes".
Q17: "Could you have been wrong about that?".
A17: [the witness's answer does not really matter]

Cross-examination tackling the witness's ability to identify the man:

Q18: "What the man did in the bank was completely unexpected?"
A18: "Yes".
Q19: "And quite frightening?"
A19: "Yes".
Q20: "When the man stood in front of you at your counter position, he said that he had a weapon?"
A20: "Yes".
Q21: "And he threatened you with violence?"
A21: "Yes".
Q22: "You say you were terrified?"

A22: "Yes".
Q23: "His mask had become a little dislodged?"
A23: "Yes".
Q24: "Nonetheless, it still covered a lot of his face?"
A24: "Yes".
Q25: "His eyes were exposed?"
A25: "Yes".
Q26: "Though after the event you were unable to say what colour his eyes were?"
A26: "That is right".
Q27: "The man was only in front of you for a matter of seconds, after all, wasn't he?"
A27: "Yes".
Q28: "When you identified the man at the identification procedure as being the man who came in the bank, you were mistaken, weren't you?"
A28: "No, I was not!"

By the time you get to that crucial last question, you have *already established* the main facts that support your suggestion that the witness is mistaken. All the other questions (the ones you asked first) mean that when the witness comes to disagree with your final point, it does not matter so much. You can see how the structure of your questioning is helping you, how it combines with you undermining the witness, and how *your case that the witness is mistaken* is looking stronger.

It is often thought that every "challenge" part of the cross-examination has to be left to the very end and dealt with in a single batch of questions. There is no requirement to do this. It can lead to the conclusion of cross-examination being quite cumbersome. It might not make as much sense to your tribunal. In this situation, you typically end up putting a series of challenges, and there is a whole section of your cross-examination where the witness is disagreeing with you a lot. In turn, that may leave your tribunal under the impression that you have made a series of rejected points. You will have lost some control. Instead, spread the challenges out throughout the cross-examination. Deal with the challenge as you deal with that chapter of the evidence.

Dealing with Previous Inconsistent Statements

It is part of everyday life that we assess how far to accept what people are saying to us; what to believe and what not to believe. That goes for courts and tribunals, too – whether they are judges, magistrates, juries or any other kind of tribunal. You appreciate already that as an advocate it may be part of your job in a case to show why the other side's witness should not be believed, whether because they are untruthful or mistaken. An important part of that task is to identify whether the witness has said anything on a previous occasion that is different from what they have told the tribunal. Every advocate needs to understand how to confront a witness in cross-examination with a previous inconsistent statement.

Usually this comes about when you are cross-examining a witness who has previously given a witness statement to the police. Perhaps you are defending and you have had the witness statement served by the prosecution and the prosecution have called the witness as part of their case, for example William Hawkins in our case of *Rex v Tegan Plant.* Or perhaps the prosecution served you as defence counsel with the witness statement of someone the prosecution decided after all not to call as a witness; however, you have decided to call them as part of the defence case, and now the prosecution wish to cross-examine them on their witness statement. Those are just two examples. In fact, it could be any previous inconsistent statement from the witness made anywhere that you might wish to cross-examine the witness on.

We ask you to consider two important aspects of this:

1. There is a process that you need to follow in court if you wish to confront a witness with a previous inconsistent statement. In other words: "how-to?";
2. That process is cumbersome, and you should really only embark on it if the previous inconsistent statement is about a topic that you consider really matters in the case. In other words: "should you?".

We will look at each of those in turn.

How to Cross-Examine on a Previous Inconsistent Statement

This procedure is governed by statute, the Criminal Procedure Act 1865, sections 4 and 5 which together set the procedure that you must follow.

Section 4 is headed "As to proof of contradictory statements of adverse witness" and states:

If a witness, upon cross-examination as to a former statement made by him relative to the subject matter of the indictment or proceeding, and inconsistent with his present testimony, does not distinctly admit that he has made such statement, proof may be given that he did in fact make it; but before such proof can be given the circumstances of the supposed statement, sufficient to designate the particular occasion, must be mentioned to the witness, and he must be asked whether or not he has made such statement

Section 5 is headed "Cross-examinations as to previous statements in writing" and states:

A witness may be cross-examined as to previous statements made by him in writing, or reduced into writing, relative to the subject matter of the indictment or proceeding, without such writing being shown to him; but if it is intended to contradict such witness by the writing, his attention must, before such contradictory proof can be given, be called to those parts of the writing which are to be used for the purpose of so contradicting him: Provided always, that it shall be competent for the judge, at any time during the trial, to require the production of the writing for his inspection, and he may thereupon make such use of it for the purposes of the trial as he may think fit.

Let us continue on the basis that we defend the case of *Rex v Tegan Plant* and that the prosecution witness William Hawkins has said in evidence-in-chief that the car he saw was green. This is problematic for the defendant because it supports the prosecution case against him: Amy Barber's car, which has the defendant's fingerprints on it, is green. But we also know that in William Hawkins's witness statement, in which he gave an account a long time previously and just after the incident itself, he did not say the car was green; rather, he said it was white. We intend to cross-examine on that inconsistency.

Sections 4 and 5 of the 1865 Act describe a procedure that goes like this:

Q1: "In your evidence to the jury, you have said the car that the man got out of was green?"
A1: "Yes".
Q2: "You are certain of that?"
A2: "Yes".

[In Q1 and Q2 you are being fair to the witness by giving them an opportunity to think again about their evidence on that point. This introduction also serves to signal to the judge and to the prosecutor that you intend to cross-examine on a previous inconsistent statement]

Q3: (Addressing the judge) "Your Honour, may I ask that the witness's statement is passed to him?"
Judge: "Yes".

[The usher will pass the statement to the witness. In our case, William Hawkins has made one statement to the police. If he had made two or more statements, you would need to be clear which of his statements you would like to be passed to him.]

Q4: "Mr Hawkins, what have you just been passed?"
A4: "My witness statement".
Q5: "Does it contain your signature at the bottom of each page?"
A5: "Yes".
Q6: "Was the statement made on 19 November 2026?"
A6: "Yes".
Q7: "Please could you look at the top of the first page. Can you see that there is a declaration there?"
A7: "Yes".
Q8: "What does the declaration say?"
A8: (reading aloud) "This statement is true to the best of my knowledge and belief and I make it knowing that, if it is tendered in evidence, I shall be liable to prosecution if I have wilfully stated in it anything which I know to be false, or do not believe to be true".
Q9: "You signed that declaration, didn't you?"
A9: "Yes".
Q10: "When you signed that declaration, you understood the importance of the declaration?"
A10: "Yes".

Q11: "Please turn to the second page of your witness statement on the first line. Can you see the sentence beginning with the word 'The'?" [Pause while the witness find that part of the statement.] Do you see that now?"
A11: "Yes".
Q12: "Please read that sentence to yourself in silence and tell me when you have done that".
[Pause while the witness reads the line to himself. It is the line stating "The car was small and white and had two doors".]
A12: "I am ready".
Q13: "Having read what that sentence in your witness statement says, do you still maintain that the car you saw was green?"
A13: "No, I do not. It was white".
Q14: "Please read that sentence aloud for the jury?"
A14: (reading aloud) "The car was small and white and had two doors".

Case Theory:
What would your approach be if, in answer to your Q13, the witness replies something like, "Yes! I know what the statement says but looking back I am quite clear that the car was green!" On our facts, you are likely somewhat limited in what you do. Remember your instructions, that Mr Plant was not there and therefore he cannot give you any instructions about what colour the car was; nor do you have any evidence that Mr Hawkins is lying, or even any basis for suggesting that he might be. You therefore cannot directly suggest to the witness Hawkins that he is lying or even wrong.

You may nonetheless test the witness's evidence. If he gives you an answer like "Yes! I know what the statement says but looking back I am quite clear that the car was green!" you could question him about these facts:

- *His statement was made on the same day as the incident;*
- *In it he said that the car was white;*
- *In it he does not say that the car was any colour other than white;*
- *He has never since made a statement to the Police saying that the car was any colour other than white.*

Then follow those factual questions with the conclusion question: In his evidence today (and you can calculate how many years and/or months since the date of the incident it is that his evidence is now being given), is the witness really saying for sure that the car was not white? Who knows what he will say. But this is probably the best you can do.

In your career you will encounter other situations, unlike our scenario in *Rex v Tegan Plant,* where you are able to formulate a sensible case theory that the witness is lying. You will have a reasonable basis for suggesting that they have changed a significant detail from the witness statement deliberately when giving their evidence. If this is your case, you must put it directly to the witness at the end of the procedure. Not only is it fair to the witness to give them the chance to respond, it is right that you should make your position very clear in front of the tribunal, so that the tribunal fully understands why you have just taken them on this detour about what is in the witness's statement, about why it matters.

Should You Cross-Examine on a Previous Inconsistent Statement?

This is always the big question! We have just seen, in our example of the cross-examination of William Hawkins, that such questioning always carries risks. It is a judgement call you have to make each time whether to cross-examine on a previous inconsistent statement.

One thing is for sure: if the previous inconsistent statement relates to a matter of insignificance, then leave it alone. Cross-examination like this on a point that really does not matter might only succeed in proving to the tribunal that you are a too-smart lawyer who is only trying to trip the witness up. That is not how you want your tribunal to view you.

Putting previous inconsistent statements takes time. You must go through the correct and lengthy procedure. Is it worth it?

Traditional "Golden Rules" of Cross-Examination?

You may sometimes hear it being said that there are two traditional "golden rules" of cross-examination which are so fundamental to the skill that they are part of the building blocks:

1. Never ask a question too far;
2. Never ask a question to which you do not know the answer.

These are both elements of the "defensive" nature of cross-examination. They must have been repeated as advocacy advice more times than anything else. They are both rules that help prevent the reckless advocate from doing more damage than good. It goes without saying that we hope that by reading this book you are taking strides along the path away from recklessness.

Never Ask a Question Too Far

This is a very sound rule. It demonstrates that you, the advocate, always need to remain detached and calm in cross-examination. You always need to be evaluating each question and each answer. You need to be on the ground working your way through the evidence. At the same time, you need to be up above, able to look down and see the whole of the terrain below you, because you need to know if the path that you are so expertly clearing is bringing you to a cliff edge – if so, stop!

How do you know if a question is going to be *the question too far?* Measure each question and answer against the test "have I done enough?" This test requires you first to have a well-thought-out overall plan for the case (in other words, a sound case theory). What do you want to establish? What are you seeking to undermine? When your cross-examination is in full flight, you constantly need to be balancing "have I done enough" versus "am I going too far".

Each question you ask, no matter how closed the question is, gives the witness the opportunity to respond. It is a further opportunity for them to have their say, and that opportunity brings with it the potential for trouble. It may allow the witness the opportunity to explain away something that is inconvenient to them, or to return to a fact that you prefer is consigned to the dustbin.

And the rule is never more important than when you are doing well, when every answer is exactly what you want. The temptation is to think that this golden run is going to continue. The temptation is to think that the witness is going to keep giving you the answers you want.

That is when you need to think "have I got enough" and not "can I get more". Earlier in this chapter, we said that cross-examination should not be a gamble. It is tempting to roll the dice just one more time. But if you have enough – STOP.

Here is a set of questions that could go too far. Going back to our cross-examination of the witness Hawkins in our case of *Rex v Tegan Plant* about his observation of the car. Let us repeat our questioning from a few pages back:

Q1: "You were outside Martin's Mart Corner Supermarket, weren't you?"
A1: "Yes".
Q2: "You saw the car pull up, didn't you?"
A2: "Yes".
Q3: "You observed that the car had two doors, isn't that right?"
A3: "Yes".
Q4: "Your evidence is that this car was white, isn't it?".
A4: "Yes".

You will have noticed that that last question is asking the witness to confirm his evidence that the car was white. During the witness's evidence-in-chief by the prosecutor, he has said what is in his witness statement about the colour of the car, that it was white. On our case theory, it suits us that the car is described as white because the car on which our client's fingerprints were found was green. And remember that our client instructs us he was not even there, so he does not know anything about the colour of the car – white, green or anything else.

This last question is pointedly not framed in such a way as to give the impression that we are asking the witness once again to think about the colour of the car. We are anticipating potential disaster if we ask that question instead. We run the risk of this happening:

Q4 ALTERNATIVE: "And the colour of the car that you saw was white?"
A4 ALTERNATIVE: "Well, yes. [Pause] Though now you make me think about it, I suppose it could have been another light colour, maybe green or something".

Another example of a question too far is the question that you simply do not need to ask. These questions have established that the evidence is that the car was white.

Whilst it might be tempting to ask, "The car wasn't green, was it"? you do not have to. And imagine how you would feel if the witness paused, looked at you and began to say "now you come to mention it …".

Never Ask a Question to Which You Do Not Know the Answer

This is another defensive rule. It has to do with control. Do not run the risk of giving the witness the impression that they are being permitted to say whatever they want. It is a rule that you should keep at the forefront of your mind as an easy-to-remember rule of the defensive nature of cross-examination.

If we think of one of the aims of cross-examination being the control of the flow of information, it is vital that you know what that information is going to be. You want to be the one in control of the narrative. You cannot control the narrative if you are not in control of the evidence that the witness gives.

This is a simply stated rule which, if kept at the forefront of the mind, will help prevent the new advocate wandering off into uncharted territory. It will help you focus on controlling the witness with closed, leading questions. Have it as one of your golden rules.

These two golden rules are valuable. A little later in this chapter we will also see why the advanced advocate does not always follow them! But whilst you are building your skills, do not ask a question to which you do not know the answer.

Preparation, Planning and Structure

The final foundation skills for you to acquire are preparation, planning and structure.

Preparation

Even the most basic of cross-examinations requires preparation. And the preparation does not begin with the formulation of questions but with a reading and understanding of the whole case.

It is often said that you start your preparation by writing your closing speech and shaping your cross-examination around that closing speech. Are there any advocates out there that truly do this? It is a huge duplication of work. It is a complicated way to go about case theory and case preparation. The speech you write based on the papers is going to have to be written again at the end of the evidence. We discuss this further in the chapter on submission advocacy.

What you need to do first is to read all the case documents so that you understand what the case is all about. Then when you come later to prepare your cross-examination, you are not tied to some imagined closing speech, but rather you are guided by some fairly simple questions that you will have answered by the time you have read the case. Those questions are:

- "What am I trying to achieve?"
- "What does the law require in order to achieve what I want?"
- "What does the evidence currently say about those requirements?"

- "What facts do I need to establish?"
- "Which facts do I need to challenge?"

This is the application of case theory to preparing cross-examination. We will look at these questions in turn.

What Am I Trying to Achieve?

In a case which is proceeding to trial, "what am I trying to achieve" is the verdict that suits the party you are acting for. The verdict you are seeking depends on which side you are instructed.

What Does the Law Require in Order to Achieve What I Want?

"What does the law require" relates to the things you need to prove in evidence (or cast doubt on) in order to succeed. You also need to take account of the burden and standard of proof. If the other side has the burden of proof, then it is up to them to prove it; but if you have the burden of proof, then you need to, for example, if you are prosecuting a criminal case, prove the ingredients of the offence charged and the identity of the defendant as the offender.

The reality is that whichever side you are acting for, you will always need to know which side needs to prove what. Only then can you target your preparation appropriately.

What Does the Evidence Currently Say About Those Requirements?

You will need to consider what the evidence currently says about the facts that need to be proved. This will begin to help you refine what the issues in the case are based upon all the evidence that you currently have. If you are defending in a criminal case, this will cover basics like whether the defendant admits presence at the scene, but also whether the prosecution can *prove* he was at the scene. Is this in issue between the parties? Do the prosecution have sufficient evidence to prove it?

What Facts Do I Need to Etablish or Challenge?

Sometimes lawyers talk about "good" facts and "bad" facts at this stage of the preparation. Perhaps that is too simplistic. Instead, look at the evidence and ask yourself this: in order to establish the objective that I have already identified, which bits of the evidence do I need the tribunal to form a view on and what view do I need them to form? On a realistic view of the situation, what chance do I stand of getting the tribunal to form the view that I want them to form?

This is the thought process by which you begin your preparation. How you choose to do it is entirely personal. You may write out pages and pages of notes. You may annotate a PDF. You may print out the papers and read them with a high-lighter pen in hand. You may make lists of bullet points grouped by subject. You may just read and think. However you go about it, this is the preparation stage.

Planning

Now you plan. This is the point at which your preparation becomes more detailed. You know the evidential place where you want to end up, so this is where you begin to plan the questions in relation to each evidential area. This stage requires you to prepare how you will ask the questions and what you will deploy in the course of the cross-examination. Which exhibits will you use? Get the detail ready about which page numbers and paragraph numbers you will be asking the witness to look at. Will you be playing some CCTV footage to the witness – which section of the footage? Can you get it lined up so that it is ready to go at the right part? Some advocates think of this planning stage as including "stage directions". Your notes will not only be the areas of questioning but also notes to yourself about the mechanics of what you are doing. You want it to be seamless and you want to show your mastery of the case papers at all times.

Structure

Then you come to structure. Structure has two elements. The first is the internal structure within each topic you want to deal with. The second part is the order in which you are going to approach each topic. There is no right or wrong answer to this element of the structure. It is a bespoke element dependent upon each case and each witness. It requires thought and preparation each and every time. As you do more cases, you will establish patterns of preparation that make the task quicker over time.

What do you start with? We go back to the question of what it is you are trying to achieve, what is it that you are hoping to get out of the witness? You may have one absolutely standout killer point. Do you use that first? This may unsettle the witness. It may leave their credibility in tatters, which you can build on during the rest of your cross-examination. Or do you save it for the end? This allows you to finish on a strong point. That may be the thing that the tribunal recalls most about the witness.

It could be that you have some useful detail you want to elicit from the witness. Is that going to be better achieved before you have deployed your more devastating, attacking point?

Use the effective method of leading questions to control the narrative. Add to your evidential picture by gaining useful evidence for your case. Plan your route to assisting the tribunal to decide whether the witness is honest, accurate and reliable. Know where you want to be and take the witness and the tribunal with you.

Control Your Pace

The final foundation stone: do not forget that you are responsible for the pace. Even more than in examination-in-chief, the temptation is to fire questions at the witness. Resist the temptation. Let the points land, let the judge take the note.

Cross-Examination in Civil Cases and Criminal Cases Heard by Judges

In civil litigation, the core principles of cross-examination are broadly the same as those used in criminal proceedings. The subject matter, however, can vary enormously. You might spend half an hour questioning witnesses about the fine details of a road traffic collision that unfolded in a fraction of a second. At the other end of the spectrum, you may find yourself engaged in several hours of cross-examination in a complex contractual dispute involving years of commercial dealings and extensive documentation.

A key difference to keep in mind is the nature of your tribunal. In civil cases you are usually addressing an experienced district or circuit judge – not a jury, and not a bench of lay magistrates. In other words, your tribunal is someone who has spent many years in legal practice and has observed countless cross-examinations. While you must still address inconsistencies and put your case fully, be aware that a professional judge will often grasp the point you are making far more quickly than a jury would. You will find that if you labour a point unnecessarily, all you will do is test the patience of your tribunal. This would be a distraction from your main aim, which is to keep the judge focused on the value of the points you are making and on the evidence that you are uncovering.

That said, the balance can be subtle. Effective cross-examination in civil practice requires you to understand the judge before whom you are appearing and to tailor your approach to their expectations and working style. This is not so easy to do as you begin your career, and it will help to seek out advice from other advocates about your judges.

A similar point can be made in relation to criminal trials and hearings conducted in front of district judges in the magistrates' courts. Like the district judges in the civil jurisdiction, they are professional judges who will likely understand intuitively the direction that your cross-examination is taking, and you should take a similar approach. The position regarding the future of crown court trials seemed uncertain during the Labour Government's period of office in the mid-2020s. Proposals were put forward to create a procedure whereby some trials may be heard by judge alone without a jury. This would represent a significant change for criminal practitioners who would need to adjust their presentation style from jury advocacy to judge advocacy. This may have a somewhat counterintuitive result. It may be that the more junior criminal practitioners, with fresh and recent experience of magistrates' court advocacy in front of district judges, would adjust to this new style of crown court advocacy more readily than practitioners who have years of jury trial experience.

Advanced Technique

The first rule of advanced cross-examiner club? Break one of the golden rules. Remember one of the foundations of your cross-examination skills:

Do not ask a question to which you do not know the answer.

This golden rule is absolutely a safety-first approach, a basic safeguard. It may not actually work with what you are seeking to achieve. The position for the more advanced advocate is subtly different:

Do not ask a question without first thinking through the possible answers you might get and what damage any of them may do to your case.

The advanced advocate appreciates the reality: it is not truly possible to know the answer to every question you are going to ask. If you did, you would have a knowledge of the future that would enable you to have the lottery numbers each and every week. Even if your client, from their knowledge of the witness, has told you what they think the answer will be, you cannot know for sure. You sometimes must ask a question to which you do not strictly know the answer. You must enter into the void – a little.

The most skilled cross-examiners are not necessarily the wittiest or the most eloquent. These elite advocates possess two essential qualities that heavily inform their approach to cross-examination: *imagination* and *empathy*. It is the qualities of imagination and empathy that will allow you the vital advantage of *anticipation*. They combine to give you the ability to drop yourself into the scene or event that the witness is giving evidence about and look around. What do you see? Who is there? Who is not there? What is everyone doing? Why?

Recreating this scene in your imagination is more powerful than any AI simulation. And that is because you can layer empathy over the imagined scene. You can begin to think about how others would react. What do you think the range of reactions would be? Do the reactions that people are describing fit the scene as your imagination and empathy tell you the scene was like? Or is something not quite right about what the witness is saying?

It is by this method that you begin to anticipate what answers may be to certain questions that you will pose in the course of your cross-examination. And it is by this method that you evaluate in your preparation and planning the potential damage that one answer may bring versus the reward that another answer may bring. It is by that assessment that you can decide whether to ask the question – and how to ask it. It is a judgement call. At our fundamental level, we learned not to ask a question to which we do not know the answer. Now we are learning not to ask a question to which you have not anticipated the potential answers.

That then leads us to the next advanced application of your cross-examination skills. Anticipating the potential answers allows you to plan your cross-examination in order to block each of the potential answers as you get closer to the ultimate point.

Blocking Unfavourable Answers Before You Get Them

This requires anticipation of the answers along the way and controlling the narrative by use of closed leading questions to block each turn so that by the time you get to the ultimate destination you have reduced the risk of an answer that is bad for you. You cannot eliminate all risk, but you can control it. And control is your best weapon.

The perfect place that you want to end up is the place where the witness has been so boxed in that there are really only two potential answers to the question and each of them is of benefit to your client's case.

The classic example of this comes with a police witness who has not recorded an important detail in a notebook or statement. You start by building the picture showing why it is important to record things in the note. You establish that the note was made contemporaneously to the events it describes. You get them to confirm that they know the importance of such records. You layer in any relevant statutory requirement. You then get them to confirm the detail. You highlight the relative importance of the detail. You get them to acknowledge their awareness of the importance of the detail. And then you get to the note and the absence of the detail and by the end of it they are left with only two choices – either it did not happen or they neglected to record it.

You may not know which way they are going to choose, but you have anticipated a range of answers and then steered the factual stages along the way so that you control the destination as being advantageous to you no matter what.

We can look back at the cross-examination of Mr Hawkins where he was asked about his previous inconsistent statement. The advanced advocate would anticipate that Mr Hawkins might adopt his previous statement as correct or might reject the contents of the written statement. Before engaging the "previous inconsistent statement procedure" and getting him to look at his witness statement during your cross-examination of him, the advanced advocate would ask a series of questions along the lines of:

Q: "You made a statement to the police?"
Q: "That statement was made in the hours after the incident?"
Q: "What you had witnessed was fresh in your mind?"
Q: "You realised that it was important to give the police as much detail as you could about what you had seen?"
Q: "And it was important to be as accurate as possible, wasn't it?"
Q: "After giving the statement, did the officer read it back to you?"
Q: "Did you read it through yourself?"
Q: "You then signed it?"
Q: "By signing it you were stating that its contents were true and accurate, were you not?"
To the Judge: "May the witness be shown a copy of their statement".

This is a handful of questions that are asked in anticipation of the witness either accepting that his account in his witness statement is more likely to be correct or rejecting his account in his own witness statement. You could not know in advance what the answers are going to be when you confront the witness with the inconsistency, but you have anticipated the possible answers and prepared the groundwork by getting the witness to bolster the accuracy of what they write in their witness statement.

Open Questions

Up to this point, the whole building blocks of cross-examination have been the leading question. Whilst leading questions are forbidden by the rules of evidence in examination-in-chief, non-leading questions are not forbidden in cross-examination. And there are times when you can deploy them to devastating effect.

This once more requires you to have done all the groundwork and anticipated all the possible answers. Any hint of risk, either in the lead-up work or in your assessments of what could be said, and you absolutely do not go near asking a witness to explain themselves, but there are times when asking "why?" can be absolutely devastating.

It is one of the few instances when the witness's inability to explain is going to be the pinnacle of your hard work. But this can very easily fall into the category of a question too far. If the witness explains, if you have not shut off every avenue available to the witness, it can undo all your work.

Never gamble. Always err on the side of caution. But if you are in that moment and have the confidence in your work building up to the point, asking an open question which the witness cannot answer is a tool in the armoury. Only do it if you have truly anticipated every possible answer.

The Difficult Witness

Every well-prepared advocate will come up against the difficult witness: the witness who does not answer your question. Turn this to your advantage. When the question goes unanswered, or when the witness answers the question that they wanted to be asked, simply ask the question again in exactly the same way. If that does not get an answer, ask it a third time, this time politely indicating that the witness has not answered the question. On the fourth go, politely point out to the witness that this is their opportunity to answer the important question that they have not yet taken up and ask the question again.

There comes a point when the witness's failure to answer becomes a good point for you in itself. It signals to the tribunal that the witness has no answer or wants to hide the answer. It undermines them as a reliable witness.

Final Points

An important additional point is the tone of voice. You have to be prepared to cross-examine in a range of tones. Bombast may work occasionally but not in every situation and with every witness. There are times when you want them to help you; shouting at them is not going to help that. In fact, shouting at them is never going to help.

Use your tone, your language and your pace to assist in the control of the witness. Vary the way you speak. But do not overdo it. Be polite and pleasant, not fawning and smarmy. Be assertive and strong but never shout or be impolite.

Control but do not bully. Be confident but not cocky. Be understanding but never shy of dealing with everything.

The final, underrated skill of the expert cross-examiner is knowing when not to. You should never be eager to cross-examine every witness that the other side have paraded in the case. Only ever cross-examine with a purpose and an intent, done to a plan.

Ask yourself these two questions:

1. "Do I *have* to challenge this evidence?"
2. "Do I have *anything to gain* from this witness?"

If the answer to both these questions is no, make the wise choice and back away. The best form of defence, when it comes to cross-examination, is to take the decision not to cross-examine.

5 Re-Examination

Re-examination is the process by which you can ask questions of your own witness once all cross-examination has concluded. The purpose is to clarify or further explore anything that has arisen during the course of cross-examination. The form of questions in re-examination is the same as the form of examination-in-chief, that is to say, non-leading questions.

Fundamentals

The temptation to lead your witness in re-examination is in some ways even greater than the temptation to lead in examination-in-chief. You have just listened to your opponent ask a series of leading questions that have led to the point where you are going to ask questions in re-examination. Because you are not in the "examination-in-chief" section of the witness's evidence, your mind can deceive you into thinking that the rules of examination-in-chief do not apply. Also, your mind is used to hearing the leading questions of your opponent, and it is easy to simply get to your feet and replicate what has just gone before you. It is very tempting to ask the question in a way which leads the witness to the answer that you want. Do not do it!

The defining nature of re-examination is that the areas you ask about have to arise from the cross-examination. You cannot ask about any and all aspects of the evidence. Your re-examination has to be prompted by the questions asked and the answers given in cross-examination.

How-To

Not Leading

The technique in re-examination is not to lead. The challenge is that the witness has already given their evidence, so how do you go about re-examination in a non-leading way? What would have happened after the cross-examination of Miss Ullger? If the witness has been cross-examined to the point that they have perhaps accepted that they did not see the full face of the person that they have identified as the offender, it can instinctively be tempting to ask a question such as:

DOI: 10.4324/9781003602019-5

Q1: "You have said that you did not see their full face, but you did see their eyes and distinctive limp, didn't you?" (leading)
A1: "Yes".
Q2: "And that's how you have subsequently identified them?" (leading)
A2: "Yes".

Better questions might be these:

Q1: "You have said that you were not able to see their full face; what could you see?"
Q2: "Could you see anything else?"
Q3: "Other than their face, was there anything else that enabled you to identify them?"

Do not set out with only damage limitation in mind

Be sure to adopt the right mindset. It is sometimes tempting to think of re-examination as being all about repairing the damage done in cross-examination, but this is the wrong approach. If damage limitation is your mindset, you will almost always end up focusing on those topics where your opponent has done the most damage to your case. In doing so, you may not be able to do much about certain specific points, and you may not in fact be able to repair the damage. There is a great risk that if you focus your re-examination on damage limitation, you might only appear to be highlighting the strength of the points made by your opponent.

A "damage control" re-examination might do your case even more damage. What has been said in cross-examination has been said and cannot be un-said. It is *out there*. You cannot turn back time. If you ask more questions about a topic touched on in cross-examination, will you end up harming the credibility of your witness more than it has already been harmed? This can happen if the tribunal of fact gets the impression that the witness is modifying their evidence to suit the questioner. Will re-examination repair the witness's credibility or damage it further? There is a great risk of causing further damage.

Do not think of re-examination solely in terms of trying to counter the points made in cross-examination.

Before you re-examine, ask yourself if you even should re-examine

Before you begin to re-examine, it is very important to ask yourself two questions:

1. "Do I need to re-examine?"
2. "Is it going to improve the quality of the evidence?"

It is always a good idea to pause before beginning to re-examine. Do not leap to your feet as soon as your opponent sits down. Give yourself a second or two. Get to your feet and give yourself another second or two. If need be, pour a glass of water to give yourself a couple more seconds. All of this should not take more than a few seconds, but there is no rush. Let your mind focus on the task at hand – whether and how you will go about it.

The Correct Mindset

Rather than engaging in damage control, what should your approach be? For re-examination, the mindset you want is to focus on areas where there has been misunderstanding or incompleteness in the witness's evidence. This could be where the witness has misunderstood the question, or where attention has been given by the cross-examiner only to part of the witness's evidence.

You know the nature and detail of your own case, and this will inform your view about whether re-examination is necessary. By the time you have got to your feet, you have been able to view the cross-examination of your witness as an observer, not a participant. This has allowed you to recognise where perhaps a question has been misheard or misunderstood by the witness.

Ideally, you will be in a position where you have recognised that here, at the end of cross-examination, *as things presently stand*, the evidence may be confused or confusing. Your focus should therefore be on clarifying those features of the evidence that, in your judgement, need some further explanation.

Sometimes you want to ask questions that put the answers given in cross-examination in the correct context.

In re-examination, you may want to repeat the question that was asked in order to ask for further clarification. Just repeating the question may prompt the witness to realise the error or incompleteness in their answer. You can also take the opportunity to ask further questions in clarification:

Q: "You were asked how long you had seen the man's *face* for"

- "How long did the incident last?";
- "Where were you looking during the incident?";
- "What could you see of the robber?";
- "When did you first see his face?";
- "What other features about him did you observe?".

There is some scope for getting a witness to repeat evidence that they have already given but keep this to an absolute minimum. There are times when you want the witness to repeat that a key part of their evidence is still maintained, for example that they recognised the defendant as the robber; however, it is much better to do this as the conclusion to a series of questions. Your goal is to provide the best context and reasoning that leads up to the ultimate point. Get the witness to explain how it is that they recognised the defendant, not just that they did recognise him.

Note-Taking

Having a good note becomes of paramount importance in how you re-examine. Once you recognise during cross-examination that a witness has been asked a question which they may have misheard or failed to understand properly, you should make a note of *the question and the answer.*

How you generally take notes will be a matter of personal preference for you. Some advocates write each question and each answer as best they can. Some incorporate the question into the answer as a narrative note. Some handwrite their notes, others type. Your notes of the cross-examination are likely to be continuous, or a "running note" of what the witness has said.

Whatever method you use to take your notes generally, make sure, however, that you write or type the specific question and answer if you consider that the topic may be something that you want to re-examine on – this will help you formulate precise questions.

You also need to work out *how* you are going to make the notes of matters you need to deal with in re-examination. Will you make these notes on a separate page of your notebook or in a separate Word document on your screen? Will you just keep them as part of your running note, and use a highlighter, or draw a box round them, so that you can easily locate them when you begin to re-examine? Your system is what works for you. Just make sure you keep a note of the question and answer relating to matters you may wish to re-examine on.

Civil Cases

In the civil courts, re-examination is governed by common law principles and by the Civil Procedure Rules. It is generally approached in a restrained and highly purposive way. Its function is confined to clarifying or explaining matters that have arisen from cross-examination, and advocates must not use it to introduce new topics, bolster credibility impermissibly, or undo concessions properly made.

Civil judges are typically robust in enforcing these limits, reflecting the emphasis of the Rules being on efficiency and discipline in the presentation of evidence. Re-examination is therefore expected to be concise and tightly focused, addressing only genuine ambiguities or misunderstandings created by the opposing party's questioning.

That approach is reinforced by the overriding objective in Civil Procedure Rule 1.1, which requires the court to deal with cases justly and at proportionate cost. In practical terms, this means that re-examination in civil proceedings is often even shorter than in criminal trials (if conducted at all), with judges willing to curtail questioning that does not materially assist the resolution of the issues.

The court's active case management powers, including control over the evidence and the manner in which it is given, shape how re-examination is conducted. Advocates must therefore be strategic and selective, using re-examination not as a safety net but as a precise tool to ensure the court has a clear and accurate understanding of the evidence relevant to the matters it must decide. As in criminal practice, it is generally better not to undertake re-examination at all, because it can make a bad situation even worse. It is for you as the advocate to make this judgement call.

Advanced Technique

If you do not have to re-examine, then do not. If you think you might have to re-examine, think about it. Unless you really have to re-examine, then do not do it. There are a number of reasons.

Sometimes, you just cannot repair the damage. It is better to focus on the good material that you have, rather than try to chase a point that you have already lost.

If the witness has not been undermined too much, then trying to achieve perfection in re-examination may give the appearance that you are overly worried about the points that have been made against you in cross-examination. If you give the impression you are not confident in your case, your tribunal may wonder why they should be confident in it.

Re-examination always brings a risk that the witness may say something which is even more damaging to your case. Remember that you cannot lead the witness and to that extent you have less control. Only seek to correct or clarify something you are confident the witness will correct or clarify. Re-examination is not a time for exploration and adventure.

Be very aware of not seeming to force a witness at this stage to a certain conclusion or piece of evidence. Remember that sometimes a concession that the witness may have made about a certain point may in fact be something you can use later in the trial, perhaps in your closing speech, to bolster their overall credibility; making concessions shows that the witness is fair. Not every concession weakens the witness; it may boost their independence and credibility in the eyes of the tribunal. Conversely, the advocate who is seen to be trying too hard to shape the evidence in re-examination may be perceived by the tribunal of fact as no longer assisting the tribunal but chasing a preferred narrative.

Give real thought to your manner during re-examination. The demeanour of the advocate should always remain calm – expressionless, almost. That calmness is most required in re-examination.

The witness has just been cross-examined. It may have been uncomfortable for them. They almost certainly felt under attack. Now is the time for your voice to be their anchor point. You must be calm. You must be even. You must be slow-paced. Create that oasis of calm. Allow the witness the space to recalibrate and concentrate on the evidence. This is the moment when you absolutely cannot afford to look flustered. As with your demeanour during evidence-in-chief, you should remain calm and unobtrusive. Do not signal to the tribunal that the cross-examination was a disaster for your case.

6 Expert Evidence

In this chapter we will consider the fundamentals of expert evidence, what it is and how an expert witness is different from a witness of fact. Then we will break down our How-To section and our Advanced Technique advice into two sections that you will likely have to deal with as an advocate: examination-in-chief of experts and their cross-examination.

Fundamentals

Expert witnesses are witnesses who have two important characteristics. The first is that they have expertise in a particular area, an expertise that derives from scientific knowledge or perhaps technical skill, training or experience. This expertise must relate to something that the tribunal of fact is likely to need some help in understanding because it is outside their general knowledge and experience of life, plus it relates to questions of fact that they will need to decide. The second characteristic is that experts are permitted to express their opinions that follow from their findings.

A jury does not need an expert to tell them how to place a call or send a message from a mobile phone, for example; but they would need expert evidence if the trial needed to consider issues relating to how a call or message is sent from one handset to another or how mobile signals bounce from mast to mast if the person in possession of the phone is moving across the country.

The second characteristic of an expert witness is that, exceptionally, they are allowed to express an opinion. In our case *Rex v Tegan Plant*, the bank employee Miss Ullger is not an expert witness; she is an eye-witness who is telling the jury the facts about what she saw, heard and experienced of the attempt to rob the bank. Miss Ullger is an example of a witness of fact, and advocates must ensure that she gives evidence about the facts as she observed them. She may not give her opinions about the facts that she observed.

The reason for that restriction is that it is the jury's job alone to form opinions about the facts of the case. They can do that using their common experience of life. This is exactly the reason why we have juries; they do not need expert help to decide how much of Miss Ullger's evidence they should accept or reject, or how much weight they should attach to what she says. The trial process, allowing for examination-in-chief and cross-examination of the witnesses to test the evidence, is sufficient to enable the jury to do their job.

DOI: 10.4324/9781003602019-6

The scientist Harry Farooqui, on the other hand, is an expert witness. You will recall that he analysed body samples. Mr Farooqui knows nothing of the facts of the case from his own personal experience. He cannot recognise Mr Plant. He did not see the car pull up outside the New Dilhorne Bank. He did not see whether the robber walked with a limp or not. Mr Farooqui is simply presented with a sample taken from a car door handle and a sample taken from Mr Plant, and he compares them with each other having first applied DNA extraction techniques to the samples. He is involved in the case simply because the case calls for his expertise, and he makes a witness statement about his findings and conclusions.

His expertise goes way beyond what might be expected from a jury. If the subject area of his evidence were in dispute, and if he were called as a witness, Mr Farooqui would be allowed to give evidence to the jury about the expert opinions that he draws from his factual examination of the samples.

It is inevitable that a jury hearing expert evidence will learn about a topic that otherwise in their lives they may never have any experience of. Your task as an advocate is to make sure that the evidence is presented sensibly, clearly and easily so that the jury have no difficulty understanding it and understanding how they may use it in their tasks.

Can the Expert Help the Jury?

Here we are really considering whether the expert's evidence is relevant to the case. All evidence placed before the court must be relevant to the issues it is considering, and that applies equally to expert evidence. Taking our case *Rex v Tegan Plant*, you may have seen how Harry Farooqui's evidence is relevant to the jury's considerations. This is because on the facts of the case:

a) The prosecution has sufficient evidence that allows them to assert that Amy Barber's car was used by the gang of robbers to try and rob the bank;
b) Some DNA was later recovered by scenes of crime officer Afiya Lamai from the front passenger door handle of the car;
c) The prosecution says that it is a reasonable inference to be drawn that the DNA is the defendant's DNA;
d) If the jury accepts that, this supports the prosecution allegation that the defendant had used the handle to open the car door;
e) Which in turn supports the prosecution allegation that the defendant had travelled in the front passenger seat;
f) And that the journey had taken place on the day the New Dilhorne Bank was the subject of the attempted robbery – when the defendant alighted from the front passenger seat and went inside the bank.

All well and good. We understand why the scientific evidence is relevant to the case. But in the defence statement, Mr Plant is now saying something that he did not say in the interview with the Police: he now accepts that the DNA on the door handle may be his, and he gives an explanation about how it may have got there. You will be reading carefully, though, and you will have noticed that in his defence statement, Tegan Plant does not appear to be accepting that the DNA from the door handle is definitely his DNA, so this is still very much something you will have to prove by using Harry Farooqui's evidence.

Even a New Advocate Can Expect to Handle Cases Involving Expert Witnesses

Do not think that expert witnesses are only involved in complex cases. Advocates can expect to encounter expert witnesses very early on in practice. Most personal injury cases will require some form of expert. Virtually any criminal case can require an expert to assist the jury, whether that be in the form of medical evidence, scientific evidence that provides direct evidence of the identity of the offender, or evidence that relates to the interrogation of mobile phones or other digital devices. These are just some examples.

Is the Expert Really an Expert?

Guard against the mistake of reading an opinion in a witness statement and then "back-calculating" that the witness who made the statement is an expert. That is the wrong way round. Always start with the question of whether the witness is an expert, and only if they are, go on to consider the value of any opinion they have expressed. If they are not an expert, then their opinion is meaningless to the trial and very likely irrelevant and inadmissible.

Some criminal trials have been seriously derailed, and some convictions overturned on appeal, because the expert's credentials were not checked thoroughly.

Get an Expert in the Correct Discipline

Your first step is in identifying the correct discipline that you (or the jury) will need expert help with. You must obviously instruct an expert who has authority to comment and give an opinion on your case. This may involve some research on your behalf. Is it a psychiatrist you need, for instance? Or a psychologist? Or a neuropsychiatrist? Identifying the correct discipline is critical and will involve you doing some basic research on the differences between the various types of experts and reading a selection of CVs from experts in those fields.

Reading the CVs can assist you in understanding how the experts describe their areas of expertise. They should also be very open about the type of work they have been involved in and their court experience as experts. The other research you should undertake is to ask other lawyers for their experience in similar cases.

Sometimes that will lead to you realising that you may need two different experts in overlapping fields. If that is the case, make sure part of their instruction includes asking each of them about the proper sequence, that is to say, whether either of them needs to consider what the other says before reaching their own conclusion.

For example, a psychiatrist may want to see the expert toxicology results before deciding what impact drugs may have had upon a person's mental state.

What Kind of Instructions Should You Give an Expert?

Once you have identified the type of expert who you need to instruct, you will want to be able to advise on the nature of the instruction to give them. This involves you considering giving advice about the material they need to see. se Will the expert need any case documents, and if so, which ones? Will the expert need to see any records, such as medical records? Which other reports that may bear upon the issues will they need to see?

The expert should be provided with a letter or terms of their instructions. This will come from your instructing solicitor, but you should expect to work closely with them on the drafting of the terms of instruction. In so far as the case preparation aspect of this is concerned, you should advise on the issues in the case the expert should be asked to address. This will often be an overarching instruction (for example, to consider the defendant's mental state or the causation of an injury). You may have subsidiary questions about specific aspects. When you have an expert, take the chance to explore fully how far they can help you.

The expert may be instructed to consider whether it is possible either to advance positively a particular aspect of your case or to counter an aspect of the opposition's case. Or both. If you are countering an expert report served by the other side, do not simply advise your solicitor to ask your expert to comment on the written report of the other side's expert. You should still give consideration to whether there is some positive case that the expert can advise may be advanced.

In order to do this effectively, you should try to be involved in the instruction of your expert from the outset. What the expert is asked to consider is very important to the success of their evidence. If at all possible, you should advise on the area of expertise required and then the questions and hypotheses that the expert is invited to consider. Experts can be expensive, and if you can get everything you need from your expert in one report without the need to pass the expert further requests that cost more money, all the better.

The instructions should be drafted on the basis that the other side may see them. The questions to your expert can be direct and specific, and you may instruct the expert by identifying any hypothesis that you would like them to consider, but do not draft your questions in a way which asks the expert to come to a particular conclusion.

Once you receive the report you need to review it and consider whether there is anything else at that stage that you need to go back and ask the expert. Reading the report, however, is a skill in itself. Even on your first reading of the report, you need to begin to understand its contents. Read it with proper research tools open on your laptop or tablet and search for every word that you do not know and even those that you think you might know. Annotate the report at this stage so that every time you pick it up you know what the words mean and you know the sense and meaning of the whole thing.

Have a Conference with Your Expert

No matter whether you have been involved with your expert from the outset or if you are going to meet the expert for the first time on the day of trial at court having been instructed late and with the attendance of the expert already arranged, you must be sure to speak with your expert. It is much better if you can discuss the case with them in advance of the trial, but any time you are calling an expert, you need to make sure that you speak to them. Never call an expert without having spoken with them about the case.

There are a number of things you need to achieve in your conference. At the top of your list is making sure that you have understood the report correctly. The discussion that you have with the expert at this stage needs to be in terms that a non-expert will understand. This may not be too difficult because, of course, you yourself are not an expert! But you have read and digested the report and at least you will have understood it as much as you can just from the written word.

Avoid jargon and technical language in your conference. Every time jargon or technical language crops up, get the expert to explain it in simpler terms. By this method you will help yourself understand the evidence and how to explain it, and you will also be showing the expert that they need to communicate the subject matter in ordinary language. Your end point is to ensure that your tribunal of fact understands the evidence properly and in the way that best presents your case to them.

This is essential for your own understanding and preparation, and you would take this approach with any evidence, expert or not. If your witness is new to their role as an expert, then your conference becomes even more important to you. It serves an additional purpose: to help you assess how they will perform in front of your tribunal. You may have the world's leading authority in a particular field, but that expertise counts for little if they cannot communicate their conclusions clearly and intelligibly to a jury.

Your task is, therefore, twofold when dealing with your expert in conference. First, ensure that the expert can express their evidence in language that your tribunal will understand and be able to follow. Second, satisfy yourself that the expert is going to be able to explain and defend their conclusions effectively.

You will also want to explore with the witness whether they have any experience of the expert instructed on the other side. Often the world in which many experts operate will be a small one. Find out what the opposing expert is like in terms of their standing within the field and their personality.

Your Ultimate Decision

Your conference with your expert will help you make an important strategic decision about your expert witness: will you in fact call them to give evidence after all?

Sometimes you instruct an expert only because the other side has served their own expert report. In those situations, you might decide to use your expert solely to help you prepare a strong cross-examination of the opposing expert, without ever putting your own expert in the witness box. Whether you actually call your own expert may then depend on how well your cross-examination goes. In other situations, your expert may give you useful points, but you might judge that if you call them, the other side will be able to exploit weaknesses during their cross-examination. In that situation, you have to weigh the risks and decide whether calling the expert will ultimately help or harm your case.

These are decisions about trial tactics. These are decisions for you. They are not decisions for your expert. For sure, they are decisions that you should make in conjunction with other lawyers on your side and, importantly, with your client; but ultimately, the decision rests with the person who has control over the shape of the entire case – and that is you, the advocate.

In a nutshell, when in conference with the expert, ask yourself these questions:

1. "Have I understood their evidence?";
2. "How am I going to get everyone else to understand it?";
3. "How do I deal with the other side's report?".

How to Examine an Expert Witness in Chief

Build Your Own Understanding of the Expert Evidence

Understand. Prepare. Prepare some more. Check again that you understand. And then start to plan.

Expert reports can be lengthy documents. They can be dense with technical material. They can be very dull. This very dullness can be a barrier to your concentration and understanding, so approach your reading with a fresh mind.

When you are preparing your examination-in-chief of your expert, consider making yourself a glossary of every single technical term that is used in the report, explained in clear and simple language. Especially do this if the expert field is an area you have no experience of from previous cases. This will assist you in assisting the jury with their understanding. The internet is a wonderful tool that can help you. If you understand the evidence, you can get the tribunal of fact to understand it.

Each structure may be a little different. Your examination-in-chief plan may have to include a section dealing with hypothetical scenarios or assumptions. You may want to allocate time to ask about what another witness has done or the conclusions that they have come to. Your preparation gives you control.

Designing the Structure of the Examination-in-Chief

It is rarely useful if you simply ask your expert to recite the entirety of their report. A general opening question such as "so, Mr Farooqui, tell us everything you know" would be both lazy and clumsy. That would also be so even if, with more targeted questions, you were really asking the witness to just state with their voice what their report says in writing. These approaches risk translating a dull report into a dull lecture.

(Apologies to experts! We are not saying that *you* are dull; you certainly are not. It's just that any lecture on any topic at any time has the potential to be dull. It is the advocate's job to prevent that from happening.)

When you prepare your examination-in-chief, you will want to create a structure for it. That structure could begin with eliciting from the witness a summary of their particular expertise and an overview of what it is they do. This will allow the jury to see that the witness has authority to speak about their topic.

Perhaps you will then want the witness to state why they are involved in the case at all: what topics or questions relating to the case have they been asked to consider? Ask the witness to describe the material that they were provided with when they were asked to write their report. Highlight the key parts of that material. You may want to deal with the technical work they have done. Then you may come to their conclusions and opinions.

The important thing is that you need to plan your structure with your end point in mind. That end point is making sure that the jury have a full and clear understanding of everything that you want them to grasp. This means that the structure you create may be different from how the report is laid out. It also means that you will be editing again, editing out those parts of the report that the jury will not need in order to understand the evidence.

Do not forget the skill of signposting. We discuss signposting a lot in this book. When you are "translating" a technical written report into ordinary spoken English for the court, signposting is essential to help the jury recognise where each set of questions is heading and when you are moving topics.

Planning Questions for Technical, Complex and Key Issues

Once you have settled on the overall structure of your examination, turn to planning how you will present the expert evidence to your tribunal. Begin by identifying the areas that are either technically complex or central to your case. These are the issues the jury must truly grasp. Your task is to plan how you and the witness will communicate those points clearly and effectively. This is the essence of your role as an advocate.

A crucial part of that planning involves what we will refer to as the *mechanics* of advocacy. We discuss this in the chapter on submission advocacy and speeches. The mechanics of presenting expert evidence are just as important. People absorb information differently, and with a jury, you have no insight into how each of the individuals will process material. You must reach all of them at once, which is no small challenge. If your tribunal is a judge, you may have the advantage of knowing their preferred way of receiving information from past cases, and you can adapt accordingly.

Think carefully about how you will use exhibits to maintain interest and aid comprehension. Photographs, diagrams and charts can introduce variety and help the expert evidence "land" with the jury. They must be able to see how the expert's conclusions fit within the wider body of evidence they have already heard.

At this stage, step back and scrutinise your preparation. Look at your structure, your intended content, and your planned method of presentation. Be critical.

Identify any weak points. Ask yourself: *does this tell the story I need it to tell, and will it hold the tribunal's attention?*

Even then, your preparation is not complete. When you take the expert through their evidence in court, you must listen carefully and adapt to their answers. Expert witnesses usually know their reports well and can recount their material reliably, which allows you a measure of confidence that they will follow your line of questioning. But because their evidence may be contentious, you must explore disputed areas through meticulous, non-leading questions.

This requires a different approach from the one you might use with a factual witness. The emergency question "What happened next"? – which can be useful with lay witnesses – has limited value with experts. Instead, you need a bank of focused, open questions such as:

Q: "What did you do?"
Q: "What did you find?"
Q: "Why was that important?"
Q: "What did you conclude?"

These are the sorts of tools that allow an expert to explain their reasoning without being led.

Formulate a precise body of questions that will take the witness through both the technical material and the key issues. Your empathy and imagination, which help you guide a factual witness, will not serve you in the same way here. Expert evidence demands bespoke, carefully crafted questions that get to the heart of the matter without suggesting the answer. Because of the technical nature of the material, this must be planned in advance. You will not be able to improvise it in the moment.

Some of your questions will inevitably be more directional, not leading but designed to guide the witness into giving the necessary explanation. These may be as simple as:

Q: "Can you explain that in more detail?"
Q: "What does "DNA" mean?"
Q: "Can you give us an example of how that can happen?"

In short, plan not only the route through the evidence but also the specific questions you will ask when the terrain becomes most complex or most important.

Communicating the Evidence to the Jury: Presentation, Pace and Adaptation

When you are dealing with the witness in court, always remember pace. Slow the witness down. They know their stuff. You know their report. But this is not a conversation between the two of you where you can short-circuit things because of your knowledge. What is by now very familiar to you will still be totally unfamiliar to your tribunal; do not rush them to understand. You cannot race through the less important bits. Take it slow. That is why you never just set the expert off and let them lecture. Always control the pace and always be prepared to interrupt with a question to slow the pace down.

Advanced Technique for Examining an Expert Witness in Chief

With most witnesses of fact, you are aiming to be almost invisible for the jury or the tribunal. You want the witness to be front and centre of the show. When the jury receives conflicting accounts of the facts from the other side's witnesses, you want it to be your witness's account that the audience remembers.

Examination-in-chief of an expert is a little bit different. One of the things that you want to achieve is that the tribunal thinks of you as the person that has helped them the most to understand this difficult area of the evidence. You want to achieve that, to help the jury understand, but this is also an opportunity to bolster your credibility before the jury. You and the witness are very much joined together as one in this aspect of the case. You want the jury to think that you have mastered this material, have done the most to help them understand it and speak with authority about it.

Once you are confident in the skills required to obtain and elicit evidence from an expert witness in the courtroom, you can really turn your attention to the presentation of the evidence. You can work with your expert witness prior to trial on presentation material for the jury – what material by way of diagrams, images etc. can your expert provide that will help the jury understand their evidence. Here we are amplifying what we have called the *mechanics*.

Presentation material has two benefits. We already appreciate that different people understand and absorb material in different ways, so presentation material can really help you reach the full range of jurors effectively. Second, if crafted with care, it becomes your silent advocate in the jury room: a clear, concise summary of your essential points that the jury can carry with them into their deliberations.

It is important to pre-empt cross-examination when dealing with expert witnesses. Do not leave obvious points to be made by your opponent. Deal with weaknesses as well as strengths. Make sure that you have identified any limitations in your evidence and deal with them. A conceded weakness can be a strength in terms of credibility.

Try to conclude your examination-in-chief with a handful of questions that succinctly convey your best point, expressed in clear terms that are easy to understand. If you can manage all that in your final questions, you will have expertly dealt with your expert.

How to Cross-Examine an Expert

Foundational Preparation for Expert Cross-Examination

This is going to sound slightly repetitious, but your fundamental task is always going to be preparation. You have to know the expert subject material very well.

Read the report of the expert that you are going to cross-examine. Read your own expert's report again. Read any literature that is referred to in the body of the reports. Prepare and conduct your expert conference as we have described. All of this is just the foundations upon which you can prepare your cross-examination.

Where you have your own report and the report of the other side, devise a way of comparing the two reports so that you can identify precisely the points at which they diverge. You can do this by drawing up tables and schedules, or perhaps by creating a flow chart or a checklist. You will have to find the method that works for you, but always identify the points at which the two reports diverge. If you can do this, you will quickly identify the points that you need to win.

Ask for everything. Have sight of everything. See for yourself the notes that the expert has made and the records of any examinations that they have carried out. Make sure you have seen everything that they have seen. Compare what is in the report to what is in the notes.

More than with any other witness, however, do not chase every point in court. You may simply look like you are desperate. You must over time refine your judgement. If there is an error in the notes, only expose it and rely upon it if it makes a material difference. If it is an error that has no real consequence to your task or the jury's task, then leave it where it is, in the notes.

Identifying and Analysing Points of Divergence Between Expert Reports

Having identified the point at which the experts diverge, now focus on the why. Is it methodology? Is it error? Is it because of an assumption that either one of them has made? Identify the issue in this way and you will have planned your line of attack. The attack may not be just to show the expert is wrong; indeed, that will happen rarely.

The main focus of your cross-examination is going to be undermining the conclusions put forward by the other side and their assessment of the evidential position. Rather than being a demolition job of the expert, your line of attack is more likely to show the limitations of their conclusions. Can you show that they have gone too far or not far enough?

Executing a Focused and Controlled Cross-Examination Strategy

The approach that we are describing will bring to your cross-examination a good deal of focus. A focused and disciplined approach to cross-examining an expert keeps the process efficient and effective. Because most issues will be agreed until the point where the expert reports diverge, you will rarely need to explore earlier matters in detail. Your preparation already ensures that your questioning remains concise, which is essential when dealing with dense expert material.

It is crucial to maintain absolute focus throughout the examination. Experts will always know more about their field than you do, so your advantage lies in staying tightly anchored to the specific issues you have identified. If you drift into broad or general discussions, or move into areas you have not prepared, the expert will inevitably be more comfortable than you and will find their way out of any difficulty. Keeping the examination centred on your planned points is therefore essential.

Control is maintained through closed, leading questions designed to produce simple yes or no answers. The aim is to minimise opportunities for the expert to explain or expand, relying on your existing cross-examination skills to keep the witness contained.

If you have a positive case to put, it must be put to the expert. Typically, you will first challenge or undermine the expert's premise or conclusion before advancing your own proposition. As with factual witnesses, you may also have helpful material from the expert that you wish to highlight. A common and effective structure is to begin with the points that assist you, then move to undermining the expert's reasoning, and finally put your positive case.

Although expert evidence can appear complex, effective cross-examination rarely is. The key is to identify the central issue, focus relentlessly on it, and maintain the discipline to stay within the areas you have planned.

Common Pitfalls and Misguided Lines of Attack to Avoid

It is important to recognise the common pitfalls in cross-examining experts and to avoid falling into misguided lines of attack.

Before challenging an expert's status, you must be certain that the court could genuinely doubt their expertise. In almost every case, the witness will indeed be an expert in their field. If you launch this attack without a solid foundation, you risk signalling to the tribunal that you have little else to rely on.

You should also resist the temptation to create a hierarchy of experts. It can be appealing to argue that your expert is superior to the opposing expert, but the proper way to demonstrate this is through the substance and quality of their evidence, not through academic credentials or institutional prestige. The tribunal will be persuaded by the content of the testimony, not by which expert you are saying has the more impressive degree.

If you do attempt to establish a hierarchy, limit this to matters that a lay person can easily understand. This may require you to push back against your own expert's preferences. The fact that your expert believes their university department is superior does not mean that point will assist you. Unless the difference is so stark that any jury would immediately grasp it, for example where one expert holds a Nobel Prize and the other holds a third-class degree awarded last year. You see how extreme we have had to make this example in order to demonstrate the point. Comparisons are unlikely to help and may irritate the tribunal, who will want you to focus on the real issues.

Finally, avoid attacking an expert's methodology unless you have strong, well-supported grounds for doing so. By methodology, we are referring to the science or techniques that the expert has used. Whilst you may decide to cross-examine about things that were not done, only cross-examine that a particular technique is superior to another if that is generally accepted as the settled science. A weak or speculative challenge to methodology will only undermine your credibility and distract from the substantive points you need to make.

It is easy to imagine that cross-examination of an expert is going to have to be lengthy and complex. As we say, the best cross-examinations are nothing of the sort. Identify the main issue and focus on that. Do not disappear along misguided lines of attack.

Civil Cases

In civil practice you will find that the Civil Procedure Rules are very much concerned with proportionality, and so your usual means of challenging expert evidence as a civil practitioner will be in written format only, namely Part 35 Questions. These are written questions that one party may put to another party's expert (or to a single joint expert). Their purpose is to clarify the expert's report, not to cross-examine or to force the expert to change their opinion. The questions must be proportionate, focused and submitted within 28 days of service of the expert report unless the court orders otherwise.

Experts are usually not in attendance at trial to save costs, with the joint statement between the experts having sufficiently narrowed the issues pre-trial, such that the trial judge can make a determination on the remaining issues in dispute.

However, there are cases where the experts are unable to agree on key issues, and the value of the case justifies the experts attending trial. In such cases, you have to immerse yourself in the experts' area of expertise, so as to be close to being on a similar level of understanding of the topic as the experts themselves. It is the nature of civil practice that you often develop a speciality, e.g. become known for representing claimants in industrial disease matters. You may find that, over time, you almost know as much as the expert does about e.g. noise induced hearing loss or vibration white finger.

You may also find that the trial judge allows what is intriguingly referred to as "hot tubbing" of experts. This involves the experts giving evidence at the same time (concurrent evidence) as to their ideas and opinions in a direct interactive discourse between the experts and the trial judge. In this procedure, you may of course still ask questions of the experts, but the process will be closely controlled by the trial judge, who may ask questions first.

"Hot tubbing" is nowadays encountered less often than it used to be. Much more common now is what is frequently called "simultaneous evidence". This is where both experts are sworn in and they are cross-examined back-to-back on the same issue by each party to the proceedings. This is easier for the judge because they can let the advocates lead on the cross-examination, following which the judge may also have some questions of their own.

Advanced Technique for Cross-Examination of Experts

Explore the negatives. A useful line of cross-examination involves exploring what was not done: the tests that were not carried out, the material that was not available, and the steps that were not taken. There is almost always some way in which the expert could have put themselves in a better position. It might have been preferable for them to visit the scene rather than rely solely on photographs, for instance; to have had a greater quantity of body tissue to examine; or to have assessed the defendant much closer to the time of the incident.

There is always something to explore, particularly when the burden and standard of proof work in your favour. If you are defending, the burden may be on the prosecution to convince the jury so that they are sure that their expert's approach is almost perfect and unimpeachable. This allows you to cross-examine even when your own expert – whom you will not have served – is in complete agreement with the other side's report that you are challenging.

You should choose carefully the negative that you intend to focus on, ensuring it is relevant and potentially significant. You will almost always be able to identify such a point, but you must avoid relying on trivial or inconsequential omissions.

This method of preparation and presentation also allows you to cross-examine without running the risk that you will be doing more than presenting your scenario for the expert roundly to reject. This method provides structure and purpose beyond merely putting your case.

If you have one strong point, but only one, then examining the negatives can be an effective way to build towards it. You begin by establishing a series of omissions in the foundation of the expert's opinion. You then show that some or all of these missing elements would have improved the reliability of the expert's conclusion. Once that groundwork is laid, you connect those omissions to your key point. You develop that point fully and then return to the omissions, emphasising that they not only could have produced a more reliable opinion but may also explain why the opinion being advanced by the expert is flawed.

It is important to remember that the aim of cross-examining an expert is often not to force them to admit they are wrong. More commonly, the goal is to create space for your positive factual case or your own expert's opinion to be seen as viable. You are opening the door to alternative explanations. For this reason, knowing when to stop is crucial. You will rarely finish having completely defeated the expert. That is the stuff of courtroom drama fiction. You must form the judgement to stop once you have achieved exactly what you need. Continuing beyond that point brings two big risks. First, you give the expert an opportunity to recover lost ground. Second, you make it easier for your opponent to close the gaps you have created during re-examination.

Think of it this way: challenging the expert's omissions in cross-examination creates room in the evidential picture. Securing a few strong positive points lowers the baseline against which your case is judged. The combination gives your argument the space it needs to sit comfortably within the acceptable range. Once that gap is wide enough, stop – there is no advantage in stretching it further.

Remember that your expertise builds in the same way as your expert's does. By continually learning and by experience you will become expert at examining and cross-examining experts. As you begin to establish a degree of knowledge in a particular area and that is an area which comes up a lot in your area of practice, begin to get ahead of the game by reading the latest literature in that field. If you are a personal injury practitioner with a particular client base that sees you instructed in low-velocity impact injury, develop your own learning in that field. One note of caution, though – you will never be an expert in that field, in the same way as the actual expert is. You are a lawyer; you are rarely a scientist or a doctor as well.

A more limited version of this is to search the name of the expert that you are going to cross-examine. You are looking to see if they are published authors in this field. If they are, and their journal entries are relevant to the report they have prepared, it is worthwhile reading them. It may produce some material for your cross-examination, but it is just more likely to equip you with that little bit of extra knowledge and an appreciation of the thought processes of the witness you are about to cross-examine. It's an aspect of thorough preparation. Did we mention the need for preparation?

7 Submission Advocacy 1

Submissions to a Judge

In this chapter, we are going to deal with submission advocacy to a judge. We are going to approach the subject in a very general way, with the skills that are applicable across a wide range of different submissions, whether that be an application to exclude evidence, an application in civil proceedings, or submissions to an appeal court.

Submission advocacy is not a competition to see how much material you can pile on the judge's bench. You do not place every fact and every legal argument before the judge and say, "Have a look through all this and take whatever you like". Your job is to create one well-crafted dish: you decide what you are making, you select only the ingredients that genuinely belong in it, and you present the finished product in a way that is clear, appetising and easy for the judge to digest.

Find Your Voice

The heart of any great speech or submission lies in discovering your own voice – both in spirit and in sound, so we start with your actual voice, the sounds that come from your mouth. The first requirement is audibility: if your audience can't hear you properly, they will stop listening. Courtrooms come in different shapes and sizes. Sometimes your audience will be within almost touching distance; other times you will be so far away you could almost fit a tennis court between you and your audience. Whatever the layout of the courtroom, you absolutely must be heard. Speak in a voice that is loud enough for everyone in the room to hear. Do not mistake this for shouting; what we mean is having the ability to project your voice.

If you would benefit from some training in the skills of voice projection, do some research and acquire the skill. It will be money well spent. Remember that your audience may be in a room that looks and feels most unlike a courtroom. Coroner's Courts, to take one example, try very hard to shed the imposing "courtroom" image and they may be quite small. They may be an example of a room where you would deliberately not speak as loudly as you might in a large courtroom.

The ability of your audience to absorb what you are saying is not just about your volume. It is about your clarity, too. This does not mean you should analyse your accent and eliminate it. Far from it. We are not living in the 1950s. It is not about adopting the voice of the aristocracy or adopting "BBC English" – unless this happens to be how you speak anyway, in which case that accent is authentically "you"

DOI: 10.4324/9781003602019-7

and you should stay with it. It is about recognising that sometimes an accent can be more difficult to follow when it falls upon ears that are unfamiliar with the sounds. Make sure you enunciate the words clearly and distinctly, but do so in *your* voice, not a different voice which you are artificially putting on for your audience.

Some of the richest and most fabulous voices to listen to are not bland, uniform accents; rather they are accents that have the richness that comes from variety. This is worth repeating: use your voice that is authentically "you". Authenticity is one of the most persuasive tools that you have. An audience that instinctively finds you authentic is going to be more likely to give you their attention – and here is the most important thing: they are also more likely to think that the points you are making to them are credible. Your submissions or speech will be soundly based, you will have researched and prepared thoroughly, and you will have confidence in what you are saying. Do not let your submissions fail because you are delivering them badly.

You will want to pay attention to the physical sound of your voice, for sure; but you must also find your voice in the way you perform your advocacy. Advocacy is a deeply personal skill. What may work well for someone who you recognise to be a fabulous advocate is not necessarily going to work well for you.

Fundamentals

Structure ... and Preparation

Structure is everything. Structure, as we have already seen, always begins with preparation.

You need to master both the facts and the law of your case. Before you begin to think about what you are going to say and how you are going to say it, you need to know what the evidence is, what facts are established; what, if any, facts are in dispute; and what the legal framework is. The extent of this knowledge is going to vary from case to case and from submission type to submission type.

This means that you must read, analyse and record all the salient evidential material. How you analyse and record is going to be different from how someone else does it. Some cases will be fact-heavy and require schedules and chronologies to make sense of it all. Others, as is often the case in appellate advocacy, will have a largely settled evidential picture. By this we mean that no one disagrees any more about the facts, and the issues are mainly about whether the law has been correctly applied. But whatever your case and wherever it is being argued, you absolutely have to make sure that the facts and the evidence are at your fingertips from the moment you begin your preparation.

How do you do this best? It will often assist if you start noting page references from the very outset. Where there is something that you appreciate has the potential to be of key significance in the case, make a note for yourself as a reminder about where it is found. A little like a revision note, this can help embed the source in your mind. And it allows you to incorporate the references into the notes you make for your submissions or any other written documents you produce in support of your arguments.

Once you have the facts and evidence assessed, you need to master the law. Even if you think you know the law, double-check it. There are probably whole books devoted to techniques of legal research. For the purposes of this chapter, there are just a few observations that may be of assistance.

First, begin with solid commentary, not the raw cases or statutes. Let the people who have already done the hard work do the heavy lifting; you can piggy-back their insights. Read journal articles and textbooks. These are your base.

Second, read around the topic. One drawback of digital research is that on a screen you often do not see the paragraph that came before the extract in the practitioner text that you're reading right now. You do not see the subject headings on the page either, or the material before it or after it. There are many times when that will not matter, but there are also times when it does.

Often you need to see beyond the words currently appearing on the screen for context or in order to expand the way you are thinking about something. It is not a bad idea to go to the print edition or the PDF version of the chapter that your research takes you to. Let the search engine take you there but give your eye the freedom to wander around the words.

Third, use digital tools. Use artificial intelligence. But use it in a way that makes you the final arbiter as to whether something is correct or not. If there is a reference to a case, find and read the case. Make sure the digest you are given is actually what the case says. And that the case actually exists.

Finally, identify what the fixed law is. Then work out where the edges are, where the points have yet to be decided. The fixed point is your guide; the edges are your opportunity.

Having done this preparation, you should be able to ask yourself three questions (and also answer them):

1. "What is the rule?";
2. "Where does the rule come from?";
3. "How does the rule apply to the facts/circumstances of this case?".

And so you now move from the preparation of research to the preparation for presentation. This is all about the structure. We now slightly adapt the three questions that we have asked ourselves above:

1. "What is the legal question the judge must answer?";
2. "What order do I want the judge to make?";
3. "What must the judge find in order to rule in my favour?".

How-To

A Universal Structure

We can now develop an almost universal structure for you to follow when putting your submissions together:

(i) Introduction;
(ii) Legal framework;
(iii) Relevant factual/legal matrix;
(iv) Positive argument;
(v) Counter argument;
(vi) Conclusion.

We will now consider each element separately.

(i) Introduction

Begin by telling the judge what the application is all about and what it is that you are seeking to achieve. This should be concise and direct:

> Judge, this case involves a commercial dispute between former partners in an engineering firm, and we seek today an injunction that prevents the defendant from working in the same industry.

Or:

> My Lord, it is our submission that this confession was obtained in circumstances that may render any such confession unreliable and we invite you therefore to exclude it from evidence.

Or:

> May it please Your Honour, the defendant falls to be sentenced for the offence of robbery, and the aim of these submissions is to persuade Your Honour to impose a suspended sentence of imprisonment.

By doing this, you make the judge aware of exactly where you are seeking to take her in your submissions and what you want. There is no reason why submissions should be a suspense thriller. Your address to the judge should not be a mystery!

(ii) Legal Framework

Set out the legal fundamentals first: address the judge about the test that she has to apply, about the relevant statute and about the leading case or cases. Do not be afraid to state the obvious, just do not seek to explain or demonstrate the obvious. By way of example, if a court is determining something to the criminal standard of proof, you need only say "Your Honour would need to be satisfied so that you are sure". It requires no further explanation or embellishment.

At this step, really confine yourself to the leading authority that establishes clear principles. Time and time again, the judiciary is critical of the over-citation of authorities. You should never cite a case for the sake of it. In this part of your submissions, you should only rely upon a case that establishes a fundamental principle.

(iii) Relevant Legal/Factual Matrix

Now knit the key facts of the case into the legal framework. Only mention facts and evidence that genuinely drive the legal issue. Remember the point from the start of this chapter: do not unload everything you know or everything you have read. You are here to persuade, not to show off.

This will inevitably involve you making selections. It is crucial that you do this. When it comes to the facts, ask yourself, "is this fact relevant to the decision that the judge is going to have to make?" If it is not relevant, do not waste any time on it. When it comes to authorities, ask yourself, "Is this case the reason why the judge will be persuaded one way or another in the case?" If the answer is no, leave it out.

The judge does not need to know how you got here. It is not a mathematical examination where it is important to show your workings out. It is about you persuading the judge to do what you want her to do. Keep it simple. Keep it focused. Keep it concise.

(iv) Positive Argument

This is where you want to draw the first three sections together. You explain how the facts that you have set out will engage the relevant law in a way that the judge will feel properly justifies her granting the order you seek.

This is the section where you may introduce a wider selection of decided cases which help further an understanding of the principles involved. The focus should be on the law in the cases, not the facts of those cases. Do not cite cases just because they have some factual features in common with your case. Cite precedents that assist with the court's understanding of the relevant law. Only cite authorities that actually advance your legal argument.

When setting out to persuade the judge, do not simply set out the facts and then point to the relevant law as though drawing a straight line between the two. Effective advocacy goes further. You must explain *why* the outcome you seek is the right and just result in the particular circumstances of the case. This is the point at which you move beyond merely listing the factual and legal ingredients: you should aim to *show* the judge how and why they fit together to form a coherent, convincing argument that leads naturally to the conclusion you want the court to reach.

In advancing your positive arguments, do not be afraid of making concessions where it is proper to do so.

(v) Counter Argument

Anticipate what your opponent is going to say and prepare to deal with it. Of course, you may be responding to their oral submissions or perhaps you have had advance written notice of their arguments. Either way, you always need to be prepared for what the other side will say and deal with it in your submissions, even if you are the first to address the judge.

The most critical thing here is that you do not simply say that your opponent is wrong; instead, you should *demonstrate* why they are wrong. Give the judge the reasons why your opponent is incorrect. Give reasons which the judge can easily adopt when giving her judgement.

Your legal research will have identified all the cases that the other side may seek to deploy in their arguments. Always bring any authority that is against you to the attention of the court and then distinguish that case from your current legal position or explain how it is that other authorities put a different emphasis on the law.

(vi) Conclusion

End with a clear statement as to what you want the judge to order. Add a sentence that answers the judge's real question. This should explain why she should do what you want her to do.

With this structure, you will bring clarity to both your preparation and your actual submissions.

What About the Act of Delivering the Submissions?

The most dominant feature of submission advocacy to a judge over a closing speech to a jury is the fact that the judge can and will interrupt you. She will ask questions. She will debate with you. This impacts two aspects of submission-based advocacy.

The first is that you have to deal with interruptions from the judge. When a judge asks you a question during your submissions, you have to do two things – you have to listen to the question, and you have to answer it directly.

Always answer the judge's question at the time when it is asked. Never reply by saying, "I will come to that" before moving on to whatever you were going to say next. Even if your intention was to deal with the point behind the judge's question later in your submissions, recognise that the time is now. Answer the question at the point in time it is asked, even if you add that you will deal with it in more detail later on.

The second is that you must listen to the interjection. We do not just mean listen to the words, although you certainly must do that. You should listen to what may be *behind* the question: why is the judge asking this, or saying that? The interjection may give you a big clue as to the way the judge is thinking. It may signal the direction her thoughts are going. It may be telling you that she has a settled view on an aspect of your argument that you either need to adopt or navigate around. The judge may be telling you which aspects of the argument trouble her the most.

Be Dynamic Not Scripted

All of this means that submission advocacy to a judge has to be an organic and dynamic form of advocacy. Give your submissions room to grow: you have to be able to change and adapt them according to the interactions that you have with the judge.

You simply cannot prepare your submissions by having a written script to which you rigidly adhere. It is absolutely essential that you have notes in a format that gives you the freedom to depart from what you have written whilst still allowing you to maintain the relevant information about the facts and the law, including citations, at your fingertips. What you need is not a *script*, but a speaking *note* which allows you to adapt and change your approach whilst you are on your feet, prepared in a way that your eye can easily find what you need when you need it.

You will develop your own approach to making your speaking note as useful as possible, but common techniques include: using clear headings; setting out your submissions in bullet points; highlighting case names and references, or typing them in bold; and preparing fuller notes for key sections – such as writing out the two or three sentences of your closing remarks in full. This is an example of the mechanics of advocacy that we deal with elsewhere.

Signposting

Signposting is an essential element in submission advocacy just as it is elsewhere. You can begin the section of positive argument in your advocacy by saying to the judge:

> I have three submissions in support of the application. Dealing with the first submission…
>
> Now turning to my second submission…

If you have not framed your argument in this way, help the judge know that you are moving on by using the technique of signposting with phrases such as:

> Dealing now with the leading case…
>
> I turn now to my submissions on the facts…

Submissions should be framed in a balanced and reasonable way. Oral submissions, particularly those where you are disagreeing with your opponent, should avoid hyperbole and adjectives. It makes no difference to the substance of your submission if you *disagree* or *strongly disagree*. It does not persuade a judge if you say that your opponent is *wildly wrong*. You should instead aim to demonstrate that your opponent is wildly wrong.

Modes of Address

One of the pitfalls for the advocate is the mode of address for the judge. It may be that from day to day the judge you appear before will be in different divisions or be at different levels from first instance to appellate. A criminal practitioner in England and Wales can be before a district judge in the Magistrates' Court ("Judge") one day, a circuit judge in the Crown Court the next day ("Your Honour"), and end the week in the Court of Appeal ("My Lord, My Lady").

Get the mode of address correct. Whatever form your notes take – written or typed on paper, or digitally on a screen – have the correct mode of address written somewhere obvious on every single page. More than once. Have it in bold at the top of every page. Every single time your eye goes back to the page, give your mind a reminder as to what the correct mode of address is.

Civil Cases

In civil cases the structure of your submissions should follow the test set out in the Civil Procedure Rules or in case law, e.g. *American Cyanamid* [1975] AC 396 for interim prohibitory injunctions, and as then interpreted by further case law. The White Book is your best friend in this regard!

Particularly for assessments, examiners will want you to cover all limbs of the test. In practice, you may choose to focus your submissions on one particular limb of the test where the test is expressed in the alternative, e.g. setting aside default judgment. However, do not forget to consider whether you have compelling arguments under both limbs. In short, raise as many lines of argument as you realistically can within the time available, starting with your best points.

You will have the chance to practise many types of submissions on a Bar course, and you will also practise application-based submissions if you undertake the SQE. You will be studying both criminal and civil law together when undertaking your qualifying course, and there can be a temptation to treat both sets of advocacy similarly and so end up being overly bombastic in your submissions in front of your tutor acting as a district judge or circuit judge. However, they are not a jury, and so there is no need for emotive language. Nevertheless, you must still make your submissions persuasive and interesting, through your tone and also through perhaps finding that compelling point that nobody has raised before.

Advanced Technique

Do not fear the judicial intervention. Rather than being a hurdle, it is an opportunity. It presents to you a valuable chance to resolve in your favour a question that the judge has. You may take the question and then frame both it and your response in a way which supports your arguments.

There are a number of ways that you can achieve this. If the judge raises a concern, use it to reinforce your case: show how your submissions resolve that concern, and once it is resolved, that there is no remaining reason for the court to decide against you. If the judge asks a hypothetical question based on different facts, reaffirm the reasons why the actual facts support your proposition. If the judge raises with you an area of potential weakness in your case, be prepared to confront that weakness and deal with it.

Advocates who stray into overly dramatic language will often be met with the stern judicial response "Don't treat me like a jury, Mr Booth!" That is not, however, to say all advocacy and rhetorical devices are to be abandoned. Judges are, after all, still human beings. They are susceptible to arguments made in attractive ways.

The language you use should be clear and precise, but your submissions should never be dull. Make it your job to engage with the judge. The device of repetition can be as effective with a judge as it can be with a witness or a jury. Reduce your key point to a single phrase. Then find two other ways of saying the same thing but with different phrases. Then weave those three phrases through your submissions. Each time, you will be reinforcing your key point.

We come back to the idea that you do not simply lay out everything before the judge and tell her, "you decide!" You want to build the narrative. Each element of your submission is telling a story. A story about what the law is. A story about what the relevant facts are. A story about why the law, when applied to those facts, means you win. Those are the stories that you want in the judge's mind as she comes to determine her judgement. A list of facts and authorities is dull, whereas a complete narrative is compelling. (Incidentally, you noticed how we used the device of repetition there to reinforce our point to you?)

That last paragraph used the phrase "you win". Your mindset should never be that you are arguing *against* the judge. One of the most important skills in submission advocacy is knowing that the time has come to concede a point when the judge is plainly right. Your credibility as an advocate is as vital as the credibility of any witness. Approach your submissions with the attitude that you are assisting the court to reach the correct decision. If you concede appropriately when it is right to do so, the judge will pay far closer attention on those occasions later when you stand your ground. You win the argument by getting the judge on your side, not by pitting yourself against them.

8 Submission Advocacy 2

Opening and Closing Speeches

In this chapter, we will look at speeches, the focus being on speeches in jury trials, but we also deal with speeches in civil cases. Opening and closing speeches are very good examples of submission advocacy, but they are a type of submission advocacy that have some very distinct features.

You will see that there are similarities between opening and closing speeches. There are also similarities between speeches in criminal cases and non-criminal cases. But each type of speech is different, both in what you are saying and what you are hoping your speech will achieve. Critically, you will be careful to match what you are saying and how you are saying it to your specific audience. You must be able to adjust your content and style, sometimes in significant ways. Look at it like this: if you are making a closing speech to a criminal jury in Bristol as though you are speaking to three Lady Justices in the Court of Appeal in London, you will not do well.

Jury advocacy is very different from advocacy to a judge or tribunal. It is important to remember the distinctions between the two of them but never forget that judges are humans too. (At least they are for now. The world has not yet brought us AI judges – but if that time comes, you would need to be ready to adapt your approach to accommodate it.)

There are transferable skills and principles that you can use when composing and delivering your submissions to juries and judges, whether the speeches are mainly about law (to a judge) or mainly about facts (to a jury). You will spot some areas of overlap in the guidance that we are setting out here and in the previous chapter.

We begin with some introductory advice common to all opening speeches. We have in mind a jury trial, but it will often be equally applicable to judges or other tribunals of any kind.

Fundamentals of an Opening Speech to a Jury

Fundamentals

It is often said that the prosecutor is a "minister of justice". This phrase is used to convey the idea that prosecuting involves adopting a fair attitude to the job. The job should be done properly and with professional determination; it is not about

DOI: 10.4324/9781003602019-8

securing a conviction at any cost. Indeed, prosecutors who give the impression that they are unfair will often find that the jury rebels against them.

You may aim to be persuasive in how you open the case to the jury, but at this stage your focus is mostly about introducing the case to them and setting out why the defendant is being prosecuted. You describe the evidence upon which the prosecution is based.

Criminal justice is about the dispassionate evaluation of evidence with cool heads and thoughtful minds. It is not your role to be emotive, to try and persuade the jury by appealing to their feelings. In your opening speech, your persuasive ability will come through in the way you reason things out.

There has been a view growing in the legal world since the early 2000s that a prosecutor's opening speech should not really address the law in any great detail. Our advice is that you should keep it brief.

Looking at our case of *Rex v Tegan Plant*, it would be usual to say something about the burden and standard of proof, that Tegan Plant can only be convicted if the Prosecution has made the jury sure that he is guilty. We pause there to state that this only needs to be referred to. You do not need to wax lyrical about the burden and standard. Tell the jury what it is. Then move on.

What you absolutely do not want to be doing is giving the jury a mini law lecture breaking down into its constituent elements the offence of robbery contrary to section 8 of the Theft Act 1968 and by explaining how a defendant's actions can only be an "attempt" if they are "more than merely preparatory" to the commission of the full offence. Did you find that your eyes started to glaze over as you got to the end of that last sentence? That would likely be the effect on the jury, too.

Instead, talk about what Tegan Plant did, talk about the facts of the case in a way that naturally highlights the key elements of the offence that you need to prove in order to give the jury the ability to convict him. In our case, that is quite straightforward. A jury is going to understand that someone who enters a bank and makes verbal demands for money, without actually getting away with any money, has not actually robbed the bank but rather has tried (or attempted) to rob them.

There is one other rule to know about. Sometimes a trial will begin with a question of law undecided. You will have read in the *Plant* case documents, for example, that the defendant has a number of previous convictions that you, the prosecutor, say are good evidence of his bad character. This is a specific area of law governed by section 101 of the Criminal Justice Act 2003: unless the defence agrees to you telling the jury about those previous convictions, you will need the permission of the judge to do so. Sometimes a judge will postpone any determination of a question whether to let you adduce a piece of evidence until later in the trial. If that happens, then you should make sure that you do not tell the jury anything about it in your opening speech.

How To Make an Opening Speech to a Jury

There is a common thought that advocates are failed or *wannabe* actors, and that we always make ourselves the star of the show. Not so! If anything, we are like ghost writers. We tell other people's stories in a mixture of their words and ours. Never is that more so than in an opening speech.

The vast majority of opening speeches in criminal cases are made by advocates acting for the prosecution. This is the opportunity for you as prosecutor to tell the story or build the picture of the case. Sometimes, people think of it as a jigsaw: the evidence and the law will make up the jigsaw pieces, but your opening speech is like showing the picture on the box. Your aim is to show the jury how the pieces fit together.

A prosecution opening speech should do four things:

1. Tell the jury the overall story that the case is about;
2. Introduce the jury to the evidence that they are going to hear;
3. Allow the jury to understand why the prosecution says that evidence points to the guilt of each defendant (or, how you "put the case against each defendant");
4. Explain to the jury a little of the law that will apply to the case if you feel this is necessary.

The defence has the right to make an opening speech in criminal cases. The time to make an opening defence speech is after the end of the prosecution case and before the defence calls any evidence. In England and Wales, it is only very rarely that the defence takes advantage of that right. Where the defence gives an opening speech, the purpose is much the same, namely to highlight what the defence case will be and to provide an overview.

In addition, in England and Wales, sometimes a judge will invite the defence to address the jury briefly immediately after the prosecution has opened the case. This is not a full opening speech but is to identify the issues in the case so as to assist the jury. This tends only to happen in the more complex and lengthy cases.

Keep the Jury's Attention

When you rise to your feet for the first time as the prosecution advocate in a trial and properly start to speak to the jury, you will find that the jury are at their most attentive. The members of the jury have just walked into the courtroom, possibly for the first time in their lives; one by one they have each taken the oath to try the defendant fairly; and they have heard the charges against the defendant being read out. They will have had a welcoming address from the judge giving them a brief introduction to their duties. They may have received a leaflet from the judge or from the court officials in the building which deals with similar matters.

But when you address the jury with your opening speech, that will be the moment when everything will crystallise for them: now is the time that they find out why they and everyone else are there. Now is the time for them to begin the work that they have been assembled together to do. The jury will give you their fullest attention.

This is a great opportunity for you. Do not waste it.

Do not begin by telling the jury what the indictment says or what the charges mean. Do not launch into an explanation about the burden and standard of proof. Instead, introduce all the advocates and explain who is representing which parties in the case, then get the jury's attention straightaway by telling them what the case is all about in two or three pithy sentences. The jury want to know what this case is all about.

> Shortly before 5 pm on 19 November a masked man burst into the New Dilhorne Bank in Marple, approached the lone bank employee and shouted words to the effect of "Give me the money or I'll shoot you". The Prosecution say that the masked would-be robber is this defendant, Tegan Plant. He has been identified by the bank employee as the person who was responsible for the robbery and has been linked to the stolen car that was used as the getaway vehicle.

So begins our opening speech in our criminal case scenario of *Rex v Tegan Plant.* You do not want to descend into sensationalism or resort to hyperbole in your speech; but you do want to create a degree of interest. You have the jury's attention, and you need to keep it!

Perhaps the phrase "burst into the New Dilhorne Bank" begins in a few words to paint a picture in the mind of the jury? Embed the phrase "Give me the money or I'll shoot you" in the memory of the jury now and you will have told them, almost immediately, everything they need to know for them to understand why you are saying this is a kind of robbery.

Take the jury to what the case is really about. Tell them that the issue for them to decide is not really whether the bank employee was robbed, but whether it is this defendant – the man sitting in the dock right in front of the jury – who was that robber. Identification is, of course, the big issue in the case. Give the jury a brief summary of how this is to be established in the evidence.

You have not told the jury everything about the case in those opening few sentences, but they now know enough to get them engaged in the story.

"Miss Ullger Will Say"

Then move on to the evidence that the jury are going to hear. But how do you do this? We will look first at how *not* to do it. Sometimes you might hear an opening speech which turns from one witness to another, introducing their evidence with a phrase such as,

> Miss Ullger will say...

This approach is deficient for a number of reasons. First, it encourages you to introduce too much of what the witness says, and you are likely to fall into the trap of summarising large chunks of each witness's evidence. Your speech may start to get heavy with detail, and the jury may worry about how much they are supposed to be remembering. If they are worrying about that, they will stop listening to you.

Second, the "Miss Ullger will say" style might make you jump from topic to topic in a way that is confusing for the jury. This is because when you finish summarising Miss Ullger's evidence, what about the next witness – and the next, and the next? The trouble is that each witness may not necessarily have experienced things in chronological order. If you try to talk about the evidence in this *witness-by-witness* style you can easily get sucked into giving a disjointed account of what happened. It will make sense to you because you know the case very well already, but a jury who are learning about the case for the very first time may struggle to understand.

Third, repetition of "the witness will say" can also begin to sound very tedious. We have used that phrase a few times now already in the last couple of paragraphs – do you find that you have begun to notice it more? It begins to take over. When the jury hears for the tenth time what a "witness will say", they will be bored or confused, or both. Bored and confused is absolutely not what you are aiming for.

Fourth, this approach risks becoming something you later regret. If you are explicit from the very start about what each witness is going to say, you may well create a weakness in your own case. For the alert juror, nothing will highlight more effectively that something is wrong with your case than when your witness does not say what you have expressly told the jury they *would* say. (Incidentally, this is exactly the reason why you do not hear many defence opening speeches.)

Summarise the Case

So far, we have looked at what you do not want to be doing in an opening speech. Instead, it is much better if you provide the story that the evidence is going to tell, with reference to how it is that the witnesses themselves experienced it. Do not tell the jury what the witnesses are going to say; instead, summarise what they saw, heard and felt. This makes what you are saying somewhat personal to the witnesses, but it still maintains your role as someone who is helping the jury see the image on the front of the jigsaw lid.

> William Hawkins was outside the New Dilhorne Bank in Marple. He saw a car travelling too fast for the conditions pull onto the pavement and he saw a man wearing distinctive clothing and a mask jump out of the vehicle and run into the bank. He noted that the male walked with a limp. He also saw that the car registration contained the letters XCM, which he made a note of in his phone. The male who ran into the bank was wearing a stripy top and balaclava. The witness thought at the time that the car was a white coloured car.

Once you have introduced a factual narrative of the case in general outline terms, you can begin to develop some detail in your opening speech about why the Prosecution is saying that they can prove the guilt of the defendant. Or rather, how *you* are going to prove the guilt, because as far as the jury are concerned, you are the prosecution advocate and so *you are the Prosecution.*

How do you set out this detail, and what of the details do you want to include? A criminal lawyer might say that you have a *prosecution case theory*, and that now in your speech you will be *setting out the prosecution case against the defendant*. We have prepared a document headed "Prosecution Case Theory" to show you the sort of thinking that criminal lawyers have in mind when preparing cases. We have also prepared a "Defence Case Theory" to show the other side, too.

The reasons why you say that the defendant is guilty should be set out in clear and concise terms. You do not have to tell the jury about all the evidence that they are going to hear in the trial. Doing that would be much less helpful than making sure that the jury understands what conclusions you seek them to draw from the evidence. To assist the jury best, you may wish to be clear about the most important issue(s) you expect them to be trying in the case: where do you expect most of their focus to be in the trial?

You will gather from reading the case documents in *Rex v Plant* that the central issue in our case is whether the defendant was the robber. In other words, it is an identification case. There are two main strands of direct evidence that you are placing before the court to show this: first, the successful identification of Plant by an eyewitness at a properly conducted identification procedure; and second, the DNA evidence against him.

This evidence is supported by the fact that the defendant walks with a limp, as did the robber. You will know that there are other pieces of evidence that you will be deploying alongside the identification procedure evidence and the DNA evidence. But you do not want to be giving the jury long lists. You will have to make a judgement call about how much you tell them in your opening speech.

No Law Lectures

Next turn to anything about the law that you feel you must say. In the way we describe above, perhaps you might deal very simply with what you need to prove (the ingredients of the offence), what the defendant is saying in answer to it (the defence raised), the role of the judge and the burden and standard of proof.

As we say, this is absolutely not the opportunity for a law lecture. If you make it sound complicated, the jury will think it *is* complicated. Above all, you want the jury to appreciate that showing the guilt of the defendant is a simple and straightforward task. You will give an overview of the law that is even more brief than the overview that you gave of the facts.

Now this is really important: no matter what anyone else ever tells you or does, do not begin with the law. You will lose and confuse the jury before you even begin. The jury are unlikely to be fascinated by the law. The facts will be far more gripping and dramatic.

End with a straightforward summary of the prosecution case which draws the main evidence together in order to make clear what the prosecution say that this defendant has done.

Keep It as Simple as You Can

This simple template for an opening speech will serve you well throughout your career:

1. Headline;
2. Narrative;
3. Case;
4. Law;
5. Summary.

Civil Cases

In civil practice, opening speeches at trials are a rarity, and may at most be a short summary of the key issues remaining in dispute. There is, of course, much skill in such speeches, namely in distilling all of the points which have arisen in a case that may have taken three years to get to trial into a short, succinct summary of a few minutes' length.

As an advocate in a civil case, you need to be ready to deal with the possibility that the trial judge will have a provisional view about the law that they want to explore before hearing the evidence. One of the distinctive points of civil cases is that the trial judge may decide a legal issue in such a way that (at least some) witness evidence becomes unnecessary.

Advanced Technique for an Opening Speech to a Jury

You are not a newsreader. You are an advocate. Talk *to* the jury, not *at* them.

Keep It Simple and Straightforward

We expect that there is a reasonable prospect that you, the advocate, are well educated and well read. A law degree or a law conversion course has never been an easy ride. The Bar and SQE exams are hard. You have, without doubt, shown great ability in your journey to become an advocate. You have no idea, however, what level of education the members of the jury have. You have no idea of their backgrounds. It is not a case of comparing you against them because the very point we are making is that you know nothing at all about them. But they will observe you very closely over the duration of the trial as you begin to do your job. To some extent, they will get to know you. Do not fall into the trap of thinking that if you use big words and flowery language they will see you as more eloquent and persuasive. They will not. Instead, communicate clearly with understandable language. That is not to say you patronise the jury. Just keep things elegantly simple.

In the introductory remarks in our opening speech, we plan to say to the jury:

Let's just look at that in a little more detail.

This way of speaking serves two purposes. The first is that it introduces a hint of a conversational tone which helps you connect with the jury. The jury members may have arrived at court for their jury service with an impression that barristers are stuffy, old-fashioned and aloof. Instead, they will find that you are including them in what you are doing. You are not telling them or commanding them; rather, you are explaining to them that you and they will be looking at the case together. They will find that you are helping them. Secondly, this kind of expression serves as a useful signpost – and use of signposts merits a little more detailed consideration in the context of jury speeches.

Signposts, Reinforcement and Themes

As we have already said, signposts are an effective tool in all submission-based advocacy. Signposts allow you to tell the listener that you are moving from one topic to another. They help the listener to understand what they are about to listen to. The jury will make sense of what you are saying because they understand the context leading up to it. Judges whom you are addressing will be thankful to you for the same approach.

Signposts also act as a reminder to you that you need to pace your speech exactly right so that the jury can follow you, that you need to vary the tone from one portion to the next in order to make it easy for the jury to follow you. Each time you come to a signpost, pause. Then move on.

You are making sure that you keep their attention, and that is important to you; but since they are listening to you, they will appreciate that you are making it easy for them.

Reinforcing key concepts strengthens the overall persuasiveness of your argument and helps anchor the most important elements of your case in the minds of the jury. For instance, we use this expression in our opening speech:

> The Prosecution say that the masked would-be robber is this defendant.

Might there be other occasions in your speech where you could emphasise the point "would-be robber" again? You can imagine why a jury might think that this phrase is ideal to describe the man exactly. Perhaps a variation on the theme, such as:

> that man, the would-be robber, who the prosecution say is this defendant, …
>
> so it is that the Prosecution say that there is direct evidence that the would-be robber is the defendant.

The basic pattern there is "would-be robber" and that connection that the would-be robber is this defendant. Given that the main issue for the jury is identification, this description, this concept, is key to your case. You will want to be careful not to overuse the technique of reinforcement; rather, the important thing is to use the same words or phrasing without necessarily being identical each time and not so much that it becomes mere repetition.

A similar technique is to have a theme that runs through your speech that you can tie to different parts of the evidence. Here we use the idea of signs to describe what we mean:

> The evidence that the would-be robber had a limp is a signpost that points to this defendant.
>
> The identification evidence is a signpost pointing to the conclusion that the defendant was the would-be robber.
>
> The DNA evidence is a sign along that road that leads you to the conclusion that the defendant was the would-be robber.

Do Not Avoid the Difficult Bits

A difficult decision often arises when you are drafting your opening speech. What to do about the difficult bits? A lot of advocacy revolves around the judgement calls that you, the advocate, will have to make. This is one of those judgement calls.

It is often best to deal with any potential weakness in the Prosecution's case upfront. There are discrepancies and inconsistencies in the witness accounts about the robbery. You do not have to necessarily highlight what they are in opening (you might choose to do so in certain circumstances) but it is worth signalling to the jury that they can expect some inconsistency and begin to lay the groundwork as to why that might be the case.

This is what advocates call "insulating the witnesses". You are anticipating an attack from the Defence on the witness, so you are insulating the witness first. Your aim is to make sure that when the attack comes, it does not have quite the effect that the Defence intends.

Here is one example from our opening speech in *Rex v Tegan Plant*:

> Both the eyewitnesses were under the stress of witnessing something that was both fast moving and traumatic. You should consider that when looking at what they say and any differences that there may be in the evidence that they give.

You know that your witnesses are not entirely consistent on the topic of the colour of the car. View this not as a weakness, not as a problem, but as an *issue*. This issue exists as one among many issues that the jury will be considering. Have in mind that most of these issues can, looking at the evidence, be decided firmly in your favour (or more precisely, in the prosecution's favour).

You may well make the judgement call that if you deal with that one isolated issue when you open the case to the jury, then you can achieve a number of objectives. First, you will actually bolster the credibility of the prosecution case: it can be seen as a strength to recognise your weakness. You are also showing yourself to be reasonable and fair and someone the jury can trust to be straight with them. Second, you can in your speech begin to suggest how the jury should approach the issue in your favour. Third, it means that when the jury come at the end of the case to consider what verdict to return, subconsciously they will feel that that particular issue has been present from the outset. It is not something the defence have unearthed and presented with great fanfare. The jury will feel that the issue has never been a surprise to them and is not, after all, a point of any great importance.

Emphasise Points That Will Resonate with the Jury

There are some aspects of the evidence which sometimes you may think will achieve a particular resonance or importance in the overall dynamic of the case. In *Rex v Tegan Plant*, an example of this may be the defendant's response to being told about the positive identification by the witness. See this in our opening speech:

> The defendant was interviewed by the police after the positive identification by Miss Ullger. When it was put to him that he had been identified he replied, "Oh bollocks".

This is where you begin to be the advocate, by which we mean not just the author, but the teller of the story: the teller of the story with the spoken, not the written, word. Your delivery of this part of your speech might include, perhaps, a little vocal flourish.

Consider the scene. You are standing fully robed in a courtroom and performing your role as a barrister. The jury are not going to expect you to use such colourful language. Play on that. Use pace and vary your tone. Use your voice to give voice to the story:

> The defendant was interviewed by the police after the positive identification by the witness. When it was put to him that *he* [emphasise <u>he</u>] had been *identified* [emphasise <u>identified</u>] he replied … [pause]."*Oh bollocks*" [emphasise <u>oh bollocks</u>].

Fundamentals of a Closing Speech to a Jury

Be clear about whether you are entitled to make a closing speech at all. The prosecution may always make a closing speech if the defendant is represented by an advocate. If the defendant is unrepresented, then in the magistrates' court the prosecution may make a closing speech only if the defendant has introduced evidence other than their own. In the crown court, the position is subtly different in that the prosecution can make a closing speech if either the unrepresented defendant has called someone else to give evidence about the facts of the case or the judge allows it.

The defence may always make a closing speech at the end of a trial. If both parties are making a speech, then the Prosecution go first and the Defence second.

You must take care to make sure that you do not mention in your closing speech anything that has not featured in the evidence in the trial. This obligation requires you to be careful. It is very often the position that a prosecution witness expresses something in a certain way during their evidence in court which is different from how they expressed it in their witness statement. This all matters because hardly ever will the witness statement itself be presented as evidence in the case. It follows that if you refer to what it says, there is a risk you will be introducing inadmissible evidence.

The witness may go further when giving evidence to the jury in court and say something that is different from what they wrote in their witness statement, and you may consider that you want to highlight the difference when cross-examining the witness. Let us imagine that you are defending in our case of *Rex v Tegan Plant*, and you note that Mr Hawkins has said in evidence-in-chief that the car he saw pull up outside the bank was green.

> *Defence Case Theory:*
> *Potentially Mr Hawkins's evidence that the car was green is damaging to your client's case because it may support the prosecution case that the car the would-be robber was in was Amy Barber's car, where the client's fingerprints were found – which was green. You may consider that this matters because in his witness statement he said the car was white and he does not say green. You may therefore wish to cross-examine Mr Hawkins on the fact that in his witness statement made much nearer the time of the incident he said "white" and not "green". Your aim is to show that the recent evidence that the car was "green" is less credible and less reliable.*

Cross-examining on the witness statement in this way then qualifies you to refer to the green/white difference in your closing speech. The point we are making here is that where you do not cross-examine on the difference, you may not refer in your closing speech to what the contents of the witness statement are on this point.

Sometimes, of course, you may notice a difference between what the witness statement says and what the witness has said in evidence to the court, and you may consider that the difference does not matter, and you decide not to ask the witness about them: here, too, you must take care not to mention in your closing speech what the witness statement said.

How to make a Closing Speech to a Jury

You might think that there is not much difference in your approach between an opening speech and a closing speech. We think that they are very different. They are so different that, whilst we have set out for you a kind of template for an opening speech in our case of *Rex v Tegan Plant*, we consider that it is impossible to set out a general template for a closing speech.

Why Is There No Template?

It is because the evidence is different in each case you do and because everything about the case will be different: not just what the witnesses have said, but how they have said it and how they have come across in court. The dynamic with the judge will be different. Your opponent will have put things in a different way. The jury may have asked a question which has focused minds in all sorts of directions.

When you were writing your opening speech, you knew the material that the speech was going to be based on as it is all set out in the statements and the exhibits. There are no surprises. The closing speech is going to be shaped by what has happened in the trial.

Advocates sometimes conduct re-trials, for example if the jury was unable to agree on a verdict. You might think: same trial, same evidence, same closing speech. No! Everything will be different. Every closing speech you make in your career should be an absolutely bespoke piece of advocacy, unique to the case. If we compare your closing speeches to suits, think of them as being tailor-made, not off-the-peg.

It is often said to advocates learning their skill that they should be able to write their closing speech in advance of the trial and that this will form the basis for the advocate's case strategy. We dealt with the reality of this in the chapter on cross-examination.

Planning in this way could be an excellent way to focus your mind, anticipate issues and plan your strategy and your approach to the trial. But our view is that this approach is not going to work if your aim is to produce an outstanding closing speech, certainly not if you deliver the speech that you wrote at this point. For sure you can think in advance about your speech and plan it in outline, but you cannot actually write it before a word of evidence has been spoken in court.

Often the reason why advice is given to write your closing speech first is to instil in the new advocate the necessity of preparation; you must always identify what the good points are and also what the issues are that you will need to deal with. That is sound advice. But *write* your closing speech in advance? Impossible if you want to do it well. The closing speech has to reflect what has happened in the room, not what is written in the papers.

Preparation Is Key

The most important aspect of your closing speech is preparation. Whilst you will not actually be writing your closing speech when you first sit down with the case documents, you should certainly be thinking about it from a very early stage in your involvement in a case. This is because nearly everything you do in the course of a trial is a step on the road to the closing speech. At every step you should be thinking about the final destination: what you are going to say in your closing speech. Think about what you have to say and how you are going to say it. Think about the phrases you will use, the framing you will adopt.

You will need to find a method of recording your thoughts in preparation for your closing speech at this early stage. You might be able to retain and order all your thoughts in your mind (good if you can; we cannot). You might jot notes down as they occur to you, whether that is in a paper notepad or a Word document on your laptop. You might prefer to leave yourself voice notes to listen to on your way home each day from trial. Whatever your method, you must find a way of retaining your thoughts from the first moment you start reading the case documents right up to the moment you ask the last question of the last witness. The way you make your notes will assist you immensely when composing the final draft of your closing speech. Your future self will be very grateful.

The Mechanics of Making a Speech

Now comes the important part: how you write your closing speech. This is not to do with content or delivery; rather this is to do with mechanics. And somewhat unhelpfully, this is something you will largely have to find out for yourself, although we can help you find your way.

By "mechanics" we mean the practical arrangements that allow you to have your speech organised and accessible to you during delivery in court. We mean the preparatory actions that make effective advocacy possible.

You can write the whole speech out word for word and read it. (But be aware: if it sounds like you are reading it out from the page, and you sound monotone and dull, your audience will very quickly stop listening to you!) You can write bullet points. You can write your speech out word for word and then convert that into bullet points. You can try to memorise the words. You can read it from paper or from your laptop screen. But however you prepare, how will you organise your notes and materials to ensure that when you are actually delivering your speech, everything flows smoothly? You are going to be focussed on the jury, and you want them to be focussed on you; you cannot afford any interruptions.

If you do have written notes, make sure you are not just staring at them: the jury will want to see your face, not the top of your head. And this means that you must have a way that your notes are organised and easily visible to you. Do not have just scraps of paper in your hand that you are fiddling with, dropping and mixing up.

Along the way, you will have to demonstrate the ability to perform submission advocacy in circumstances when there is no opportunity to write things out word for word. You will undertake submission advocacy, including opening and closing speeches to a judge, where the experience will be interactive, and where they will interrupt. You cannot script that.

The foundational skill we invite you to learn is the skill of working from bullet points. Your exact method will develop and refine itself over time. The optimum method that you find to deliver a closing speech will be personal to you; however, at the start of your career, when you are handling the simpler work typical of a junior advocate, treat it as a chance to develop the ability to deliver a closing speech in a way that uses your time efficiently and – crucially – helps you become less dependent on a script.

Being efficient is important. The time will come when you have to conduct a speech after a short trial. You may only have a very short time to gather your thoughts and make your notes. You still have to be able to deliver a poised and eloquent speech.

Training yourself to avoid heavy reliance on a word-for-word script will also help prepare you for the times when a judge will be asking you questions and you need to be able to shape your submissions to the changing landscape of the hearing.

Making notes for a speech in bullet points does not mean that you will not write out word-for-word certain parts of it. There may be something that you need to deal with in a precise way. You may be describing a piece of expert evidence, for example, where you need to have the precise terms of the evidence in an accurate way. Or it may be that you have thought of a particular way that you want to express your submissions where each word of the sentence is important. If so, simply place these complete sentences in the body of your notes, so that you have the security of knowing they will be there when you need them.

Writing out sections of the speech is often of value at the beginning and the end of your submissions. It can help settle you into the speech if you have the opening line or two written out. Having the final couple of lines written out can help you finish on a strong, eloquent note which will be the last words that sit in the jury's minds, or the mind of the judge. When you are a new advocate, this can help anchor you and make you feel more confident. As we discuss below, these sections become a key part of the content of your speech.

The method you finally settle upon to get yourself organised when giving your speech will be the method that most suits you and the way you work. You can see why we say it is largely something you will have to figure out for yourself.

Structure and Signposting

Your speech needs structure. It cannot be a rambling stream of thoughts about the case. You need to provide a structure and then the verbal cues to where you are moving on. This is a version of signposting, which we discussed a little earlier in this chapter and elsewhere throughout this book.

Perhaps you could add into a closing speech in *Rex v Tegan Plant* verbal cues such as these:

> Members of the jury, can we now turn to the evidence of identification?
>
> So let's leave the evidence relating to the ID there and consider what the prosecution say about the defendant's previous convictions.

Use a signposting technique similar to the one you would use in examining witnesses. Think about when you read a document. You are helped by paragraphs, headings and, in longer documents, chapters. (That is how we are trying to signpost our content for you in this book.) Think about achieving this effect in a speech. Tell the jury when you are moving from one topic to the next in a way that fits into the narrative of your speech.

The structure requires a degree of discipline. Do not jump around from point to point. Also consider carefully how the points sit together. If a piece of evidence has its greatest value in connection with one aspect of the case, the same evidence may not be worth returning to when you are dealing with another topic where its relevance is of less impact.

Deal with Negatives As Well As Positives

The jury will always be anxious to consider fully the credibility of a witness, but your credibility as an advocate is very important. If you are defending, do not ignore the strength of evidence. Acknowledge it and then counter it if you reasonably can. This last part is very important. You are not going to win every battle in the case, so ask yourself whether any particular battle needs fighting at all. Acknowledge that the Prosecution may have persuaded the jury of something that your client denies, but seek to place that within the context of the case and show why that does not mean the Prosecution have proved the charge against your client.

When dealing with what may be a weakness in your case or a strength in the case of the other side, think about the point in your speech when you should deal with it. One thing which is certain: do not deal with it at the end of your speech. You may want to include it in the middle of the speech, surrounded by better points. There are times when you may want to get it out of the way early on, even beginning with it and seeking to turn it into a positive.

> Members of the jury, having heard the witness you may have come to the conclusion that the defendant is not likeable, you may have thought he is exactly the sort of person who would do this terrible thing, but that is why the witness has come to the mistaken conclusion that it is the defendant. The witness has done what you must not do, and jumped to a conclusion.

If you make the decision to confront an issue and deal with it at the outset, do so recognising that there are many who will remember most closely the first thing and the last thing they are told in any speech. That may not be to your advantage.

Themes

Decide the theme which will go on to decide the structure. Are you going to deal with events chronologically as the events unfolded? Are you going to replicate the chronology of the case as it was presented in court? Are you going to deal with events as chapters of evidence? Or by issues in the case?

Again we make the point that the approach you take will be bespoke to the case. There is not a wrong or right answer; there is only the answer that you make a conscious decision to adopt.

Be Accurate

In your preparation, make sure that you have two things absolutely right: the law and the evidence. When dealing with the evidence, ensure you are accurately quoting or summarising it. If in doubt, check with someone. Check with your opponent or your instructing solicitor. Even check with the judge. Do not lose credibility by having to make a correction after you have finished. But if you do happen to get it wrong, accept the blame and put it right with the minimum of fuss.

In the vast majority of trials in England and Wales, the judge will have discussed the legal directions with the advocates before closing speeches begin, and she will usually give the jury legal directions before the advocates' closing speeches take place. In many jurisdictions there are standard directions that judges will adopt and sometimes adapt to deal with the specifics of the individual case.

When you are addressing the jury, echo the language of the judge. Do not simply repeat the exact framing; do not just quote. But use very similar phrasing and tie it to the facts of your case when you explain why the jury should decide things your way. In that way, your submissions to the jury will chime with what the ostensibly independent figure of judicial authority is telling them on the same topic.

The Burden and Standard of Proof

When it comes to the burden and standard of proof, you need to strike the balance between not boring the jury with repetition and reminding the jury of this quite important aspect of the case. If you are defending, by all means focus on dropping in reminders such as:

> Have the prosecution made you sure?
>
> Is that evidence something you are happy to rely upon to the extent that you feel sure?

But if you make your speech all about the burden and standard of proof, and nothing more, you are telegraphing to everyone that you have not got very much else to say.

When prosecuting, consider how you can make the burden and standard your strength and ally:

> [After a summary of the evidence] That combination of evidence, independent and corroborated, is the kind of thing you look for in your daily lives when asking yourself whether you are sure. It is why the prosecution invites you to say that you can be sure of the defendant's guilt in this case.

What Not To Do

There are a couple of things you really do need to avoid. The first is sarcasm, particularly sarcasm at someone else's expense. It can be funny and it can be an effective way of communicating a message; however, it is just as likely, if not more likely, to come across as bullying or condescending, or both.

Remember that the jury will be directed by the judge to try the case calmly and dispassionately according to the evidence they have heard. If the jury think you are trying to get them to do something else, if you are belittling a witness in the case, you will lose credibility.

The second thing to avoid is being boring. If you deal with every single aspect of the evidence, you are likely to be boring. Your closing speech is not a replay of the entire trial. It is the edited highlights that you need to make your best points. And that means focusing on your best points, not every point.

Think of it this way. The speech is like the newspaper or online report of a sporting event like a football match. It is not every word of commentary that describes each kick of the game.

Learn to Edit

This brings us on to the foundational skill which is that you need to learn to edit. Speeches are an exercise in judgement, as is a lot of advocacy. Really do concentrate on developing and relying upon your best points. When you stray into minor, inconsequential points, the risk is that your audience will think you are desperate. If you make a point which is obviously devoid of merit, you lose credibility with the jury. When you focus on your best points, then your every word is pointing the jury in the right direction.

Civil Cases

Closing speeches at trial are equally as important in civil cases as in criminal cases. The key point, though, is to remember who your tribunal is. The longstanding District Judge or Circuit Judge hearing the trial has heard all of the same evidence as you and has understood it as much as you (or more than you!). Therefore, again, it is a matter of distilling the key points from the evidence that help your client, while addressing as best you can any weaknesses.

Advanced Technique for a Closing Speech to a Jury

Always Look to Improve

Treat your opening and closing speech advocacy like a sport or any other skill. Always look to achieve even marginal gains. What is working best for you? The speech being written out? Bullet points? Is there something that can improve how you deliver it by using a tablet or a laptop? Make improvements to the mechanics of advocacy as you go along in your career to improve your performance.

Engage in regular self-analysis: which parts of your last speech would you tweak and why?

Think about how you may use things during the course of a speech: a physical exhibit, an image on a screen, a section of CCTV or a document. If you are taking the jury to a document, always make sure you have the reference to take them to it and always give them time to get it to hand before you start talking about it.

Mental Rehearsal

There are plenty of apps that will read your written words back to you. If you have written your speech out in full, read it back to yourself and play it to yourself as well. It can really help you identify the bits which feel a bit "clunky". Some parts may read well with your eyes across the page, but simply do not sound good to the ears when being spoken. If you have time, listen to it again after a period away from the speech.

As you listen to it, edit. Strike through the bits you can now appreciate are unnecessary. If a phrase needs improving, improve it. The process of listening multiple times helps not only with the editing; it also begins to embed the speech in your mind in readiness for delivering it.

In your mind, imagine yourself delivering that exact speech in the exact court room where you will be delivering it. Imagine the words you will say, the pauses you insert, your facial expressions. Imagine everything. *Rehearse it all.* When you come to deliver the speech, you will recall more of it than you thought you would be able to and you will be able to look up from your notes more frequently and engage with the jury better. Most importantly, you will find that you will perform more effectively overall.

Errors that might creep into your speech will have crept in at the rehearsal stage, and that gives you the opportunity to correct them. You have already identified phrases that do not work well, and you can alter them.

This process of mental rehearsal will give you immense confidence, and that benefit cannot be overstated. It is a highly effective way of learning. The best thing about it is that if you practise that method of preparation regularly, it is not just that one speech performance in that one case that is improved. You will begin to recognise patterns of thoughts and situations. Whilst creating speeches at the outset might have taken you a few hours, it will over time take you far, far less time. And all the while you will be improving your effectiveness.

Speaking Techniques

As you become more confident with the content of your closing speeches, start to focus on varying your tone, pace, volume and intonation. Use pauses not only for their dramatic impact but also to give your audience time to absorb what you have said. Do not be afraid to produce a heavy emphasis on certain sections – and when you want to emphasise something, slow down.

There are times when you want to adopt a phrase which is a case-specific shorthand for an important aspect of the evidence. It may refer to the time that something takes, such as "the fatal 13 seconds" to refer to a portion of the CCTV, or "the Oxford Street evidence" to refer to everything that happened in a particular location.

Establishing this sort of phrase in the minds of the jury whilst dealing with the witnesses can then allow you instantly to associate a chapter of the evidence with the point you are making in your closing speech. This method will really help you make a point stick in the minds of your jury.

What you are seeking to do is get the jury so familiar with this expression, and this way of thinking of a piece of evidence, that when they discuss the case in their jury room, they will be referring to that evidence in the same way. They will naturally recall the key points you highlighted at the time when you referred to the evidence by that phrase. You are then able to deploy the technique of reinforcing these key points by repetition, in a similar way that we discussed above in connection with opening speeches.

A note of caution in terms of repetition. Your opponent may have used a repetitive device or motif in their speech or their cross-examination of witnesses. Do not adopt it in an unthinking way. Only adopt it if there is purpose to it. If you fall into the same shorthand, you may simply be reinforcing your opponent's point every time you repeat their key phrase! Only repeat it if you are going to rebut it.

> The defendant's previous convictions are not a signpost; really, they are nothing more than a point on the compass that is pointing you in a vague direction which the prosecution hope you will take – but it is the wrong destination.

There is another point that we would make about repetition, and it is to do with cases that have multiple parties and therefore multiple advocates. When it comes to making your closing speech, if you are the last advocate of seven to speak, you really need to have something different to offer when compared with the other six who came before you. Not the same old content, the same old delivery and the same old techniques; but, instead, a change, a variation in style and approach. You will need to work smarter to retain the attention of your tribunal.

The parts of the speech most likely to be prominent in the minds of the jury are the first things you say and the final things you say. We touched upon this with the impact you can make in your first words in an opening speech. The same applies to effective advocacy in closing speeches. This is where, no matter what method you use to write and deliver your speeches, writing your first and last paragraph out in full can be of huge benefit.

Make sure those two portions of the speech really say something to your audience. Think about how they can be impactful. You can sometimes echo what you have said in your opening paragraph in your concluding paragraph. Your final words could answer a proposition that you set up in your first words. Perhaps at the end you could take the jury back to where you started and demonstrate how the journey through your speech has brought you to the same place. You will find lots of different ways of doing something with those two portions of your speech. Just make sure that you do something which you have thought about when you fill these two valuable moments.

Finally, this. What you are hoping to achieve in a closing speech to a jury is not that the jury should feel that you have been lecturing them or persuading them. You want to aim to leave them with the feeling that you have helped them reach their conclusion. Provide them with assistance to look at things in a certain way without telling them to look at it that way.

You will often find that you can achieve this by not always stating so obviously the conclusion you want them to come to. Establish in the jury's mind that they may be helped if there were a piece of evidence which could point them in a certain direction. Then take them to the piece of evidence that demonstrates the point. Just leave it there. Do not state the conclusion. Trust the jury; they will work it out.

9 Submission Advocacy 3

The Plea in Mitigation

The plea in mitigation is the most common form of submission advocacy. It is something a junior criminal practitioner encounters on an almost daily basis. Nearly every barrister, regardless of their eventual specialism, undertakes at least one plea in mitigation in their early career.

A plea in mitigation is a submission made on behalf of a defendant after conviction (or guilty plea) aimed at persuading the court to impose the most lenient sentence that is consistent with the law. It shares many of the character traits of the legal submissions that have been discussed in our other submissions chapters. It does, however, have its own character.

In this chapter, we are going to use a plea in mitigation to illustrate some of the points that have been made in this book about submission advocacy generally. We will not use our case of *Rex v Tegan Plant* as our example. That is because Mr Plant, facing a charge of attempted robbery of a bank, would be most unlikely to be the recipient of a sentence other than custody (and a fairly lengthy one at that).

Instead, we will consider another fictional case, this time relating to the unfortunate Gordon Heyworth who perhaps has a better chance of receiving a sentence other than custody – depending, in part at least, on how good your plea in mitigation is.

You will find some simplified case documents for *Rex v Gordon Heyworth* in a chapter towards the end of this book. We recommend that you read the case documents first and then come back here and carry on reading. At the end of this chapter, you will see an example plea in mitigation for Gordon Heyworth.

Fundamentals

Sometimes at their sentence hearing, a client maintains their innocence. Typically, they may tell you this, or they may tell the probation officer when the probation officer is interviewing them in preparation for writing a pre-sentence report. It may even be that reading the report is the first occasion on which you become aware of the client's refusal to accept the verdict.

Where the finding of guilt has come about after a trial at which the client pleaded not guilty, it is unsurprising that the client does not accept the verdict. Because they did not plead guilty, they obviously cannot receive a reduction in sentence that they may be entitled to had they pleaded guilty. You will mitigate to make sure that the

DOI: 10.4324/9781003602019-9

sentence ultimately passed is properly within the guidelines, is lawful in any other respects and takes account of other mitigation that is specific to the client.

Difficulties can arise where the client, having pleaded guilty, thereafter disputes guilt completely or, more subtly, accepts that they are guilty but disputes significant elements of the case against them. To illustrate this more subtle point, imagine that in our case scenario of Gordon Heyworth our client accepts he is guilty of burgling the house, but disputes that there was any confrontation between him and the householder.

Where a client disputes guilt completely, you will need to hold a conference and confirm what they are now saying about their guilty plea and why things have changed. You will need to consider whether you can continue acting for them if you were their advocate at the hearing where they entered their guilty plea. There are ethical questions involved.

The most important ethical consideration is that you cannot say anything about the facts of the offence if the client does not admit he is guilty, other than comment on the prosecution's case. You cannot challenge any part of the factual matrix of the case. You cannot say to a judge that the defendant denies the offence during the course of your plea in mitigation if they have pleaded guilty and wish to maintain their plea.

Where a defendant who pleaded guilty still accepts guilt but seeks to contradict a significant part of the factual case against them at sentence, they may find that the judge decides to hold what is called a trial of issue – sometimes called a "Newton hearing" after the leading case in England and Wales. This may involve the prosecution calling the householder, Mr Henshaw, to give evidence on the disputed issue of the confrontation, and you calling your client (if he wishes to give evidence on this point). The judge would then determine on the evidence whether she is satisfied so that she is sure that there was a confrontation. This all happens because the judge considers that whether there was such a confrontation is a fact that would materially affect the level of sentence.

There is a big risk for the client with a "Newton" hearing. First, having pleaded guilty and accepting in principle that they are guilty, they may be perceived to have little credibility as a witness if they give evidence about "how guilty" they say they are. Second, the client may have been expecting to receive a reduction in sentence for their guilty plea, but this reduction can diminish, often to the point where it vanishes, if they lose at a "Newton" hearing.

There may be many types of documents that are relevant to your plea in mitigation. The first is a pre-sentence report written by the Probation Service based on an interview they have held with your client, on the prosecution case documents and on any other material made available to them. Sometimes the Probation Service representative will complete a short report on the day of sentence and sometimes they will deliver an oral report to the court.

What other material is available may ultimately depend on you and your solicitors: what do you consider may help the client? Has the client suffered medical issues that you will want to submit to the judge she should take into account? Has the client encountered difficulties with mental health? Is the client well respected at work with an unblemished employment record? These are just some considerations. You will want to arrange for letters or reports dealing with issues such as these to be available on the sentence date, or preferably before so that the judge has the opportunity to read them ahead of the day of sentence. Your aim, of course, is to reference them in your plea in mitigation.

If your client is of previous good character with no previous convictions or cautions recorded against them, then references speaking to their good character are essential. Often overlooked is that character evidence can be just as important for a client who does have previous convictions: such evidence would be of more limited value, of course, but it may help give a more balanced picture of the client.

Relevant to sentence and to mitigation are the sentencing guidelines. Many offences that you will be dealing with have guidelines which help the judiciary sentence appropriately and consistently. Easily found online, the guidelines will help you to address the judge and help her reach the right sentence. The guidelines often require an assessment to be made of the client's culpability and the level of harm that their offending caused. You will also need to have a sound awareness of sentencing legislation. Some offences require the imposition of a mandatory minimum sentence, for example. Sentencing of youth offenders is an area that requires specific knowledge.

When mitigating, you should be aware of the law relating to derogatory assertions in the Sentencing Act 2020. This law deals with the power of the court to make an order restricting the reporting of any assertions made that are derogatory to a person's character and which are false or irrelevant to the sentencing exercise. You should not be making submissions that are false or irrelevant. This ties in with the duties imposed on advocates to act responsibly in the exercise of our role.

How-To

Everything that has been said previously about structure applies to a plea in mitigation. The plea cannot just be a list of mitigating features of the offence interspersed with some of the relevant law and sentencing guidelines. Remember: your task is not to present a mass of information for the judge to sort through and determine its relevance. You should identify and advance what is genuinely relevant.

Do not present a biographical memoir of the defendant's life up to this point. Your role as editor-in-chief of your submissions is never more key than when you mitigate. It does not matter whether your client played Tiny Tim in the school production of "A Christmas Carol" *unless* that bears some relevance to the decision that the judge is going to make.

Let us recall the universal structure of submission advocacy from our chapter dealing with Submissions to a judge:

Introduction;
Legal framework;
Relevant factual/legal matrix;
Positive argument;

Counter argument;
Conclusion.

Our task now is to apply that structure to the preparation of a plea in mitigation in our case of *Rex v Gordon Heyworth.*

Introduction

In the introduction to your plea in mitigation, set out what it is you are trying to achieve. This is not a suspense novel; spoilers are allowed. Tell the judge what sentence you are trying to persuade them to pass:

> May it please Your Honour, on behalf of Mr Heyworth, I am going to seek to persuade the Court to impose a sentence that allows Mr Heyworth to retain his liberty and to be fully rehabilitated. The headline submission is that there exists today an opportunity for Mr Heyworth to turn his back on drug use and, if that can be achieved, to stop his offending behaviour.

Legal Framework

Next, deal with the legal matters that relate to the case. This may include reminding the judge of the relevant statutory maximum sentence for the offence or any other aspects of the sentencing regime that may apply to the case. Does the case attract a mandatory minimum term of imprisonment? If the client is a youth, what changes are there to the range of available sentences? Does the client benefit from a reduction in sentence for a guilty plea? Are there any sentencing guidelines that apply to your case that the court must have regard to? Are there any other laws that apply relating to the imposition of particular sentences?

In our case of *Rex v Gordon Heyworth*, there is a sentencing guideline for the offence of dwelling house burglary. You may briefly summarise the legal framework in this way:

> The court has a pre-sentence report. The court has also been directed to the sentencing guidelines for the offence of burglary. The court will want to consider the issue of credit for a guilty plea, the overarching principles guideline, the guideline dealing with the imposition of community and custodial sentences, and the statutory regime concerning the suspending of custodial sentences.

Relevant Factual/Legal Matrix

Thereafter, you will begin to blend the factual material into that legal framework. This is often going to be in two distinct categories: material specific to the offence and material specific to the offender. The offence-specific material will relate to the information that assists the court in determining how seriously the offence is viewed according to any sentencing guidelines that are in force, balancing the aggravating and mitigating features of the offence. The offender-specific information is the defendant's personal circumstances, such as are relevant to the sentencing exercise. We repeat: it is not the client's entire biography.

Often, when dealing with offence guidelines, the court is directed to consider the offender's culpability and the harm caused. We might deal with culpability in the following way:

> Turning to the offence specific guideline for dwelling-house burglary. It is submitted that this offence falls within the category of medium culpability as there was not a significant degree of planning, perhaps best illustrated by the fact that Mr Heyworth was not wearing gloves. It is accepted that this was not simply a spontaneous offence involving limited intrusion into the property. It is therefore submitted that the offence would be rightly categorised as falling within category B, that is to say medium culpability.

Positive Argument (and Any Counter-Argument)

You then move to present your best arguments in favour of the sentence that you are seeking to persuade the court to pass. This may include reasons why the court should not pass other sentences that are available to it.

Your approach will differ slightly from most other types of legal submissions because sentence hearings in England and Wales are less adversarial than other aspects of criminal litigation and submission advocacy. The prosecution does not really argue in favour of a sentence. That means that you are not really expecting to counter the other side's arguments. Instead, you are dealing with a decision that the judge may have to make, and you are helping her make it:

> Before the court today is a man who began to address his conduct when he entered his guilty plea. That was his decision and perhaps his first step. The pre-sentence report recognises the issues that need addressing. Mr Heyworth states that he is in a position where he wants to address those issues. He has three significant factors present in his life. First, his partner, Becky, who sits in the public gallery today, is willing to support him and who is herself a motivation for him to change. Second, he has the prospect of work should he be in a position to work. Third, he is well aware that he placed himself at peril of losing his accommodation.
>
> A man with a desire to engage with probation, with the support of his partner, with stable accommodation and with the prospect of employment is best placed to succeed with probation intervention.

Conclusion

Conclude with a concise summary as to why it is that the sentence should be that which you contend for.

> It is submitted that the court should today provide Mr Heyworth with the opportunity of working with probation during 28 RAR activity days allied with a drug rehabilitation requirement. Whether that is a stand-alone order or connected to a suspended sentence, Mr Heyworth will know the consequences of breaching that order. But the court can impose such a rehabilitative sentence today – not just with the hope that it will stop his offending conduct, but with the realistic prospect that it will.

Overall Structure of a Plea in Mitigation

The summary for a plea in mitigation may therefore be seen as follows:

1. Tell the judge what sentence you will argue for;
2. Set out the sentencing framework, including any sentencing guidelines;
3. Overlay offence-specific matters and then personal mitigation to the framework;
4. Argue for the sentence you seek, whilst possibly discounting other sentences;
5. Conclude by inviting the judge to pass the sentence you are aiming for.

As with all submission advocacy, signposting is an invaluable tool. We see it above where the advocate would say "turning to the offence-specific guideline". The advocate may go on to say, "now dealing with his previous convictions" or "we now move to deal with his guilty plea". Just little verbal cues that say, "we are changing direction a little".

With a plea in mitigation, you are not seeking to persuade the judge to do something they do not want to do. You are not persuading them towards leniency. You are seeking to persuade them they are passing the right sentence. In order to achieve this, there are some fundamental "dos and don'ts".

Do not shoot for the stars

You absolutely want to achieve the best outcome for your defendant. The key word there is "achieve". That is different from trying to argue for the best but unrealistic outcome. Make reasonable concessions, particularly where the classification or categorisation of the offence is concerned. Reinforce that the judge can trust you and rely upon you before you begin to take her where you want her to go.

In our mitigation for Mr Heyworth, the desired result is that the client retains his liberty and gets the assistance he needs. A judge is never going to just fine him or give him some form of discharge, and submissions that are geared to those outcomes would be unrealistic.

Do Not Bring Emotion into Play

A judge moved to tears will do one thing – take a step back, take a moment or two to recalibrate and then make sure they are sentencing with their head and not their heart. You do not want a judge to think that she is being soft if she passes a particular sentence. You want the judge to think that she is passing the right sentence.

Humanise the Defendant

Whilst you are not making a plea for sympathy, it does no harm to remind the judge along the way that this is not a scientific, formulaic process. Remind them that they are sentencing a human being. Use the defendant's name rather than just calling them "the defendant" all the time. Notice in the quote from our mitigation above that when referencing Mr Heyworth's partner we were careful to direct the judge's attention to the person in the courtroom. This makes the person a real, living figure in the judge's mind.

Do not Blackmail the Judge

You will see a lot of pleas in mitigation that effectively say, "if you send him to prison, he will lose his job and his house" or "think about what that means for the poor children". A plea of this nature will often be met with the response "well he should have thought about that before he went out burgling houses".

Do not make submissions which give the impression that you are blackmailing the judge. Turn the negative consequence into a positive assertion. It is not "he will lose his house if he goes to prison" but it is better expressed as "if he retains his liberty, he will get to keep his accommodation which is recognised in the PSR as an important stabilising factor in his life".

End Positively, Not Cautiously

Another common error is to end submissions with a catch-all line which says something like "If Your Honour is against me and sends the defendant to custody immediately, please make it for a short a time as possible". Instead, have confidence in your submissions and convey that confidence. Finish with a clear restatement of the sentence you seek and why it is that the judge should pass that sentence.

Do not undo everything that you have argued for by acknowledging that the judge could be right to ignore all your powerful points. Do not leave the final thing in the judge's mind that sending your client to prison is the right thing to do. If you do have to deal with the possibility of the judge dealing with your client in a different way to your primary submission, deal with that in the main body of what you have to say; do not finish with it.

But Do Have an End to Your Submission

Select your good points. Do not repeat them over and over. Then end.

Advanced Technique

We begin the Advanced Technique section of this chapter with a discussion about sentencing notes. This is mainly for the reason that a written sentencing note is only really required in cases of complexity. A judge should be able to pass sentence in most cases on the basis of the documentation provided in the form of reports, a prosecution opening and a competently delivered plea in mitigation. The preparation of sentencing notes places an additional burden on the advocate that is only really required in more serious and complex sentences.

The prosecution may provide two different types of documents for the purposes of sentence. One is a written opening that deals with the factual matrix of the case and then gives assistance with the sentencing framework, such as the maximum available sentence, guidelines, etc. The other type of note is limited to the sentencing framework.

A defence sentencing note should be in the format of a skeleton argument, which we discuss in more detail in our chapter on Written Advocacy. Its main purpose is to summarise the submissions that you are going to make to the court about the relevant guidelines and about the type of sentence that may be imposed if your client may be subject to unusual sentence types such as discretionary life sentences.

A sentencing note should be concise, even more concise than you intend to be when you address the judge in open court. Do not descend into detail. Provide a framework which assists the judge in following your oral submissions. Effectively done, you can use a sentencing note as an early opportunity to persuade, but it is only going to be the first step on the road. It is not a substitute for the well-crafted and delivered oral plea in mitigation.

Advising in Advance

The advanced advocate begins the process of preparing the plea in mitigation as soon as possible. Advise on what steps need to be taken in advance of the hearing. Ask your solicitor to gather character references, obtain medical reports and seek information from any other services that will be relevant to your submissions and that will help your submissions to succeed. Ask yourself: do I need this extra material, and what am I going to say about it that will work towards achieving the ultimate goal of my mitigation.

Think Like a Judge

Think like the judge. Identify what is likely to worry you as the judge and how you can reassure the judge about it. Have at the forefront of your mind the key recognised objectives of sentencing such as deterrence, protection of the public, punishment and rehabilitation. Direct your submissions so that it is clear why the sentence that you are arguing for is in line with each of those considerations.

Approach your task with the idea in your mind that the judge is likely to be risk averse. She is not going to want to release a defendant back into the community if he is going to reoffend the day following his release. Advanced submissions seek to eliminate that idea of risk. Do not suggest that you are inviting the judge to take a chance but demonstrate why it is that the sentence that you are arguing for is the right sentence, not a light sentence.

Reinforce Your Submissions

Echo and repeat key phrases, particularly from any sentencing guidelines that apply. In the guidelines that are used in England and Wales, there are certain phrases used that you can repeat in the body of your submissions without necessarily referring to the precise guideline each time you do. Phrases such as "community orders can fulfil all of the purposes of sentencing" or "is it unavoidable that a custodial sentence be imposed?" or "can the defendant be safely managed within the community" are examples of phrases that you can slip seamlessly into your submissions, and which will act as an anchor for the judge when she wants to include your submissions into her reasoning process.

If you have thought like the judge and echoed the language of the relevant sentencing material, your submissions and the judge's sentencing remarks will in all probability be very similar in their content. Your submissions should be halfway towards what the judge needs to say when sentencing.

Whilst always maintaining credibility, look for supporting material in unlikely places. Do not think of all "bad facts" as just all bad. In our example case of *Rex v Gordon Heyworth*, the defendant has a set of previous convictions. Look beyond the convictions and the sentences to see that, although he has a relatively long record, he has never previously had the opportunity that the Probation Service is proposing in this pre-sentence report now. That is not "spin" but a sound point in support of your submission.

Think about every mitigation. Think and prepare. Those five minutes on your feet could change someone's life.

***Example Plea in Mitigation in the Case of* Rex v Gordon Heyworth**

Note 1: We advise you to look up the sentencing guideline for dwelling-house burglary and read that carefully. Be aware that sentencing guidelines are updated and changed from time to time, and so the guideline used in this case may have changed since the date this chapter was written. The guideline indicates sentence starting points and ranges for examples of burglary offences, and it classifies them by reference to "culpability" factors and "harm" factors.

Note 2: Defendants who plead guilty receive what criminal lawyers call "credit" by way of a reduction in the sentence they are given by the court. A guilty plea at the first hearing which, in Gordon Heyworth's case, was at the Magistrates' Court would attract a reduction of one third. A guilty plea in this case entered at the next hearing, which was at the Crown Court, would usually attract a reduction of 25 per cent.

> *Note 3: Changes introduced by the Sentencing Act 2026 included (a) sentences of imprisonment that are no longer than 3 years in duration may be suspended and (b) sentences of imprisonment that are not more than 12 months in duration must be suspended unless there are exceptional circumstances relating to the offence or the offender.*

May it please Your Honour, on behalf of Mr Heyworth, I am going to seek to persuade the court to impose a sentence that allows Mr Heyworth to retain his liberty and to be fully rehabilitated. The headline submission is that there exists today an opportunity for Mr Heyworth to turn his back on drug use and, if that can be achieved, to stop his offending behaviour.

The court has a pre-sentence report. The court has also been directed to the sentencing guidelines for the offence of burglary. The court will want to consider the issue of credit for a guilty plea, the overarching principles guideline, the guideline dealing with the imposition of community and custodial sentences, and the statutory regime concerning the suspending of custodial sentences.

Turning to the offence-specific guideline for dwelling-house burglary, it is submitted that this offence falls within the category of medium culpability as there was not a significant degree of planning, perhaps best illustrated by the fact that Mr Heyworth was not wearing gloves. It is accepted that this was not simply a spontaneous offence involving limited intrusion into the property. It is therefore submitted that the offence would be rightly categorised as falling within category B, that is to say, medium culpability.

When it comes to the question of harm on the guideline, it is submitted that there are features in more than one category of harm as there were persons present on the premises when the offender was present. It is, however, submitted that the presence of others is envisaged within category 2 harm because that category also deals with violence being threatened or physical injury being caused to the victim, which must envisage their presence. It is conceded that this case involves Mr Heyworth having threatened Mr Henshaw and that the correct approach would be to place this within category two harm. This would also reflect the level of loss caused to the victims and the disturbance to the property caused by the thorough search described by the victim.

On the offence-specific guideline, therefore, it is submitted that the starting point for sentence would be 1 year and 6 months' custody, with a range between 6 months' custody and 3 years' custody.

The offence is aggravated by the fact that it was committed at night. It is also acknowledged that Mr Heyworth has previous convictions that involve theft, and whilst they are not for burglary, it is accepted that the record further aggravates his position.

Mr Heyworth does have the benefit of a guilty plea. It did not follow an admission in interview, nor was it entered at the first hearing before the Magistrates' Court; nonetheless, the guilty plea was entered at the first opportunity before this court. It is not submitted that he is entitled to a full discount of one third, but there is no reason why the defendant should not be afforded 25 per cent credit for his plea.

Taking a starting point of 18 months' imprisonment for a first-time burglar, it is submitted that the offence does not warrant a sentence exceeding three years once all relevant factors are considered, even before applying credit for the guilty plea. The resulting sentence therefore falls within the range that may be suspended.

Looking at the guideline dealing with the imposition of community and custodial sentences, the questions for the court are whether it is unavoidable that a custodial sentence be imposed and whether that sentence can be suspended. Going to the very heart of that is whether there is a realistic prospect of rehabilitation in the community and whether there is a high risk of reoffending or harm.

The court is sentencing a man who commits offences for one reason and one reason only: his drug addiction. There is an inescapable logic to the fact that if that addiction is conquered, the factors driving his offending will be removed. His offending behaviour has escalated in the last five years since the breakdown of his relationship and his use of Class A drugs. In that time, he has served custodial sentences, and they have not arrested his drug taking.

Before the court today is a man who began to address his conduct when he entered his guilty plea. That was his decision and perhaps his first step. The pre-sentence report recognises the issues that need addressing. Mr Heyworth states that he is in a position where he wants to address those issues. He has three significant factors present in his life. First, his partner, Becky, who sits in the public gallery today, is willing to support him and who is herself a motivation for him to change. Second, he has the prospect of work should he be in a position to work. Third, he is well aware that he placed himself at peril of losing his accommodation.

A man with a desire to engage with probation, with the support of his partner, with stable accommodation and with the prospect of employment is best placed to succeed with probation intervention.

May I return for a moment to Mr Heyworth's record of previous convictions. Whilst that list does him no credit, one thing is immediately clear: he has never previously had the opportunity to engage with the Probation Service on focused work designed to rehabilitate. His previous sentences have been short custodial sentences with no time for meaningful work, or they have consisted of punitive community work. The factors are now in place which the Probation Service needs in order to conduct meaningful rehabilitative work with Mr Heyworth. Should that work succeed, his risk of re-offending is drastically reduced – and the whole of society gains from that.

It is submitted that the court should today provide Mr Heyworth with the opportunity of working with probation during 28 RAR activity days allied with a drug rehabilitation requirement. Whether that is a stand-alone order or connected to a suspended sentence, Mr Heyworth will know the consequences of breaching that order. But the court can impose such a rehabilitative sentence today – not just with the hope that it will stop his offending conduct, but with the realistic prospect that it will.

10 Questioning Vulnerable Witnesses

Vulnerable witnesses will feature in any court or tribunal where witnesses are required to give evidence, whether that be in family, civil, commercial, crime and every discipline in between. The court system is adept at helping witnesses who are vulnerable to give their evidence. This means that you, the advocate, must be familiar with the rules and make sure that you are able to question vulnerable witnesses appropriately.

We would say at the outset that the questioning of vulnerable witnesses is a big subject area. One chapter in any book like this cannot hope to achieve much more than a summary and introduction. Though this is not taught on vocational courses, you will find that many professional associations hold frequent training courses, and that is when you can expect to take part in a thorough training programme.

Fundamentals

There has been substantial progress in our understanding of the needs of vulnerable witnesses in recent years. This chapter can do no more than give a few practical hints and tips. The must-have resource is the Advocates Gateway[1] and the many Advocates' Toolkits which are available there. You will find extensive assistance in handling vulnerable witnesses such as young witnesses, those with autism or hearing difficulties, and those who present with mental health difficulties.

All advocates should refer to those Toolkits before dealing with vulnerable witnesses. In addition, local advocates' associations, e.g. the Circuits, often hold training sessions to help new advocates learn the right way to question vulnerable witnesses. These are mandatory in some instances, though they are essential to any advocate who is looking to improve their abilities.

The Difference in Approach Between Criminal and Civil Cases

In criminal cases, there are specific statutory provisions which provide for a range of special measures. These measures include being screened from the defendant whilst giving evidence in court, giving evidence with the assistance of an

1 https://www.theadvocatesgateway.org/

DOI: 10.4324/9781003602019-10

intermediary, giving evidence by link, sometimes from a venue outside the court building; and recording evidence-in-chief and cross-examination in advance of the trial taking place.

The reason for special measures existing is to help witnesses who are deemed vulnerable to give their best evidence. Witnesses in some categories are entitled to special measures as of right, in the sense that the court is given no discretion. The main provisions are sections 16 and 17 of the Youth Justice and Criminal Evidence Act 1999.

Unlike in criminal proceedings, it is not the case that any witnesses in civil proceedings are entitled to special measures as of right. There are no statutory provisions that are similar to those in the Youth Justice and Criminal Evidence Act.

Advocates must nonetheless recognise that vulnerable witnesses may face barriers that compromise their ability to participate fully and give their best evidence, and they must be prepared to assist those witnesses. To this end, the Civil Procedure Rules Part 1 now contain a Practice Direction 1A[2] that requires judges to assist vulnerable witnesses. The Practice Direction states that the court should "ensure so far as practicable that the parties are on an equal footing and can participate fully in proceedings, and that parties and witnesses can give their best evidence".

Practice Direction 1A provides specific guidance on identifying vulnerability and what steps the court and advocates should take to address it. A person is considered vulnerable if personal or situational factors (temporary or permanent) could adversely affect their understanding of proceedings, ability to express themselves or ability to comply with court requests. Examples include age, physical disability, mental health conditions, communication difficulties, cultural or social circumstances and the impact of trauma or fear arising from the case itself.

Advocates in civil cases should assist the court in identifying vulnerability early and be prepared to propose proportionate adjustments. The court may make ground rule directions to ensure that a witness's participation or the quality of their evidence is not diminished by their vulnerability, thereby furthering the overriding objective of dealing with cases justly and proportionately.

Such directions may include protecting contact details, arranging special measures such as the giving of evidence remotely, or modifying how cross-examination is conducted to reduce distress. Advocates in the civil courts must be familiar with these procedural tools and be ready to make applications on behalf of vulnerable witnesses to ensure appropriate measures are in place.

There is a Bench Book that the judges use, and the judge in your case will be consulting that for guidance on the need for special measures in particular situations. Whilst it is not directly your responsibility as an advocate to address the issues in the Bench Book, it would certainly help you prepare targeted submissions on the topic of special measures if you are familiar with the guidance that the Bench Book provides.

2 https://www.justice.gov.uk/courts/procedure-rules/civil/rules/part01/practice-direction-1a-participation-of-vulnerable-parties-or-witnesses

How-To

When questioning a vulnerable witness, you have to be prepared to adapt everything from the way you word questions to the tone of voice you use, from the pace at which you speak to the length of time that you take. Be prepared to adjust your approach to meet the needs of the witness; it is never the other way round.

You can only do this if there has been an assessment of what their needs are. This starts with you and your instructing solicitor. It should be based on the best available evidence to you. If you are the party calling the witness, you will be in a position to gauge to a certain extent their communication needs, from speaking to them and from speaking to others close to them. You may need to start the process. To this end, know the limitations of your knowledge. Do not, for example, assume that just because one person with autism had one form of communication needs that this will apply to someone else with the same diagnosis.

Gather as much information as you reasonably can. Get reports from medical and speech professionals where appropriate. Obtain school records if you think that is going to assist. Your role as an advocate is to ensure that the witness is able to give their best evidence, including enabling them to communicate their account clearly and effectively.

There are Criminal Procedure Rules and a Practice Direction dealing with vulnerable witnesses in the criminal justice system. They are regularly updated. You should know them well.

The Ground Rules Hearing

Whilst it is very important to consider the views of the witness involved about how they will give their evidence, what they say will not be decisive. Advocates need to be alive to the fact that a vulnerable witness may seek to minimise their communication difficulties out of a mistaken apprehension that they will not be allowed to participate in proceedings or that their evidence would be viewed as unreliable if their communication needs are identified. It is very important that you make your own initial assessment about how the witness can best be helped and then take the necessary steps to obtain any reports that may help the right decisions to be made.

In a lot of cases, this is going to involve the instruction of an intermediary to perform an assessment of the witness and their communication needs. A report from an intermediary can be of huge value in assisting with the adaptations that should be made, including specific adaptations to the form of questions. Whilst of assistance, it is important to remember that they are also not the last word.

The definitive last word is often what has become known in the England and Wales criminal courts as the Ground Rules Hearing. The Ground Rules Hearing is held before a judge who determines what the rules are going to be for the specific examination of the witness. Often an intermediary will be present and will be asked for their input. Your role as the advocate is very important at the Ground Rules Hearing.

In civil cases, on the other hand, it is not a requirement that there should be a Ground Rules Hearing; rather the court "should consider ordering" one. Once a person's vulnerability has been identified and adjustments made, the court should set ground rules for the witness's evidence, covering what evidence will be given, how advocates conduct questioning, whether special measures or support are needed, and whether cross-examination should be restricted, modified, or conducted by a representative. The Practice Direction states that special measures that are available include (but presumably are not limited to) ones such as using screens so that the witness cannot see another party to the case, video-recording evidence, using an intermediary to help the witness give evidence, and giving evidence in private.

In advance of the hearing, you may be required to submit to the court your list of proposed questions for the witness. This will be so especially if you are going to be cross-examining. The judge has an obligation to review the questions in light of the vulnerabilities of the witness and may order changes to the questions that you have submitted. Do not simply attend the hearing and produce your questions there and then. To assist with the smooth running of the hearing, the judge will want to see your questions in advance.

At a Ground Rules Hearing, you can expect the judge to make orders about how the court process will adapt to the needs of the witness. Common adaptations to the process that advocates can expect will often include directions from the judge as to how the advocates and the judge will dress; the form of questions to be asked by the advocates; the frequency of breaks; the overall length of the examination; whether the submission of questions in advance is necessary; whether the advocate should provide the topics of cross-examination; the role of the intermediary; even where the examination is going to take place. The list is far from exhaustive, and it bears repeating that the place to get more detail is the Advocates Gateway.

Questioning Vulnerable Witnesses

In our chapter on cross-examination, we indicated that the prohibition on the use of tag questions is one of the most common adaptations that are encountered with vulnerable witnesses. Remember to ask the question in this way: "Did you see the colour of his eyes?". Do not ask the question with the tag: "You could not see the colour of his eyes, could you?"

A further adaptation is to introduce formalised signposts in your cross-examination. We have recommended that this is often for the best in any case, but for cases involving vulnerable witnesses, it can be most important. When it comes to each change of topic, let the witness know what you are going to ask about next. You might start here, for example: "I am going to ask you about the day when you were outside the bank". When you have asked all your questions on that topic you might say, "I have finished asking you about the bank and I am now going to ask you about when the police came to see you".

There are basic techniques which are of fairly universal application when dealing with vulnerable witnesses:

a. Keep the language simple and the form of your question simple;
b. Do not use complicated language;
c. Do not use metaphors or figures of speech;
d. Do not ask questions that have many clauses in them;
e. Be consistent in your language. For example, do not switch between saying "the defendant" and then using the defendant's name. Instead, use the name by which the witness knows the defendant.

Keeping communication simple is key to effective advocacy. These are all the sorts of techniques that we should be using with the majority of witnesses, whether or not they are vulnerable.

Check with the witness that they have understood the question if you are not sure they have. No advocate should ever seek to take advantage of a misunderstanding, and it is the responsibility of the advocate to approach the examination of such witnesses in a way that is fair. It will not impress the tribunal of fact if you are seen trying to take advantage of a vulnerable and confused witness.

You will likely be asking the witness about what other people did or said. Check the witness's understanding of who people are when you ask about them. Always be alive to the danger of misunderstanding. In some instances, it is recommended that you get the witness to tell you their understanding of your question before answering it.

The prospect of a witness requiring adaptations at short notice is relatively rare. Effective and competent conduct of a case should identify such issues early on in the life of the case. An inexperienced advocate instructed in such a case should carefully consider whether this is a case which they should conduct or whether someone more senior should take it over.

Advanced Technique

Relatively common adaptations when cross-examining some vulnerable witnesses are that you may be prohibited from putting your case and from cross-examining on material that affects the witness's credibility, including previous inconsistent statements.

The main purpose of advanced techniques for vulnerable witnesses is to find fair ways to balance out any disadvantage to your case that might result from adapting your cross-examination to meet the witness's needs. This may be as simple as the judge giving a direction to the jury in such cases that outlines the restrictions that the cross-examining party has had imposed upon them and the potential disadvantages that this produces.

Your case will not be disadvantaged by you being prohibited from placing before the jury the material that undermines the credibility of the witness. The adaptation is merely that you may be prohibited from confronting the witness with the undermining material during your cross-examination. This is, of course, the opposite of how you would approach a witness who is not vulnerable. So what do you do instead? You should make effective use of the Ground Rules Hearing to set the answer to that.

Often the way forward is by the introduction of the undermining material by way of agreed facts (formal admissions). If you are the party that is going to be cross-examining, make sure that you produce the first draft of the agreed facts and write them in such a way that they express what you want them to say without any additional explanation. You should aim to complete this first draft in good time so that the other parties and the judge can consider them before the Ground Rules Hearing. Done with skill and to a plan, a set of agreed facts can become an even more effective tool than the cross-examination may have been.

Never make it seem to your tribunal that you have been unfairly put at a disadvantage due to an adaptation made to accommodate a witness's vulnerability. This is never the purpose of any adjustment that meets the communication needs of a witness, and so it would be wrong to suggest that. When dealing with the adaptation you should not shy away from any potential "prejudice" to your side of the case; however, it would always be wise to approach the issue from the perspective of an adaptation being understandable due to the age of the witness (or other aspects of vulnerability), for example.

Remember always that the participation of witnesses with vulnerabilities in the court process is vital. Your mindset as the advocate is not that this presents a challenge but that it presents an opportunity to prove your ability as a communicator. As an advanced advocate, you will always be innovative in the ways in which you enable witnesses to participate in proceedings.

11 Remote Advocacy

Since the Covid pandemic of the early 2020s, remote advocacy has emerged more fully than was previously the case, and it has been accepted into practice in almost all fields of law, to varying degrees. It is less likely to be taught on Bar or Solicitor training courses. Most of us have experience of taking part in video calls on a variety of platforms, at least informally if not formally too. But the transfer of advocacy to a remote environment requires adjustment to our traditional approach.

There are several ways in which you, the advocate, may appear remotely, and we will see that the skills to be developed are ones mostly of practicalities: the mechanics of advocacy.

Often the issues that advocates must grapple with are "how-to" questions that will require significant thought and planning well in advance of the hearing itself. For example, if you and the witness are both physically in court, it is easy to show a witness a document in order to ask questions about it; but if you are remote, or the witness is, how will you do it then?

What Is Remote Advocacy?

By "remote advocacy", we mean any situation where you, the advocate, are communicating via a remote link during a court hearing. Where this happens, mostly it is by video link, but it can be by audio only (telephone). It can arise in any number of forms:

a. You are physically in court, but another participant is appearing remotely e.g. a witness, other advocates, the defendant in a criminal case;
b. You are appearing remotely, but another participant is appearing in person;
c. Sometimes there are a number of participants appearing remotely.

If the judge is appearing remotely, the hearing will tend to be fully remote. Members of a jury may not appear remotely unless they are all physically in the same location together and linking in as a group to the courtroom.[1]

1 Section 51(2) Criminal Justice Act 2003

DOI: 10.4324/9781003602019-11

When Is Remote Advocacy Permitted?

We cannot set out an exhaustive summary of the legal position as to who may or may not appear remotely, in what circumstances that may be, and in which sorts of hearings; that would be a book in itself. We can, however, set out a brief legal introduction to what might conveniently be called "remote attendance".

Civil Cases

In civil law, the Civil Procedure Rules at Paragraph 1.1 give the courts an overriding objective "of enabling the court to deal with cases justly and at proportionate cost", for example by saving expense and dealing with the case expeditiously and fairly. Paragraph 1.4 instructs the court to further the overriding objective by "actively managing cases", for example by "dealing with the case without the parties needing to attend at court" and "making use of technology". This includes remote attendance by advocates. Paragraph 32.3 permits the court to allow witnesses to give evidence by video link or other means.

Advocacy is often performed remotely in the civil courts by way of telephone hearings and video hearings. Such hearings are used to deal with many interim matters, such as applications or court-directed early neutral evaluations. Presently, telephone hearings will usually be run via BT Legal Connect, and video hearings via Cloud Video Platform. Such hearings will often be listed where it would be difficult for the parties to attend in person, and, indeed, the parties can themselves request that the hearing is listed remotely for that reason.

There is a real skill in conducting such hearings. In a telephone hearing, you cannot see the judge or the other side, and it takes practice to strike the right balance – making sure you do not dominate the hearing while still ensuring you can properly present your client's case.

There will of course be oral indications from the judge as to when they want to hear from you, but, in the absence of visual clues from body language, it is possible to end up sidelined in such a hearing, which can result in the other advocate presenting themselves more effectively and their arguments more clearly. Although a video hearing allows you to see the judge and your opponent, it may be more difficult to interject when necessary than in an in-person hearing.

You must make sure you have adequate computer equipment for a video hearing. For a telephone hearing, make sure that everyone has the correct telephone number for you. Make sure that you are in a place with sufficient reception. The court will potentially proceed without you if you are defeated by technology.

Criminal Cases

In criminal cases, there is more law on the topic of remote attendance. The Criminal Procedure Rules at paragraph 1.1(1) instruct courts that the overriding objective is that criminal cases be dealt with "justly", and there is a specific starting point in the law for remote attendance in section 51 of the Criminal Justice Act 2003. This section gives the judge the power 'by direction to require or permit any person" to take part in certain criminal proceedings by live audio or live video link. This includes you, the advocate, or a witness. There is a list of types of court hearings that are "eligible" for this direction. There must be an application if any party wants remote attendance and other parties to the case must be given the opportunity to make representations about it.

The judge must consider the interests of justice, in particular the factors listed in section 51(6), when assessing the interests of justice when deciding whether or not to "require or permit" remote attendance.

There is guidance[2] from the Lady Chief Justice's office to courts about how to assess the interests of justice, and these are in part intensely practical matters. Look at paragraph 7 here:

> It will not be in the interests of justice to make a live link direction unless live link facilities are available and are in working order, and will allow all participants to hear and (in the case of a video live link) see each other clearly, with no distractions, and the person attending by live link has the necessary technology available and is able to operate it. Nor is it likely to be in the interests of justice to make a live link direction unless a member of staff is available (without unreasonably impacting on other work) to set up the live link, test that it is working, and monitor its operation.

Often, the court clerk assisting the judge will have been trained to operate the court's video-link facilities; however, if you are applying to attend remotely, you (or your clerks) should confirm this in advance – and also check the arrangements at the other end of the link.

Paragraph 7 of the guidance goes on to demonstrate that the judge will be considering a very wide range of questions when deciding whether to permit your application for remote attendance:

> Pre and post court conferences between advocate and defendant may not be able to take place effectively by live link: where such conferences are desirable a live link is less likely to be in the interests of justice.

The Practicalities of Remote Advocacy

The best advice is to take time out to observe remote hearings of the type you expect to be encountering yourself. The importance of this cannot be overstated.

Subject to that, here are some common issues that will help inform the technique you deploy. Here we focus on a situation where you are attending a court hearing remotely:

2 https://www.judiciary.uk/wp-content/uploads/2022/07/Live-links-Guidance-for-criminal-courts-July-2022.pdf at time of writing

1. Choose your venue carefully. Aim for a place where you will not be disturbed and where the background is plain and simple, not distracting. Your car is not an appropriate venue;
2. Set yourself up with your screens, your documents, your notebook and any other materials before the hearing begins. Have a glass of water to hand (you would not have a mug of coffee if you were present in court, so do not have one at a remote hearing);
3. Have well in mind how you will appear to the judge and others in the courtroom. Every remote attender may occupy their own space, or "box", on a very large screen on the wall in court: your face and upper body will be visible, large-scale, during the entire court hearing. Your smallest movements and your quietest sounds will be projected for everyone's attention, so be quiet and still. The mute function will serve you well, though remember to turn your microphone back on before you speak;
4. Show the same respect to the court as if you were present in person, and dress in the manner in which you would dress if you were in the courtroom;[3]
5. An important technique of advocacy is eye contact. Being remote puts you at an immediate disadvantage because you will not usually see the judge's face clearly. To you on your screen, the judge may be a small figure in an image that shows a view of the entire courtroom. It can be difficult to assess how the judge is reacting to what you are saying. You must also guard against being less persuasive because of the difficulty of maintaining eye contact. Minimise your disadvantage by taking these steps:
    a. Maintain eye contact with the person you are addressing by directing most of your attention to the camera rather than to the image of that person on your screen. From the other person's perspective, this creates the appearance that you are giving them direct eye contact. It is counter-intuitive to look at the camera and not the person. If you find this easy to forget, try sticking a note on the edge of your screen pointing at your camera as a reminder;
    b. When someone in court is addressing you, often the camera in court will be directed to them so that their face is easily visible to you. Whether that is so or not, make sure to display the same discreet signals of active listening which you would engage in if you were present in person;
    c. Where you position your camera is important. If you position your camera at your eye level or higher, you will appear more authoritative to others who are watching and listening to you speak. This is more difficult to achieve if you are using a laptop camera because it will often be positioned lower than your eye level. Experiment with using a stand to raise your laptop from desk level or use a separate camera that you

3 Unlike one unfortunate advocate at Shrewsbury Crown Court in England, be sure not to appear in your underwear: https://www.birminghammail.co.uk/news/midlands-news/barrister-scolded-judge-appearing-court-31756125

can position at a higher level on your desk whilst it is connected to your laptop. Alternatively, use a second keyboard that connects to your laptop which allows you to use it at a greater distance from yourself;

6. To counter any time lag, which may not even be apparent to you, speak a little more slowly and signpost your submissions very clearly. Pause briefly before moving to your next point, giving the judge time to interrupt you. Do not cut in and talk across someone who is already talking unless absolutely necessary.

Sometimes you will be physically present in court, and you will be dealing with a witness who is remote. This rarely happens suddenly. You will have notice of this, and you should prepare. If your plan involves asking the witness questions and receiving from the witness their answers, and nothing more, then perhaps your approach will be a little different compared to a situation where you are both in court. But advocacy is rarely like this, and your task is to anticipate issues and prepare for them.

Think about a criminal case where during evidence in chief you decide you want the witness, who is remote, to refresh their memory from their witness statement. How will you do this? You should make sure well in advance that there has been a process to get the witness's witness statements to the room where they will be when giving their evidence.

If you are cross-examining a witness who is remote, you may have identified that in another document the witness has said something different from what they are saying in court. You may wish to confront them with that other document by getting them to look at it, but how will you do this? It is only possible if you have anticipated the point in advance and prepared for it. What if you want to ask the witness about a plan or a map? Often this will mean liaising with your solicitor and with the court to make sure that the right documents are in the right place at the right time for the witness.

Of course, the unexpected will happen. You may need to ask the judge to pause the case whilst you get a document to the witness who is remote so that you can proceed with the point you wish to make. This should be the exception. Courts will seek to minimise delay. They may be reluctant to delay the case because of an advocate's glaring lack of preparation. Delay may even cause the point you are making to have less effect.

In civil cases, good preparation of the bundle should avoid this kind of problem. As an advocate, you should be aware before the hearing starts whether the documents that you want to refer to or cross-examine on are in the bundle and, if so, where in the bundle they are.

How would you deal with a situation where you are present in court, as is the judge, but another advocate is appearing remotely? Be aware that the remote advocate will remain seated throughout the hearing, whereas you should stand as you usually would when addressing the judge. You should be very careful to avoid interrupting the remote advocate in order to avoid creating time lag confusion. Finally, do your part to make sure that the remote advocate is fully included. If you spot that the remote advocate is trying to indicate that they have something to say, help them by drawing the judge's attention to it.

Remember that it is a contempt of court to make a recording of a hearing, whether audio, video, or by taking a screenshot. Essentially, in a remote hearing you should act as if you were physically in the courtroom itself.

12 Written Advocacy

It can seem very strange to think of advocacy being written. In fact, as an advocate, your written advocacy is every bit as important as your oral advocacy. Often, your written advocacy will be your first opportunity to persuade your tribunal. In certain circumstances, it may be your best (or even your only) opportunity to persuade. It is a skill that is overlooked but needs to be mastered in the same way as every other aspect of your advocacy.

Written advocacy comes in all shapes and sizes. The most common forms are skeleton arguments, written submissions, written applications, certain pleadings and written appeal notices. This list is not exhaustive. As your career expands, the fields of law that you move into will reveal to you their own species of written advocacy.

We first consider the difference between skeleton arguments and written submissions because there is a substantial difference. A skeleton argument should be a brief guide to assist the court in understanding the range of oral arguments that they are going to hear from you. It is called a skeleton deliberately because it represents the bare bones of your submissions. Do not use it instead to develop your points fully; rather, it is designed to be supplemented by your oral submissions.

Full written submissions, on the other hand, are not generally augmented by oral submissions. You would expect your tribunal to be able to make a determination on the basis of your written submissions alone, save for any responses requested by your tribunal on matters that it may raise.

If a court orders a skeleton argument, do not prepare written submissions.

There are a number of texts that deal with pleadings in civil proceedings and other forms of legal drafting. This chapter does not replace those texts. What we are going to do is concentrate on helping you prepare the written documents that you will need to submit for your hearings, and which you will rely on to present and advance your case at those hearings.

Fundamentals

Never rely on AI to draft your legal arguments. May we trouble our readers by giving that advice again for emphasis: never rely on AI to draft your legal arguments. If you would like a stark demonstration of what can go wrong, look in the barristers' disciplinary proceedings section of the Bar Standards Board's website.

DOI: 10.4324/9781003602019-12

Be very aware also of the issue of privilege when uploading legal documents to AI and cloud-based systems. Are you uploading personal details of clients and other people? That may get you into trouble with the data protection authorities. Check very carefully what the retention and usage policies of the site or applications state.

Consider now the basic difference between spoken and written words. One type generally goes into our audience's ears; the other, into their eyes. This book has focused a lot on our oral words because, as advocates, we must strive to make our spoken words as attractive as possible. We aim to speak words that are clear and which communicate our content with clarity. You will have noticed how frequently we use the word "simple" in this book. Simplicity helps us achieve clarity. But of course, in the right circumstances we use rhetorical devices and oral flourishes to improve our powers of persuasion. Our audience must understand us immediately if we are to achieve our ultimate objective which is to persuade them with our spoken words.

When it comes to our written words – our written advocacy – we need to start with some fundamental guidance, not about content or approach, but about how our written advocacy *looks to the eye.*

You need to make the words on the page appear attractive. This is not just a question of style. In the same way that you want to be easy to listen to and to follow when you speak, you also want to be easy to read. If your spoken advocacy is a haphazard ramble, no one is going to be able to follow what you say. Do not be haphazard on the page, either. Instead, make the page appear attractive to the eye. Your reader must want to read what is written, not shudder when their eye alights upon the page.

Layout

Use a professional and easy-to-read font. Some jurisdictions or court divisions actually specify which font and size you should use – in which case, follow the rules. If you are in a position to choose, use the sort of font that replicates the most common typesets used in textbooks. You do not want a font that oozes individuality. Keep it simple by choosing a font, text size and spacing that combine to make your document easy to read. You do not want a page of words that are packed together as a dense blob of ink.

Use a consistent paragraph style throughout the document, with consistent and correct paragraph numbering. Use the tools available to you in all document creation apps that allow you to deploy italics and other ways of emphasis. Allow for margins and room at both the top and bottom of the page. Whilst it may be tempting to use every space on the page, your reader will find a less dense landscape much easier to pick out the detail. It also allows for the reader to make notes on the face of your document (particularly if they choose to print it).

Do not ramble. Keep the paragraphs relatively short. Avoid repetition. Avoid repetition and avoid repetition. (That duplication was deliberate to prove our point.)

Signposting

In previous chapters we have highlighted the importance of signposting in oral advocacy. In written advocacy, signposting is achieved by headings and sub-headings. Have your headings highlighted in some way so that the eye can easily find them (for example, by having them in bold or underlined).

Your headings should identify what that portion of the document is going to contain. The bare minimum might identify "Introduction"; "Relevant Facts"; "The Law"; "Submissions". That is a start. It is the basics of the basics. You want to supplement those basic headings either with subheadings or more precise headings. If you have "The Law" as the major heading your subheadings may be "The Statutory Framework"; "The Leading Authority"; "Interpretation".

Writing and Editing

Your document is seeking to assist and persuade. The goal should always be that the document is concise. Your writing should have an economy of words and facts.

When you are developing your written skills, this economy requires a great deal of work to achieve. You should not be concerned by overall word count, nor should you be overly concerned about every sentence only containing a limited number of words. What you are wanting to achieve is an absence of wasted or unnecessary content. You may need to cut a word in a sentence, a sentence itself, or an entire paragraph or paragraphs. Do not be misled into thinking that spending a long time crafting some particular content is a good reason for keeping it.

This is where you will have to be your own editor. When you have completed your first draft of a document, go through it and ask yourself the following questions:

- "Is that sentence written concisely?";
- "Is every word in the sentence necessary?";
- "Is there any repetition?";
- "Is that content required to achieve the desired outcome?".

Take the first of those four questions as an example. We could have phrased it like this: "Is each and every sentence or phrase written in a way which you would describe as concise and without additional and unnecessary verbiage?" What that says in 23 words can also be said in 5 words: "Is that sentence written concisely?"

Keeping it brief is critical. Legal submissions are not the same as a work of literary fiction. They are not even a guide to advocacy which may have occasionally strayed into a more descriptive and lyrical style. Like that last sentence we just wrote.

Brevity has a number of benefits. The first is that your judge or tribunal will likely have limited time. They will be grateful for a document that they can digest in as short a time as possible. The second is that brevity will often lead to clarity. Concise sentences will be simple sentences to understand. The final advantage is that it will aid any oral submissions that you make based on the document. The "you" making oral submissions will thank "you" the author for being concise.

When carrying out this editing exercise, always have at the forefront of your mind the question, "What am I seeking to achieve?" What is it that you are hoping to persuade the judge to do? Once you have the answer to that question fixed in your mind, you can judge every fact, every submission, and every reference to law against the benchmark of whether it takes you a step closer to your goal. If it does not advance your argument, ditch it.

No Juries Here

Remember (in the main) that your audience for your written advocacy is a judge, not a jury. Some of the flourishes of language that you may use to a jury will become unhelpful with a judge. Judges are still human beings and can be persuaded by attractive advocacy, but they are going to be better helped by a document that confines itself to the issues and the analysis.

Proofread!

In terms of presentation, be sure to proofread your work. Today's technology makes everything more convenient and quicker than yesterday's technology did. Built-in spell checkers and advanced tools for identifying likely grammatical errors have been around for a long time. With the advance of artificial intelligence, where developments move apace, it is possible to upload documents and have them proofread with an ever-increasing degree of sophistication.

But the autocorrect function can still change an intended word to another word closely resembling it. Common errors such as mixing up "their", "there" and "they're" can occasionally slip through unnoticed. Automated and intelligent systems are still not infallible, and you must not rely on their results without thinking. Errors can still creep in. The resulting document will be your document, after all, and you will take responsibility for what is in it.

There is never any substitute for manual checking of the document. Errors are inevitable, and your task is to minimise their occurrence. Read your document. Find the time, if you can, to step away from your computer screen and come back to the document after a passage of time to check it again. Some people find it useful to print the document out and proofread on paper. Others may read it aloud. The important thing is to have the document as close to error-free as you can manage. Manual checking of the document allows you to refine and edit it, as well as check it.

Once you have proofread your document, proofread it again. Then again. And while you are at it, proofread it some more.

How-To

We will repeat here some of what has already been dealt with in our chapters on oral submission advocacy. There is an obvious crossover but we deal with it here in the context of written advocacy to remind you of the need to employ the techniques in your written work as well as your oral work.

What Do You Want?

When constructing your written advocacy, begin by setting out clearly what it is that you are seeking to persuade the court to do. If you are seeking to exclude evidence, make it clear that that is what you are trying to do, identify the evidence that you are seeking to exclude, and concisely set out a summary as to why it is that you contend that the evidence should be excluded.

Suggested Overall Structure

Generally speaking, your written document should then follow a structure of:

1. Summarising the relevant evidence and facts;
2. Setting out the law which you say is relevant;
3. Then setting out your submissions as to why it is that the law as applied to the identified facts leads to the conclusion that you are arguing for.

When it comes to the facts, only summarise the evidential/factual position to the extent necessary to set your document in context (the extent necessary may depend upon the previous involvement of the judge and the extent of their knowledge of the case) and then the evidence and facts that are directly relevant to the application or argument. Where it assists, provide the court with accurate references as to where they can find the material in the bundle.

Inevitably, the document will require reference to law. It is not necessary to quote in detail the well-known principles. It is, for example, unnecessary to outline the nature of the burden and standard of proof in a criminal case to an experienced criminal judge.

Use authority that really advances the case you are seeking to argue or is of direct relevance. You are not preparing to give a law lecture. You do not have to cover the development of the law. Cite authority based on the legal principles, not due to similar factual scenarios. There will always be a difference in the facts somewhere.

It can be very tempting to simply copy and paste chunks of law into your documents. Try to avoid that temptation. When dealing with statute, quote the essential words of the statute if that is required. If it is not required, simply make reference to the statute (with a hyperlink if possible). When dealing with case law, extensive blocks of paragraphs extracted from an authority can significantly break the flow of your submission. It is placing too much on the reader. Rather than extracting large quotes, summarise what is said. If there is a quote which is of particular assistance, include that in your summary. Suddenly the particularly effective and relevant quotes will pop from the page rather than be lost in the morass of seven paragraphs lifted from the original judgement.

Analyse (and Persuade)

The important part is to then draw it all together. One of the editing checks that you can do with the finished draft is to ask: how much of what you have dealt with in the facts and law section of your document is of direct relevance to your submissions? If some facts or law are not relevant, then you may conclude that it is superfluous.

You persuade judges by assisting them in the right direction. You assist by analysing. In reality, what you want to achieve is to almost write the judge's full written judgment for them. This requires you to not only advance your case but to analyse your case and set out why it is that you are right. It is not about arguing better. This is about persuading the judge that the determination that you are arguing for is the correct one.

You will inevitably have to analyse the other side's arguments or anticipated arguments. When dealing with the other side's arguments, do not simply dismiss them. Do not simply describe them. Do not fall into the trap of stating that the other side's submissions are "wrong". You need to explain to the court *why* they are wrong.

Finish with one or two sentences telling the court what it is that you want and why the court should do it.

Civil Cases

Written advocacy is of critical importance in civil practice. It is often prudent to prepare a skeleton argument for an interim application hearing (this is a hearing that is held before the main trial date and at which the judge will need the advocates' help in determining some preliminary issues). You may choose to do so if you consider the issues are sufficiently complex to justify the drafting of a skeleton argument on a key issue, for example, limitation if that is in dispute in your case, or quantum in a high-value personal injury case. Of course, you may equally find that you are ordered to provide one by the court in advance of the hearing.

The temptation in civil cases, perhaps more so than in cases in other disciplines, is to try to include every possible argument and case law reference that might ever matter in any given circumstance. Practitioners can have misplaced worries about being sued for negligence if they have failed to anticipate that one niche argument that in the end actually turns out to be central. However, this approach will not please the judge hearing your case, and there are rafts of judicial commentary from the High Court and upwards deploring skeleton arguments that contain too much detail. Remember our main advice to you that skeletons are aptly named because they should be skeletal: try to be concise, precise and succinct. Add the detail in your oral submissions.

It is worth noting that there will be a distinction between the length of the skeleton arguments that you would normally expect to submit for mock trial student competitions called mooting and in practice (which should be skeletal as we have described) and those you might submit for an assessment at Bar School. For assessments, the examiner is often looking to see whether you have covered all of the key content in writing as well as in your subsequent oral submissions, and so your skeleton may be eight to ten pages long.

It is common at a Bar School assessment in civil advocacy that your skeleton argument might represent as much as 30 per cent of the marks, and so it cannot be too skeletal. But here are the key takeaways:

a. Whether your skeleton is submitted for an assessment or in mooting or in practice, it should be an aide-mémoire and not a script;
b. Structure and organise your skeleton in such a way that the judge can easily understand your key arguments;
c. Do not just turn up at the hearing or exercise and read your skeleton aloud – the tribunal will have read it already and will consider it a waste of time that you should be reading it out.

Advanced Technique

Once you have perfected the content of your written submissions, you can begin to make adjustments to how you will *present* them to your audience. Your aim will always be to make it easy for your audience to read your documents.

There are elements to written advocacy that are like oral advocacy. One of those elements is that it is a skill which is personal to you: you will have your own style, and as you develop, your style will develop with you. There is no common style among advocates. Actually, trying to force a style that is simply not you will generally end in disaster. Always examine your own approach and stay open to improving it. Even if something *feels* like your style, question whether it is truly necessary or the best way to do things.

Consider whether you can make small adjustments to the documents to gain even a marginal improvement. This is something that you can do when it comes to headings. We have looked at the use of headings and subheadings. It is possible to make headings bolder and to make them more a part of the argument. You can replace your headings with short questions or declarations. Think of these as headlines in a webpage or social media post – judicial clickbait.

The headings for a bad character response to the prosecution application that the court should hear evidence about your client's bad character might be:

"Introduction"
"Relevant Facts"
"The Law"
"Submissions".

You can refine these by saying:
"What we are seeking to achieve" instead of "Introduction"
"What the Court needs to know about the evidence", not "Relevant Facts"
"What test does the Criminal Justice Act 2003 establish?", not "The Law"
"Establishing a propensity to be untruthful", not "Submissions".

The use of expanded questions or declaratory statements in this way still allows the reader to see the separate sections and to understand what they relate to and how your argument is developing through your document. But they also act as a more inviting introduction to the body of the text which is about to follow. They already lead the reader into what it is that they are going to read. It sets the scene.

Footnotes are a surprisingly controversial topic, however! Not only on the question as to whether they should be used at all, but also what they should contain if they are going to be used. If it is your settled personal style that you use footnotes, then simply ask yourself whether you are using them persuasively and efficiently. The only rule would be that you should use footnotes consistently to convey the same types of information. In other words, use them for a reason and use them only for that reason. You may find it more effective to include all key information within the main body of your submission. Footnotes serve a practical purpose, not a persuasive one.

When dealing with the law and legal reasoning, it is a good idea to have in your mind how the judgment would be written that gives you what you want. Where possible, form your written submissions in a way that would be easy for the judge to include in their written ruling. There are few moments when you will feel prouder than when the judge quotes your skeleton with approval when giving their judgment.

Experiment with your language and grammar. It is sometimes said that advocacy in general, and written advocacy in particular, should avoid the use of adverbs and adjectives – but adverbs and adjectives are part of how most of us communicate. You will have read in the earlier part of this chapter that the use of simple language within a concise writing style is what we recommend, but what you say should not be devoid of style, elegance and colour. Your skeleton is not machine code for a computer to read but an argument to persuade a human being. Words can be fantastic to create a visual image in the mind of the reader. An active verb can generate a striking image in the mind of your reader. It also has the advantage of economy.

Let us look at a couple of straightforward examples. You could be describing the way someone has said something, and you could use verbs and adverbs to do that. You could say that one person spoke quietly and another spoke loudly. Or you could say one whispered and one shouted. When your audience reads the words "whispered" and "shouted" in your written work, their brains will automatically translate them into *the experience of whispering and shouting*. The same works for other examples – consider *she ran quickly* or *she sprinted*. Not only does this approach convey a mental image in the mind of the reader, it also has an economy of style. You can achieve more with fewer words. That is not a bad discipline to have.

Rhetorical questions can be an effective rhetorical tool in oral communication, but we recommend that you avoid them in your written advocacy. Written advocacy always allows your opponent time to think and react. Your opponent may provide a written response in which they give a complete answer to your rhetorical question. That can be devastating. Do not expose yourself to that risk.

If you are responding to someone else's written document, make sure that you do two things. First, read and fully digest their document. Understand the arguments they have made and respond to those arguments accurately – do not base your response on a misunderstanding or misreading of their point. Second, structure your response so the reader can easily relate your document to theirs. Provide clear references in your document that allow the reader to find the relevant passages in the other document quickly and without confusion.

Finally: always finish with a calm and clear statement of your position. Power and hyperbole will not make your written submission better. Do not try and demolish your opponent. Seek simply to satisfy the judge that your argument is reasonable and right. If the judge finds that you are reasonable and right, you win. It is that simple.

13 Advocacy in the Coroner's Court

Advocacy in the Coroner's Court requires a very different approach to that deployed in the criminal and civil courts.

First, the inquest is the Coroner's inquiry into the death, and the Coroner will go first in asking questions of any witness. Second, the very nature of an inquest is that it is inquisitorial; it is *not* adversarial. Inquests are not allowed to determine liability or guilt: under Section 10(2) of the Coroners and Justice Act 2009, a Coroner's determination "may not be framed in such a way as to appear to determine any question of criminal liability on the part of a named person, or civil liability". Third, you do not "cross-examine" witnesses at an inquest. This is counter-intuitive to an advocate who is used to a traditional courtroom environment. Instead, you examine witnesses by asking questions that are relevant to the scope of the inquest set by the Coroner. Fourth, there are no "parties" to the case because there is no "case"; instead, there are "Interested Persons".

At any inquest, the Coroner (or jury when one is empanelled) must answer four statutory questions. Those questions are:

1. "*Who* was the deceased?";
2. "*When* did they die?";
3. "*Where* did they die?";
4. "*How* did they die?".

"How" is defined as "by what means". "How" is not "why". In an inquest where Article 2 of the European Convention on Human Rights is engaged, the question "how" is expanded to include "by what means and in what circumstances". Generally, Article 2 applies in situations where the state in some way may have been involved in the death by something it has done or not done.

As with all advocacy, preparation is key. The questions you ask must be within the "scope"[1] of the inquest, and should not repeat questions that have already been asked by the Coroner: if you ignore this, the witness will be told by the Coroner not

1 This will have been determined by the Coroner, either as part of a pre-inquest review (PIR), or if a PIR has not been held, the Coroner will outline this in their introductory remarks at the inquest.

DOI: 10.4324/9781003602019-13

to answer the question and you, the advocate, are likely to receive a terse reminder to keep questions relevant!

Unlike the criminal and civil courts, the manner in which you ask questions is also different. If you approach an inquest like a criminal or civil trial, you will quickly find that the coroner will stop you and remind you that proceedings are inquisitorial not adversarial. Remember this is not a court which will attribute "blame" and therefore the manner in which you ask your questions, even when you are asking difficult questions of those who have potentially made errors (even ones that caused or contributed to the deceased's death) is crucially important. Remaining calm and courteous, even when robustly asking questions, is a skill that is not only required, but expected.

Before you conduct advocacy in an inquest you should watch and familiarise yourself with the Bar Standards Board's *Resources for barristers practising in the Coroners' Court.*[2] Further, you should read the short guidance document endorsed by the BSB and SRA: "Competences for lawyers practising in the Coroners' Court".[3] These underline the fact that advocacy in an inquest should be conducted in a different style, and one you will need to adopt from the outset of your practice.

Unsurprisingly, given that an inquest is not a trial, there are no closing speeches. Perhaps most confusingly of all for those first embarking on this area of law, you are even prohibited from addressing the Coroner on matters of fact. More on this later, but for now, keep it in mind and much of what you are about to read will make more sense as a result.

Procedure

The Coroner (or in rare and complex cases, Counsel to the inquest on the Coroner's behalf) asks their questions of the witness first. This poses many additional challenges to the advocate – unlike in a criminal or civil trial, you are not in control. Mostly, the family or their representative will be invited to ask questions next.

Coroners vary considerably in how they manage the order of questioning. In some courts, the Coroner works along the bench of legal representatives, meaning that the order in which you ask questions depends entirely on where you happen to be seated – sometimes by design, but often at the well-intentioned discretion of the usher. Other Coroners set no fixed order at all, so the sequence changes from witness to witness, leaving you unsure whether you will begin the questioning. Some simply follow the alphabetical order of counsel's surnames to determine who goes first, second and so on.

2 https://www.barstandardsboard.org.uk/for-barristers/resources-for-the-bar/resources-for-practising-in-the-Coroners-courts.html

3 https://www.barstandardsboard.org.uk/static/c2e4cb09-7793-4c03-b39a84507d709932/Coroners-Court-competences-Sept2021.pdf

What is universal, however, is that you always ask questions last if it is your witness giving evidence.[4] And remember, if the Coroner asks any follow-up questions, or if members of the jury in a jury inquest ask questions, you can ask further questions of your witness to clarify any new matters raised. This can be incredibly important if you feel you need to get the focus back to a particular topic or get your witness to clarify something.

It is good practice, if the Coroner has not already done so, to introduce yourself before asking questions of a witness, explaining on whose behalf you are asking questions. This is especially important if a witness is giving evidence via a remote link and may not have been present for the original introductions in court. Be sensible about this; however, if the witnesses are sitting in court all day and you have been asking questions on behalf of the family, they will know who you are and who you represent.

In their introductory remarks, the Coroner will ask the family how they wish the deceased to be referred to during the inquest, i.e. Mr or Mrs Shahzad, first name, or a shortening of that name/different name entirely. If they say, for example, "Reg" or "Gladys" then you should adopt the same style of address towards them. In most circumstances, your witness(es) should do likewise and use the name of the deceased which the family has requested.

You will need to be flexible and adaptable in your case theory, and therefore your questioning of the witnesses. You will also have to explain to your client prior to the hearing that if the questions have already been asked you will not be allowed to ask them again just because the answers obtained were not the ones you wanted. Part of the job of the advocate in an inquest is managing the expectations of the clients. However, that does not mean you cannot explore answers already given: that is where there is the potential to turn things around for your client.

As the witness gives their evidence, work through:

- What has been covered;
- What remains outstanding; and
- What has been covered but requires further exploration.

For those who have a criminal practice, perhaps one of the strangest things about an inquest is, aside from very rare cases,[5] the witnesses all sit in court and listen to one another's evidence. Again, that requires you, the advocate, to adapt your style. If you have already asked one paramedic the chronology leading up to their arrival at the scene, you do not need to take their colleague through the same questions. If you think they may have anything additional to add or you want to check something, ask a simple question such as:

4 Rule 21(c): The Coroners (Inquests) Rules 2013.

5 See paragraph 12–51, Jervis on Coroners, 15th Edition.

Q: "You have been in court while I asked your colleague about the time period from when you were allocated this job to your arrival at the scene?"
A: "Yes".
Q: "Is there anything further you can add in relation to your colleague's evidence regarding that?"
A: "No".

However, if you want to explore what an *organisation* knew at the material time, then you may need to ask the same questions of several witnesses from the organisation. Take, for example, an inquest where the organisation is a Police Force and one police officer has denied knowing something material to the case (for example, that the driver and occupants of the stolen car had been reported as being juveniles). You want to establish what their colleague knew of that report at the relevant time:

Q: "Officer, on the morning in question you were on duty with PC Samiha".
A: "Yes".
Q: "And you were in court when I asked her about the events prior to the police pursuit commencing".
A: "Yes".
Q: "Are you content that her chronology of events was correct?"
A: "Yes".
Q: "Is there any further information you can provide to the jury in relation to the circumstances prior to the pursuit?"
A: "No".
Q: "In relation to the information that you had received about the white Fiat – what did you know when you first saw it on Court Street?"
A: "That it had been taken in a robbery the night before. That its owner had been threatened with a machete".
Q: "Had you received the report about it being spotted in the area by a member of the public being driven dangerously?"
A: "Yes, I had heard that over the radio".
Q: "Were you with PC Samiha at the time?"
A: "I cannot recall, to be honest".
Q: "Was there anything else relayed over the radio about the circumstances of the driving?"
A: "I have heard today in court that it was stated that it was being driven dangerously by suspected juveniles".
Q: "You say you have heard that in court today, do you recall that information being relayed over the radio prior to you spotting the Fiat on Court Street?"
A: "Yes I do, but when we caught up with the vehicle there was nothing to suggest either by the way it was being driven nor from what we could see inside the vehicle that these were juveniles, and therefore on reflection I don't think I gave it any thought. I was more concerned that it had been recently stolen where the young female owner had been threatened on the street outside her house with a machete".

Q: "But you were aware when following the white Fiat that on the last sighting the Fiat was being driven by juveniles?"
A: "Yes".

This questioning then allows you to go on to explore with the officer how that information should have been used in relation to the organisation's (the Police Service's) risk assessment of the situation and whether requesting authorisation for pursuit was appropriate. It is best not to jump in with a question like, "You knew, didn't you; you must have known". Invariably the witnesses are more likely to accept they had knowledge of something pertinent if you can take them through the sequence of events that leads up to this. If, however, they deny it, then you have done your job because you have laid out the groundwork by setting out the facts that are not in dispute. The Coroner or jury will draw conclusions about whether they ultimately accept the witness's denial or not.

Another peculiarity of inquests is that you only address matters that touch upon your own client's position. As frustrating as that can be, your questions of witnesses should only be within the ambit of what potentially affects your client. If you are representing the bereaved family, you are likely to have questions for all the witnesses who are being called. However, if you are representing another Interested Person[6] there is likely to be a significant amount of evidence that does not touch on your client's involvement, and you will not be asking questions of those witnesses.

Consider the following scenario: you represent a company that provides prisoner transport services which transported the deceased from police custody to court and then onward to prison. Your client is an Interested Person because it is suggested that there has been a missed opportunity to address the deceased being at risk of suicide/self-harm from the time of his arrest to his eventual remand in prison. Your job is likely to be ensuring that the best case is put forward for your client so that the jury can understand the following in relation to the prisoner transport company:

- There was a robust system in place for dealing with people with potential mental health concerns;
- That system was followed in relation to the deceased;
- The paperwork shows that that system was followed;
- The relevant and correctly completed paperwork accompanied the deceased and was handed over to the prison staff when the deceased arrived at the prison (thereby providing them with the necessary information to undertake their own risk assessment in relation to the deceased).

If the prison staff accept the paperwork accompanied the deceased and it was correctly completed, then you would have no questions of the prison witnesses. It is not your role in the confines of the inquest to explore what they then did with that

6 There are no "parties" in an inquest – instead there are "Interested Persons" (IPs) as set out in Section 47(2) of the Coroners and Justice Act 2009.

information, even if you as a lawyer consider the prison's disregard of that information completely unfathomable.

In an inquest, unless you are representing the family, you really should be guided by the maxim "less is more". The advocate who cannot appreciate that their job is only to speak if required, as opposed to because they like the sound of their own voice, will not be serving the best interests of their client, nor assisting the Coroner. Speaking less as an advocate is very often the better approach in an inquest. Unless you have requested a particular witness to attend, it is quite likely that there will be many witnesses for whom you have no questions. Even when you have requested their attendance, if the Coroner has covered everything you needed to ask, do not feel duty bound to ask anything else. You will have explained to your client the purpose and procedure in an inquest prior to the hearing. You will have also therefore prepared them for the fact that if their questions have already been asked (and answered), that is all to the good, and it shows the Coroner is alive to the same concerns.

Ensure that you ask the right questions of the right witness. For example, do not ask clinical questions of a care home assistant, who will have no medical qualifications, when the care home nurse will also be giving evidence. If you are unsure as to whether the witness is able to provide evidence on an issue, there is nothing wrong with exploring that with the witness in your questions:

Q: "The family are interested to understand whether the fact that the deceased was given more than twice the prescribed dose of chemotherapy has contributed to her death. Does your expertise as a forensic pathologist allow you to provide an opinion on that?"

A: "I would defer to the Consultant Histopathologist as to whether that overdose could be said to be causally linked to death".

You may be confident that you know who can answer which question, but what you do not want to do is miss asking it of the right person.

The Bereaved Are at the Heart of the Inquest

While no court hearing is light-hearted, inquests are naturally sombre hearings. The family of the deceased will be present. Be mindful that whilst this may be another day at work for you, the family members are having to revisit the final (and inevitably traumatic) days/weeks/months of the life of their loved one.

Some Coroners will ask whether a family member wishes to give evidence. If they do, often they will be invited to do so from where they are seated, instead of moving to the witness box. If they do not wish to say anything beyond what is contained in their witness statement, the Coroner will admit their evidence under Rule 23(1)[7] of the Coroners (Inquest) Rules 2013, usually by summarising the relevant parts.

7 Rule 23(1) Coroners (Inquests) Rules 2013. Written evidence in the form of witness statements, documents or reports can be admitted into evidence without a witness being required to prove that evidence.

If you are not representing the family but one of the other Interested Persons involved, you may be required to ask questions of the family member(s) who give evidence. Quite simply, if you can avoid doing so, then do not do it. Many Coroners accept what is often referred to as the family's "lived experience" i.e. how the family viewed what was happening regarding their loved one. There is unlikely to be any need to question this perspective as this is an inquisitorial jurisdiction.[8]

In the types of inquests in which you are likely to be instructed as a junior advocate, it is highly unlikely you will have any questions for a family member giving evidence. But if you do, make sure those questions are easily understood, relevant and asked in a sensitive manner. And keep it short.

A Worked Example

One of the ways you can revisit topics already covered, to try and extract a different answer from the witness, is by setting out the key points in the evidence of other witnesses on the relevant issue and then asking the witness if their evidence remains as it was, or whether they would wish to review their evidence in light of the further information.

Imagine a scenario where you are representing a Police Force who had in their custody a detainee who went on to take his own life. The evidence shows that throughout the deceased's time in custody there were concerns about his mental health and the risk he posed to himself in relation to suicide and self-harm. Prior to the inquest, the Coroner has instructed an expert to review all the witnesses" statements and documentary evidence in preparation for the inquest and produce an independent opinion on a particular issue. The expert is a leader in their field and none of the Interested Persons have instructed an expert to counter the contents of his report.

The expert states in his evidence that the police were under a duty to organise a mental health assessment of the deceased and it was a failure on their part not to do so. You are now in the situation where the Coroner has evidence of a possible causative failing which has contributed to death on the part of your client. However, you are aware that the evidence will show that the police at that time had no ability to organise such an assessment and were instead reliant on external healthcare professionals (or HCPs) to do that. So how in the Coroner's court do you approach this scenario?

Style is personal, and no two advocates are the same. However, you are not trying to undermine the expert's evidence (much of which is very helpful to your client). What you are aiming to do is to get the expert to review his evidence, in light of the circumstances as they were, and ultimately modify it.

8 Paragraph 26, Chapter 13 "Witnesses" – Chief Coroner's Guidance for Coroners on the Bench.

Q: "Dr X, can we go back to your review of the deceased's time in custody at the police station? You were not in court at the time, but we have heard evidence from the custody officers in charge of the deceased's care?"

A: "I have read their witnesses' statements".

Q: "Of course. However, what is not clear from within those witness statements is what systems were in place when the deceased was in custody and the options available to the custody sergeants?"

A: "I am very familiar with what mental health service provision is available in custody suites, and although it differs from force to force the deceased should have had a mental health assessment".

Q: "As you rightly say, it differs from force to force, and indeed you will appreciate it used to differ depending on which police station someone was taken to?"

A: "Yes, that's correct".

Q: "The evidence of the custody sergeants was that at that time when the deceased was in custody, they had no ability to arrange a mental health assessment as there was no dedicated mental health service in the custody suite?"

A: "I find that unusual".

Q: "Their evidence, which was also accepted by the senior lead healthcare professional, was that they relied upon the advice and guidance of the healthcare professionals who were commissioned to provide healthcare to those in custody. They were clear that as police officers, as soon as they had concerns regarding a detainee's physical or mental health, they called the healthcare professional. Do you agree that that would be a reasonable decision and process?"

A: "Yes, if the healthcare professional was commissioned to cover both physical and mental health, then that would be reasonable".

Q: "You have reviewed the witness statements and the custody record and it is clear that that is what they did?"

A: "Yes, on more than one occasion they requested a healthcare professional to review the deceased".

Q: "In those circumstances therefore, would you accept that the police did all in their power to ensure that the deceased was suitably assessed for any mental health care he required?"

A: "Yes, in those circumstances they have acted reasonably. It would appear the decision whether to organise a mental health assessment or not lay with the healthcare professional".

That all may seem very obvious and easy; however, advocates who do not adapt their style from their criminal or civil practice can regularly run into problems: the question/allegation "you are wrong" rarely works with professionals, let alone with experts. It is far better to lay the ground carefully for them to modify their answers in a way that does not undermine them or their professional judgement.

And finally, what about asking questions of your own witnesses? You may well have a checklist of matters that need to be the subject of questions, especially where issues have arisen during the course of the inquest that have not been fully addressed in their witness statements. Sometimes it may be perfectly permissible to lead your witness if it is taking them through processes and procedures and addressing any Prevention of Future Death[9] concerns the Coroner may have:

Q: "We have heard evidence that the deceased waited on a trolley in A&E for 43 hours?"

A: "Yes, due to the flu crisis we were facing an unprecedented demand at A&E and throughout the hospital".

Q: "What options were open to the Trust to ease the crisis?"

A: "All Trusts in the area were under similar pressures. The experience of the deceased and his family is not what should happen and not the experience we would wish for any patient, and I can only apologise again to the family for that. However, they were circumstances beyond our control".

Q: "Can you explain to the Coroner what measures had been put in place by the Trust to deal with the situation as it was at that time?"

A: "We were using our contingency planning to attempt to ease the pressure, but these were not exceptional circumstances; it was a weight of numbers. To close the department would have only made the situation worse".

Q: "Has anything changed subsequently to allow you to better manage a similar scenario?"

A: "We are continually exploring ways to provide better patient care. We have updated our agreement regarding information sharing with neighbouring trusts so that each acute hospital has information regarding where there may be better capacity to treat emergency patients and divert them to that hospital".

On other occasions, however, you may be deploying your examination-in-chief skills and asking open questions when the facts themselves are in issue. What you must remember is that you, the advocate, cannot give evidence. If there is a matter that needs clarifying, then either address it during the evidence of your witness's evidence or, if it needs further evidence in order to address it, ask your instructing solicitor to identify an appropriate witness and obtain a witness statement from them to deal with that matter. And make sure that that witness is available to give evidence if required.

Legal Submissions

We have already referred to the fact that at inquests there are no closing speeches. At the conclusion of the evidence, you will be invited to make submissions in relation to the conclusions[10] available to the Coroner. You may also need to make

9 Paragraph 7 of Schedule 5 Coroners and Justice Act 2009. Coroners have a statutory duty, should the relevant preconditions be met, to make a report to those who can take action to prevent future deaths (PFDs). These are known as PFDs or Regulation 28 reports.

10 The coroner (or jury) will set out their conclusion as to "by what means" (and "in what circumstances" if Article 2 is engaged) the person came by their death in Part 4 of the Record of Inquest. There is no requirement in law to use any particular formulation or particular number of words in a

submissions on the engagement of Article 2 if the evidence heard at inquest now suggests it may be engaged, and/or in respect of any concerns raised by the Coroner in relation to their duty to issue a Prevention of Future Death report (PFD).

Rule 27 of the Inquest Rules prohibits a person from addressing the Coroner (or jury) in relation to the facts in the way that you would in a closing speech in the criminal courts. However, Rule 27 is not a ban on mentioning any facts at all in legal submissions, as this is almost impossible to do, but rather a prohibition on seeking to persuade the Coroner as to what facts they should find when different factual scenarios are available.[11]

Final Points

In the Coroner's court you will have the opportunity to question and challenge expert evidence at a far earlier stage than you are likely to encounter in civil and criminal practice. Do your research and know your subject matter. For example, in inquests where there has been potential medical negligence, you need to understand and be familiar with the medical terminology recorded within the medical records and which is likely to be the subject matter of questions. There is simply no excuse for not understanding abbreviations or acronyms.

Do not be intimidated by the expertise of the witnesses of whom you are asking questions. The Coroner will request that the witnesses, when giving their evidence, provide easily understood explanations of technical medical evidence – if you receive an answer that you do not understand, then ask for clarification. This is especially important if you are representing the family – if you do not understand what is being explained, it is unlikely that they will either. If you are unsure whether you have understood, then check with the witness: "Can I just check that I have fully understood your evidence?"

Often you will be required to take a witness through what occurred and compare it to what should have happened. To do this you will in all likelihood be relying on documentary evidence such as published policies which your client (Interested Person) is supposed to have followed. Make sure you have the correct policy that was in place at the time of the event you are asking questions about.

Interested Persons have a duty of disclosure[12] and any policies relevant to the inquest should have been provided to the Coroner – who will then provide those deemed relevant to the Interested Persons. However, check in good time that you have everything you think you need. If the policies have not been obtained through disclosure and instead you wish to rely on a public document such as National

conclusion. There is a list of what are described as "short-form" conclusions, however these are not the only one- or two-word conclusions that might be used. See paragraph 40, Chapter 15 – Chief Coroner's Guidance on the Bench.

11 Paragraph 101, Chapter 15 – Chief Coroner's Guidance for Coroners on the Bench

12 The people and organisations involved in a death will usually voluntarily provide documents on request. The Coroner also has the power to compel disclosure: Schedule 5 Part 1(2) of the Coroners and Justice Act 2009.

Police Chiefs' Council (NPCC) guidance, make sure you indicate you have questions of the witness concerning that guidance and ensure the Coroner and the other Interested Persons all have a copy of the guidance in advance of the witness being called.

And finally, be careful how you phrase your questions. While the outcome of inquests can inform subsequent civil proceedings against one or more of the Interested Persons, if you appear to be attempting to settle the issue of liability in the Coroner's court, you will find yourself being reminded by the Coroner in no uncertain terms that the inquest is not the testing area for a future civil claim.

14 Advocacy Assessment Criteria

Whether you are pursuing a Bar course, the Solicitors' Qualifying Examination route (SQE) or you are a solicitor seeking your Higher Rights accreditation, you will need to pass assessments in advocacy. As we reach the end of this book, let us consider the foundation that underpins all effective advocacy for the student: the assessment criteria against which you will be assessed in your exams, and which will help you progress in your career.

In your final advocacy assessments, your task is to demonstrate clearly that you understand the criteria and can apply them with precision. That is key. The most successful students appreciate this from the very beginning of their studies – keeping the criteria close to hand, revisiting them often, and shaping every practice exercise with them firmly in mind. By doing so throughout your learning journey, you give yourself the best possible chance of excelling when it matters most.

Your Course Provider Will Provide You with the Assessment Criteria

On a course of study, you will find that your course provider will be very clear with you about what the assessment criteria are. This is because the assessment criteria have a purpose. Of course, how well you comply with them will determine if you pass the assessment, and with what degree of success. But more than that, the assessment criteria are a kind of bridge between study and the realities of practice.

The regulatory authority for each profession – the Bar Standards Board for the barristers' profession, and the Solicitors Regulation Authority for the solicitors' profession – requires there to be assessment criteria. The criteria provide a good summary of the essential skills that you will need to equip yourself with if you want to enter the world of the practising barrister or solicitor.

The assessment criteria are freely available online, and you will find them easily. They change from time to time, and for that reason, there is no benefit in us trying to reproduce them in this book. For Bar training, you will find the assessment criteria in the Bar Standards Board's Curriculum and Assessment Strategy on the BSB website. Equally, you will find the SQE advocacy assessment criteria available on the Solicitors' Regulation Authority website. The good thing is that when it comes to advocacy, you will find the criteria are pretty much common sense, and they say what you might expect them to say.

Let us take a brief look at what the criteria measure.

DOI: 10.4324/9781003602019-14

Does Your Tribunal Understand What You Are Saying?

In your advocacy assessment you might, for example, be making submissions to a judge on behalf of your client, or you might be asking questions of a witness when they are giving evidence in a trial. Either way, you must be understood by your tribunal first time. Indeed, on a bar training course the quality of your communication and delivery skills accounts for fully one fifth of all the marks for an advocacy assessment. That is worth dwelling on: 20 per cent of the total available marks are for how well you are communicating or delivering what you are saying. In an SQE advocacy assessment, your assessor will similarly be looking at your language and the way you conduct yourself, and how appropriate your engagement is with the tribunal.

What do you have to do in order to make sure you are understood? We would say the main thing is to keep things simple. It is possible to get the facts of the case so wrapped up inside your head that you lose a little control over the words that are coming out of your mouth. Before you know it, the volume of your voice has dropped, and people cannot hear you.

Maybe your short question or submission has somehow stretched longer and longer with the result that no one, including you, can remember how it started. Perhaps some conversational slang has crept in that introduces uncertainty about what you mean, such as "the guys you saw in the bar". *Guys* is an example of a conversational word that would be inappropriate language for an advocate to use in a court of law. And when you say *guys*, do you mean men; or are you referring to all the people, irrespective of their perceived gender, that the witness saw at the bar? You do not want your tribunal to be spending time trying to understand the point you were making five minutes ago, rather than paying attention to what you have been saying for the last five minutes.

All of these are typical communication errors, and they are not unique to barristers and solicitors. If you have ever given a speech at a wedding, you will have wanted to be heard by everyone, including the guests seated at the furthest table, so you will have kept your voice up. More than that, though: when you are speaking in public, whatever the occasion, what you are really doing is forcing people to listen to you. Make it interesting because not every one of your listeners will want to work hard to follow you. Can you vary your tone? Being sure never to go too fast, can you vary your pace?

If you want to build to a point, make one point at a time; one point, one question. This is a theme we have returned to several times throughout this book: keep it simple. The simpler and shorter you can make each of your points, the more likely it is that your audience will stay with you. We have all attended speeches or lectures and found our attention drifting. If you are an advocate acting on behalf of a client who is paying you money for your services, you cannot afford to lose your audience!

But also keep it engaging. Ask yourself honestly and critically: what is it like listening to you?

Listening

Whether your tribunal are listening to you depends on how well you are communicating with them.

Be aware of the subtle signs you are giving. You may choose to work from notes. This is an acceptable method, but are your eyes mostly looking down at your notes or across to your tribunal? Looking down usually means that your voice will drop and you will lose eye contact. These are outcomes that will result in you failing to engage with your audience and they will simply stop listening.

You need to be alive to signals that you can deal with, for example that unconscious furrow of the judge's eyebrow that lets you know you should expand a little more on the point you just made. If your head is in your notes, you will not spot those signs.

As you scan your notes, be conscious of the overall structure of what you are saying and what topic or submission you intend to come to next. Practise your delivery before you get to your class, or before you get to court. You do not have to memorise your content, but you do need to be very familiar with it – familiar enough so that the only reason you have for flicking your eyes down to your notes is to get a quick reminder of where you are going next. It is a quick reminder of something you already know thoroughly. Learning the confidence to do this is key. Then, when you can look up again and focus on your audience, you can deliver the next section of your submission directly to them.

We are not saying that you are a comedy act when you are in court, but the delivery technique can be similar: the best comedians deliver their gags directly to their audience, never with their heads in notes.

Keep your feet still so that you do not wander or shift from side to side. Be in control of your arm movements to prevent yourself from repeating gestures aimlessly. When you are speaking in court, you have the attention of everyone there. That is a valuable moment. Do not sabotage your own submissions with unnecessary physical distractions that take your audience away from what you are saying and stop them listening to you.

The second aspect of listening skills is about whether you are listening. A substantial part of advocacy involves the questioning of witnesses, from whom you will get answers. It may sound obvious, but you should listen to the answers. This is so important that we have repeated this advice throughout the book.

It may be that the witness gives you an answer to a question which you can pick up on and use to develop the witness's account. It may be that the witness's answer tells you that they have not quite understood you and you can quickly step in and clarify what you mean. In either situation, if you are not listening you will not notice these things and your performance as an advocate will not be as effective as you will want it to be.

The assessment criteria will require evaluation of your skills as a listener.

The questioning of witnesses is an area of advocacy where bad use of notes can be a real problem. If you write out all your questions in a list, the temptation you will feel simply to read them all out one after the other will be immense. You will find that you are focusing on your voice and not the witness's. You will ask a question because it is next on your list, oblivious to the fact that in a previous response the witness has in fact already given you the information you are asking for. The risk is that you will stop listening.

But you must learn much more than just communication skills to pass an advocacy assessment. The assessor will be looking at the structure of your questioning of the witness or your submission to the judge. Is it logical? Will the tribunal find it straightforward to follow what you are saying, or is it confusing? Are you jumping from one topic to the next and back again?

Do You Understand What the Case Is About?

You may be the best lawyer in the world, but if your grasp of the facts of your case is too loose, your advocacy will all be for nothing.

In advocacy assessments, your assessor will ask themselves whether you have understood the law and are applying it correctly to the facts of the case. Are you trying to introduce evidence that is inadmissible, for instance? Are you focusing on the facts that are relevant, rather than the irrelevant ones? If your advocacy assessment involves making submissions to a judge in a civil court, have you properly identified the legal test that the judge must apply and which facts you can deploy in your submissions that the test is satisfied (or not, depending on which side of the case you are instructed for)? Is there a really important piece of evidence that you have not referred to or asked about? This is what we have been dealing with when describing *case analysis* or formulating a *case theory*.

Case analysis is about being clear in your mind about the facts that you need to persuade your tribunal to accept. It is sometimes described as having a strategy about how you are going to win the case. Of course, in an advocacy assessment, the case is not real; it does not continue on to a verdict or other outcome. You do not get to see whether you actually win the case! Crucially, however, your assessor will be asking themselves, if this advocacy assessment were a real case, has this candidate shown that they are capable and competent in their skills performance?

Are Your Questions or Submissions Appropriate and Persuasive?

Depending on whether you are asking questions in an examination-in-chief assessment or a cross-examination assessment, the way you ask the questions will be very different. Again, this mirrors real life. Asking questions can be a large part of an advocate's job. To do it so skilfully that the witness's account lives in the mind of the judge and/or the jury is a talent that can be developed and improved all the time, long into practice.

In this book, we have taken the skills required for the questioning of witnesses, and we have set out the fundamentals for you in context. We have shown you how to move from understanding the fundamentals to performing with an advanced technique.

We have done the same for submission advocacy, the art of persuading a judge. In submission assessments and in practice, you may supply a document like a skeleton argument in advance to the judge or to your assessor. Written submissions may attract as many as 30 per cent of the marks, for example, in an oral assessment on a Bar course. We call this "written advocacy", and you will need to be good at it to pass your assessments and to succeed in practice.

When being assessed, before you even open your mouth to speak to the judge, make sure that those written submissions start you off well. Your aim is to make sure that the judge understands the outline of what you are going to say before you even begin to speak. Consider also: can you make effective use of your skeleton argument during your oral submissions? Effective use of your skeleton argument is critical when making oral submissions. Your skeleton should be an *aide memoire* rather than a script. Not by accident, this approach in Bar training mirrors directly the skills required in practice.

From Study to Practice

We hope you can see the similarity between how advocacy is assessed and the advocate's job that you want. This is not a coincidence! The assessment criteria for advocacy are chosen deliberately because they reflect the skills that your regulator expects you to have in practice.

You will need to pass many assessments in order to become qualified; that is a regulatory requirement. Of course, you cannot pass advocacy assessments by reading a book (even a book as good as this one!) It is vital that you conduct your advocacy for your assessments in the way you have been taught by your course provider.

Advocacy can only be mastered by practice, further practice and still more practice. If you are a student, launch yourself into your advocacy sessions without reservation. Embrace the fact that you will make mistakes; this is how you will learn and improve. No advocate ever stops enhancing their skills. Every advocate you ever meet will be learning all the time: learning new techniques, adapting, borrowing, tweaking, finessing. Take our book *The Skills of Modern Advocacy* with you on your journey from study to practice.

Case Papers

Rex

v

Tegan Plant

[To give context, we imagine that the trial for this case is scheduled to take place at Manchester Crown Court on Monday 27 March 2028 and that the defendant had entered a Not Guilty plea to the charges on the indictment when his case had its first appearance, the Pre-Trial Preparation Hearing, or PTPH, at Manchester Crown Court on Friday 18 December 2026]

DOI: 10.4324/9781003602019-15

INSTRUCTIONS TO COUNSEL (Prosecution version):

Counsel is instructed to prosecute in the case of *Rex v Tegan Plant*. The defendant is charged with allowing himself to be carried in a Renault Clio motor vehicle without consent and attempted robbery.

It is alleged that sometime after the car was originally stolen, he and another (unidentified) individual went in the car to the New Dilhorne Bank in the sleepy village of Marple, Stockport. Once there, the defendant exited the vehicle and went inside the bank. He approached the single member of bank staff who was on duty at the time, Isobel Ullger, and threatened her with violence, saying "Give me the money or I'll shoot you". Isobel Ullger had the presence of mind to duck down behind the screen separating her from the man and she activated the bank alarm system which caused the man to flee empty-handed.

Isobel Ullger attended a video identification procedure (VIPER) at which the defendant's image was shown along with several other men who broadly fitted her initial description of the offender. She identified the defendant.

Counsel will please note the application to adduce evidence of the defendant's bad character that the CPS Crown Advocate has drafted. It is expected that the judge at the plea and case management hearing will adjourn consideration of it to the trial judge. The application is that the defendant's previous convictions for theft, blackmail and assault are admissible at trial to show his propensity to be dishonest, his propensity to be untruthful and his propensity to demand money when not entitled to it. Some formal admissions for the trial have been drafted and served on the defence for them to consider.

INSTRUCTIONS TO COUNSEL (Defence version):

Counsel is instructed to defend in the case of *Rex v Tegan Plant*. The client is charged with allowing himself to be carried in a Renault Clio motor vehicle without consent and attempted robbery.

It is alleged that sometime after the car was originally stolen, the client and another individual (as yet unidentified) went in the car to the New Dilhorne Bank in the sleepy village of Marple, Stockport. Once there, the prosecution say that the client exited the vehicle and went inside the bank. He approached the single member of bank staff who was on duty at the time, Isobel Ullger, and threatened her with violence, saying "Give me the money or I'll shoot you". Miss Ullger ducked down behind the screen separating her from the man and she activated the bank alarm system which caused the man to flee empty-handed.

Miss Ullger attended a video identification procedure (VIPER) at which the client's image was shown along with several other men who broadly fitted her initial description of the offender. Unhelpfully for the client, Miss Ullger identified him as being the man.

IN THE CROWN COURT AT MANCHESTER T 2026/121962

CROWN SQUARE

REX

v

TEGAN PLANT

INDICTMENT

Tegan Plant is charged as follows:

COUNT 1

STATEMENT OF OFFENCE

ALLOWING HIMSELF TO BE CARRIED IN A CONVEYANCE TAKEN WITHOUT AUTHORITY, contrary to section 12 of the Theft Act 1968.

PARTICULARS OF OFFENCE

Tegan Plant, on the 19th day of November 2026, knowing that a conveyance, namely a Renault Clio motor car registration number CTH2 XCM, had been taken without the consent of the owner or other lawful authority, allowed himself to be carried in it.

COUNT 2

STATEMENT OF OFFENCE

ATTEMPTED ROBBERY, contrary to section 1(1) of the Criminal Attempts Act 1981.

PARTICULARS OF OFFENCE

Tegan Plant on the 19 November 2026 attempted to rob Isobel Ullger of money.

WITNESS LIST

NAME	DATE OF STATEMENT
AMY BARBER	19/11/26
"	20/11/26
ISOBEL ULLGER	19/11/26
"	26/11/26
WILLIAM HAWKINS	19/11/26
JOHN McCRIMMON	19/11/26
PC ALISTAIR LEFTWICK	21/11/26
SOCO AFIYA LAMAI	21/11/26
HARRY FAROOQUI	23/11/26
PC ELLA FILDES	23/11/26
"	24/11/26
"	26/11/26
"	27/11/26
Police Inspector ROSIE CANTER	26/11/26

EXHIBIT LIST

Skin sample	AL/1
Audio recording of police interview conducted on 23/11/26	EF/1
Written record of police interview conducted on 23/11/26	EF/2
Audio recording of police interview conducted on 26/11/26	EF/3
Written record of police interview conducted on 26/11/26	EF/4

IN THE CROWN COURT AT MANCHESTER

CROWN SQUARE

REX

v

TEGAN PLANT

WITNESSES

WITNESS STATEMENT

(Criminal Justice Act 1967, section 9; Criminal Procedure Rules, r. 16.2)

Statement of: ....Amy Barber.....................

Age of witness (if over 18, enter "over 18"): ....over 18....................

This statement (consisting of one page) is true to the best of my knowledge and belief and I make it knowing that, if it is tendered in evidence, I shall be liable to prosecution if I have wilfully stated in it anything which I know to be false, or do not believe to be true.

Dated: ......19 November 2026...................

Signature: ......A. Barber...................

I live at 12 High Mellor Lane in the village of Mellor, Stockport, Cheshire. High Mellor Lane is one of the two main roads running parallel to each other through the village.

Today I have been working from home. I had parked my car on my drive in front of the front door at about 9 am this morning when I came back from dropping my children at school. I use a bedroom at the back of the house when I'm working from home, and the desk I use faces out of the back window over some fields. Whilst I was working, I was using headphones for online calls, and when I have my headphones on, I do not tend to hear what is happening at the front of the house. I don't use headphones any more.

At about 2 pm this afternoon, I went downstairs to make myself some lunch, and I noticed that the hallway was colder than usual. I saw that a very cold draught was blowing through my letterbox, which was wide open. It was snowing outside, and the wind was blowing snow through the letterbox and into my hallway. There is no cover on the inside of the letterbox, and the cover on the outside had been folded up. I then saw that my little box on the hallway table was open. I was using this box to keep my car keys in, and when I'm at home, the lid is always closed. The car keys were not there. Suddenly, I heard the sound of an engine revving loudly and a squeal of wheels. In a panic, I opened the front door, and I saw that my car was no longer on the drive – it was being driven away at sudden speed off my drive and away down the road. I could not see anything of the car's occupant or occupants. I immediately rang the Police.

My car is a Renault Clio with four doors. The registration number is CTH2 XCM and it has light green coloured paintwork except for the two rear doors that were blue. No one had permission to take it. This whole incident will cause me a great deal of inconvenience. I have no idea if I will ever get my car back. I will have to hire a car now to get myself and my children about. It is very upsetting to think that someone has targeted my house and stolen my keys and my car.

WITNESS STATEMENT

(Criminal Justice Act 1967, section 9; Criminal Procedure Rules, r. 16.2)

Statement of: ....Amy Barber......................

Age of witness (if over 18, enter "over 18"): ....over 18....................

This statement (consisting of one page) is true to the best of my knowledge and belief and I make it knowing that, if it is tendered in evidence, I shall be liable to prosecution if I have wilfully stated in it anything which I know to be false, or do not believe to be true.

Dated: ......20 November 2026...................

Signature: ......A. Barber...................

Further to the witness statement that I gave the Police on Thursday 19 November 2026 about the theft of my car, I was made aware last night by PC Ella Fildes that a car matching the description of mine had been recovered from just over the county border in Charlesworth. Today I was taken to a police car pound in the Ancoats area of Manchester where I was shown a car that had been burnt from the inside. It was the same make and colour, and the registration plates on it were mine. Inside the car boot, I found my leather Lacoste gym bag that I always keep there. This is definitely my car.

It is even more upsetting now to think that someone could have set fire to my own property.

WITNESS STATEMENT

(Criminal Justice Act 1967, section 9; Criminal Procedure Rules, r. 16.2)

Statement of: ....Isobel Ullger......................

Age of witness (if over 18, enter "over 18"): ....over 18.....................

This statement (consisting of two pages) is true to the best of my knowledge and belief and I make it knowing that, if it is tendered in evidence, I shall be liable to prosecution if I have wilfully stated in it anything which I know to be false, or do not believe to be true.

Dated: ......19 November 2026...................

Signature: ......I. Ullger...................

I work behind the counter of the New Dilhorne Bank in Marple. The bank is on the corner of Stockport Road and Market Street in the centre of Marple, and on the opposite corner across Market Street is Martin's Mart Corner Supermarket. Today at about 4.45 pm, just before closing time at 5 pm, the bank was quiet with no customers. I was working alone behind the counter, and I was the subject of an attempted robbery.

I was the only member of bank staff working on the counter at the time. Because it was nearly 5 pm my colleagues were in the back getting ready to close the bank for the night. The main spotlights inside the bank were still on and the public areas were brightly illuminated. I was busy putting notes through the automatic counting machine when I became aware that the main door at the front of the bank had opened. It must have been swung open with some force because I heard it bang loudly on the wall behind, and it was this noise that drew my attention. I looked up to see a man running from the entrance door into the main atrium where I was working. The man was wearing dark trousers and a dark top. It looked like he was pretty much all in black. He was just drawing level with my counter when he called out loudly, it sounded to me like a shout of surprise or shock, and he raised both arms above his head. His shoes started to slide on the polished floor. He fell to the ground and slid on his backside along the floor and right past me towards the wall on my far right, colliding first with a potted plant and then the wall itself.

The man groaned and stayed still for a moment. He got up slowly then staggered over to my counter. He looked a bit shaken and was walking with a limp. I could see now that he was wearing a mask, but the fall must have dislodged it because it was now mostly up across his forehead. His eyes and lower face from the nose down were plainly visible to me. I could see that he was clean-shaven with no facial hair. The man leaned forwards to me and placed his hands on the countertop.

He shouted, “Give me the money or I’ll shoot you”. He then winced and slipped a little as his leg appeared to give way for a moment.

I have been asked if I could see any weapon. I could not; however, in light of what he was saying to me, in the moment I could not be sure that he did not have one. It was quite a terrifying thing to experience. I am sure he was holding nothing in his hands. I took immediate defensive action and fell to the floor beneath my seat. This took me completely out of the man’s view and out of any immediate danger from him. The man was still there, though, because I heard him shout, “I said, hand over the money”. I pressed the alarm button and put my fingers in my ears. Immediately the bank was filled with the sound of the alarm. It is really loud and is purposely intended to make any assailants flee. I heard no sound of any firearm being discharged, and a few minutes later I dared to look over the countertop and saw that the man had gone.

I believe that I would recognise the man’s face again because of the good view I had across the counter when he stood in front of me demanding the money. I had the man’s face under observation for a good few seconds and in good light. He was about five feet five inches tall[1] and had a long nose, small eyes and a small chin. I could not tell the colour of his eyes.

I will now describe the layout of the inside of the bank. When you come into the bank as a customer, you enter into a long atrium that stretches ahead of you. On your right sit the bank staff, such as myself, behind a counter. The counter runs the entire length of the wall, and there is a large sheet of clear plastic in front of each member of bank staff. This screen is bulletproof. It separates the bank staff from the customer. There is a microphone and speaker on each side of the screen so that the bank staff and customer can communicate. The door where the man came in was about six metres[2] to my left. The wall that he collided with was about seven metres to my right.

1 Our international readers may be unfamiliar with height (and weight) often being expressed in witness statements using the imperial system, not metric. five feet five inches equates to about 165 centimetres.

2 You may even find that other measurements, e.g. distance, are, however, expressed in the metric system!

WITNESS STATEMENT

(Criminal Justice Act 1967, section 9; Criminal Procedure Rules, r. 16.2)

Statement of: ....Isobel Ullger......................

Age of witness (if over 18, enter "over 18"): ....over 18.....................

This statement (consisting of two pages) is true to the best of my knowledge and belief and I make it knowing that, if it is tendered in evidence, I shall be liable to prosecution if I have wilfully stated in it anything which I know to be false, or do not believe to be true.

Dated: ......26 November 2026...................

Signature: ......I. Ullger...................

Further to the statement I gave the Police on 19 November 2026 about the attempted robbery at the New Dilhorne Bank in Marple, at 1 pm today I attended at Stockport Police Station to take part in an identification procedure. The purpose of the identification procedure was to see whether I could identify the man who I saw enter the New Dilhorne Bank in Marple on 19 November this year and who came up to me and asked me to hand over money. The officer in charge of the procedure was Police Inspector Rosie Canter.

Police Inspector Canter asked me to watch a video sequence showing the images of nine persons. She told me that the man I saw in the bank may or may not be one of the men in the images and that I should watch the sequence of images twice through in silence before indicating whether I was able to make an identification.

At 1.30 pm I watched the sequence of images twice through in silence. After that, Police Inspector Canter said to me, "I am now going to ask you whether you are able to identify the man you saw enter the New Dilhorne Bank in Marple on 19 November 2026 and who came up to you and asked you to hand over money. Are you able to make any identification?" I answered, "Yes". Police Inspector Canter said, "Can you tell me the image number relating to the man you identify?" I replied, "Yes, number six".

Police Inspector Canter then said, "I will now run through the images again and pause the sequence at the man shown in image number six". She did this. When the man in image number 6 was displayed on the screen, she asked me, "Is this the person you mean?" I said, "Yes". Police Inspector Canter said, "To be clear, is this the person you saw enter the New Dilhorne Bank on 19 November 2026 and who threatened you?" I replied, "Yes, one hundred percent. He has the same eyes and nose and face shape. I recognised him straightaway".

Police Inspector Canter then said to me that the identification procedure was at an end and that I could return home. Although PC Fildes gave me a lift to and from the identification suite, we did not talk about the case at all.

WITNESS STATEMENT

(Criminal Justice Act 1967, section 9; Criminal Procedure Rules, r. 16.2)

Statement of: ....William Hawkins......................

Age of witness (if over 18, enter "over 18"): ....over 18.....................

This statement (consisting of two pages) is true to the best of my knowledge and belief and I make it knowing that, if it is tendered in evidence, I shall be liable to prosecution if I have wilfully stated in it anything which I know to be false, or do not believe to be true.

Dated: ......19 November 2026...................

Signature: ......W. Hawkins...................

At about 4.45 pm today I was just leaving Martin's Mart Corner Supermarket in Marple when I saw something suspicious happening outside the New Dilhorne Bank just opposite. I am now aware that someone tried to rob the bank, and I believe I saw the getaway car and one of the robbers.

It had been snowing heavily all morning and was still snowing when I was outside the bank. In such bad weather, I was surprised that a car would be travelling fast in the first place. The car pulled up quickly at the side of Stockport Road next to the bank and skidded so that one of the wheels went on the footpath before the car stopped still. I was probably about 30 metres away from the car at this point.

Martin's Mart is on the corner of Market Street and Stockport Road in the centre of Marple. Market Street is pedestrianised, and Stockport Road is the main road through the village. The Bank is on the opposite corner of Market Street and Stockport Road.

I saw a man jump out of the front passenger seat when the car stopped. He was wearing long black trousers and a long-sleeved black and white striped top. The stripes were horizontal. He was all the more noticeable to me because he was wearing what looked like a black balaclava-type cover over his head. He was holding a sack in one hand that looked empty. The man ran straight into the bank and out of my sight. He appeared to be running with a limp, but the road and pavement were slippery with ice.

It was quite dark and very cold. There were streetlamps at the junction where the bank is and going up Market Street which is pedestrianised. On this night it was dark, and the streetlamps were lit except for the streetlamp on the corner right outside the bank itself. It was snowing quite hard, and it was difficult to see the registration number of the car. The last part of the registration was definitely XCM, but through the snow that's all I could see. The car was small and white and had two doors.

It was quite a dramatic set of events. I looked round to see if anyone else was watching, but I could not see anyone. I thought that I'd better try and take some photographs of the car because it all looked very suspicious. I thought my phone was in my coat pocket, so I put my shopping bags on the ground and took off my gloves so that I could reach for it. The phone wasn't in either pocket, and I was worried in case the car was going to drive off before I could take a photo. I heard the driver rev the engine a few times and then some shouting from inside the bank premises. Just as I found my phone in one of my trouser pockets, the car's horn sounded. It shocked me, and I dropped my phone into the snow. A loud alarm then went off. I picked my phone up and tried to brush the snow off, but the next thing I was aware of was the sound of a car door slamming. The car then drove away past me and sped away up Stockport Road past the Rococo Cinema and out of view.

I never did get a photo of the car, but I did type XCM in a note on my phone which is all I could remember of the car's number plate – the last part. The car was definitely a Renault Clio. It had two doors. My sister has a Clio, and so I know what they look like.

I would be unable to identify the man I saw exit the car. I presume he got back in again, which would explain the sound of the car door slamming.

WITNESS STATEMENT

(Criminal Justice Act 1967, section 9; Criminal Procedure Rules, r. 16.2)

Statement of: ....John McCrimmon......................

Age of witness (if over 18, enter "over 18"): ....over 18.....................

This statement (consisting of one page) is true to the best of my knowledge and belief and I make it knowing that, if it is tendered in evidence, I shall be liable to prosecution if I have wilfully stated in it anything which I know to be false, or do not believe to be true.

Dated: ......19 November 2026...................

Signature: ......J. McCrimmon...................

I am the manager of the New Dilhorne Bank on Market Street in Marple. I am writing this statement to confirm that the CCTV recording equipment that we have in the premises was defective on 19 November 2026. Unfortunately, it therefore did not record the incident when a man entered and tried to rob my assistant Isobel Ullger. We do not have and never have had any CCTV cameras outside the premises.

WITNESS STATEMENT

(Criminal Justice Act 1967, section 9; Criminal Procedure Rules, r. 16.2)

Statement of: ....Alistair Leftwick.....................

Age of witness (if over 18, enter "over 18"): ....over 18....................

This statement (consisting of one page) is true to the best of my knowledge and belief and I make it knowing that, if it is tendered in evidence, I shall be liable to prosecution if I have wilfully stated in it anything which I know to be false, or do not believe to be true.

Dated: ......21 November 2026...................

Signature: ......A. Leftwick...................

I am the police community liaison officer for Charlesworth, stationed at New Mills Police Station in Derbyshire. Yesterday at about 5.20 pm I was telephoned by a neighbourhood watch community volunteer in Charlesworth who reported to me they had seen a burnt-out car apparently abandoned in Chesterton Street. I went to Chesterton Street, arriving at 8 pm.

At the end of Chesterton Street by the playing fields, I located a Renault Clio registered number CTH2 XCM. A check on the police national computer revealed the registered keeper was one Amy Barber. The area had had some snow, but it had turned to heavy rain during the evening, so I decided not to try and open any of the doors. I looked through the windows, and I could see what appeared to be some fire damage as though someone had tried to set fire to the inside of the vehicle. I was aware from the police national computer that a light-coloured Renault Clio with a part registration number XCM had been reported as being associated with an attempt to rob the New Dilhorne Bank in Marple, and I considered it possible that this might be the vehicle involved, so I alerted Scenes of Crimes and stayed with the vehicle until my colleague, Scenes of Crime Officer (SOCO) Afiya Lamai, arrived at about 11 pm, by which time the rain had stopped.

WITNESS STATEMENT

(Criminal Justice Act 1967, section 9; Criminal Procedure Rules, r. 16.2)

Statement of: ....Afiya Lamai....................

Age of witness (if over 18, enter "over 18"): ....over 18....................

This statement (consisting of one page) is true to the best of my knowledge and belief and I make it knowing that, if it is tendered in evidence, I shall be liable to prosecution if I have wilfully stated in it anything which I know to be false, or do not believe to be true.

Dated: ......21 November 2026...................

Signature: ......A. Lamai...................

I am a scenes of crime officer with the Derbyshire Constabulary currently based at New Mills Police Station.

I attended Chesterton Street in Charlesworth at 11pm on Friday 20 November 2026. The weather was bad; there had been some snow and rain; consequently, there was no chance of recovery of any forensic lifts from the outside of the vehicle.

When I arrived, I was able to open the vehicle doors, which were unlocked, and examine the inside of the vehicle. The inside of the vehicle had been the subject of an arson attempt,[3] probably in an effort to hamper police attempts to recover any scientific evidence that may link the vehicle to the offenders. The seats were scorched, and the fascia had melted and become deformed. But the rain and cold weather had acted to stifle the force of the fire. Most of the fire damage was around the area of the driver's seat, and I found that it was feasible to swab the inside front passenger door handle. Doing this, I managed to recover what appeared to be a flake of skin. I labelled this swab AL/1, and I conveyed this swab to New Mills Police Station, where I placed it in the secure property store.

3 Ordinarily, you may see a witness statement from a fire officer about this, for a police officer may not have the necessary expertise to state this opinion; however, for simplicity, we are including the evidence here.

WITNESS STATEMENT

(Criminal Justice Act 1967, section 9; Criminal Procedure Rules, r. 16.2)

Statement of: ....Harry Farooqui PhD......................

Age of witness (if over 18, enter "over 18"): ....over 18.....................

This statement (consisting of two pages) is true to the best of my knowledge and belief and I make it knowing that, if it is tendered in evidence, I shall be liable to prosecution if I have wilfully stated in it anything which I know to be false, or do not believe to be true.

Dated: ......23 November 2026...................

Signature: ......H. Farooqui...................

I work for the National Forensic Service at their laboratories in Trafford Park, Manchester, where I have been employed for the last seven years and where I have developed my professionalism in DNA analysis and human identification.

I hold a PhD in Forensic Genetics from Edinburgh University and a Master's in Forensic Science following a BSc in Molecular Biology, both from Liverpool University. I am accredited by the Chartered Society of Forensic Sciences (CSFS) and I have extensive expertise in STR analysis, mitochondrial DNA sequencing, and next-generation sequencing (NGS).

I specialise in extracting trace DNA from skin flakes, epithelial cells and other minute biological samples. Often I am tasked with assessing whether DNA from a crime scene matches a profile on the UK National DNA Database (NDNAD), helping law enforcement identify and apprehend offenders. In addition to my laboratory work, I frequently appear as an expert witness in court, translating complex genetic evidence into testimony. I am a member of the Forensic Science Regulator's Advisory Panel, and I contribute to forensic research publications.

On 21 November 2026, I was asked to attend New Mills Police Station in Derbyshire to recover and analyse swab AL/1, which was in the secure evidence storage at that police station by local SOCO Afiya Lamai. I transported the sample to my laboratory at Trafford Park, where I analysed it.

I conducted DNA extraction using standard forensic procedures, followed by quantification, amplification, and capillary electrophoresis to generate a DNA profile from the submitted sample AL/1. The resulting DNA profile was then compared against reference profiles stored on the NDNAD.

This comparison identified a match between the DNA profile obtained from the skin sample and an existing profile on the NDNAD, which corresponds to Tegan Plant. The DNA match was determined using Short Tandem Repeat (STR) analysis, which examines specific regions of the genome for individual identification. The probability of this DNA profile matching a person other than Tegan Plant, assuming no close relatives are in the database, is less than one in a billion.

The DNA profile recovered from the crime scene is consistent with the DNA profile of Tegan Plant. The probability of this DNA profile matching a random unrelated individual, assuming no close relatives are in the database, is less than one in a billion. Based on my findings, Tegan Plant cannot be excluded as a potential contributor of this DNA. However, the presence of his DNA alone does not provide information regarding how or when it was deposited.

WITNESS STATEMENT

(Criminal Justice Act 1967, section 9; Criminal Procedure Rules, r. 16.2)

Statement of: ....Ella Fildes......................

Age of witness (if over 18, enter "over 18"): ....over 18.....................

This statement (consisting of two pages) is true to the best of my knowledge and belief and I make it knowing that, if it is tendered in evidence, I shall be liable to prosecution if I have wilfully stated in it anything which I know to be false, or do not believe to be true.

Dated: ......23 November 2026...................

Signature: ......E. Fildes...................

I am a police officer with the Greater Manchester Police. Today at 5.10 pm in the company of PC Caitlin Bradford, I attended at 15, St Jared's Close in Bredbury, Stockport, an address which was recorded on the Police National Computer as being where Tegan Plant lived with his mother, Nora. The purpose of my visit was to arrest Tegan Plant and convey him to Stockport Police Station for interview in connection with an allegation of attempted robbery at the New Dilhorne Bank in Marple on 19 November 2026.

I knocked at the front door, which was answered by Nora Plant. Before I had the chance to say anything, Nora Plant shouted over her shoulder, "What have you done now." Tegan Plant appeared at the door behind his mother and raised his hands in the air, palms upwards. He stepped past his mother to the doorstep and said to me, "What? What is it?" I replied, "Tegan Plant, I am arresting you on suspicion of attempting to rob the New Dilhorne Bank in Marple on 19 November. You do not have to say anything, but it may harm your defence if you do not mention when questioned something which you later rely on in court. Anything you do say may be given in evidence".

Tegan Plant did not reply but sighed loudly and turned round, putting his hands behind his back so that I could place the handcuffs on him in the approved rear stack position. I then placed him in the back of my police vehicle and, with PC Bradford, conveyed him to Stockport Police Station.

Later the same day at Stockport Police Station, I interviewed Tegan Plant in connection with the allegation for which I had arrested him. I exhibit the audio recording of the interview as EF/1. Later that evening at 7.45 pm, Tegan Plant was bailed for further police enquiries.

WITNESS STATEMENT

(Criminal Justice Act 1967, section 9; Criminal Procedure Rules, r. 16.2)

Statement of: ....Ella Fildes......................

Age of witness (if over 18, enter "over 18"): ....over 18.....................

This statement (consisting of one page) is true to the best of my knowledge and belief and I make it knowing that, if it is tendered in evidence, I shall be liable to prosecution if I have wilfully stated in it anything which I know to be false, or do not believe to be true.

Dated: ......24 November 2026...................

Signature: ......E. Fildes...................

Today I prepared a written record of the interview of Tegan Plant in this case that I conducted on 23 November 2026. I exhibit the written record as EF/2.

WITNESS STATEMENT

(Criminal Justice Act 1967, section 9; Criminal Procedure Rules, r. 16.2)

Statement of: ....Ella Fildes......................

Age of witness (if over 18, enter "over 18"): ....over 18.....................

This statement (consisting of one page) is true to the best of my knowledge and belief and I make it knowing that, if it is tendered in evidence, I shall be liable to prosecution if I have wilfully stated in it anything which I know to be false, or do not believe to be true.

Dated: ......26 November 2026..................

Signature: ......E. Fildes...................

Further to my statements dated 23 and 24 November 2026 in this case, I can confirm that yesterday morning at 10 am I spoke with Tegan Plant by phone and made him aware that there would be a VIPER identification procedure held today at Stockport Police Station in connection with the allegation of attempted robbery that he had been interviewed about three days previously. I offered him the opportunity to attend. Plant refused to attend.

At 12 pm today I collected Isobel Ullger from her home address and conveyed her to Stockport Police Station and into the company of Police Inspector Rosie Canter, the VIPER officer. I took no part in the identification procedure and waited outside the room whilst it took place. At 1.30 pm I took Ms Ullger home again. At no stage did we discuss the case.

Today at 4 pm in the company of PC Heather Thorbjornsen, I attended at 15, St Jared's Close in Bredbury, Stockport. The purpose of my visit was to arrest Tegan Plant and convey him to Stockport Police Station for a further interview in connection with an allegation of attempted robbery at the New Dilhorne Bank in Marple on 19 November 2026.

Upon arrival at Stockport Police Station, after he had been booked in by the custody sergeant, I took Tegan Plant to an interview room and conducted an interview with her. I exhibit the audio recording of the interview as EF/3.

WITNESS STATEMENT

(Criminal Justice Act 1967, section 9; Criminal Procedure Rules, r. 16.2)

Statement of: ....Ella Fildes......................

Age of witness (if over 18, enter “over 18”): ....over 18.....................

This statement (consisting of one page) is true to the best of my knowledge and belief and I make it knowing that, if it is tendered in evidence, I shall be liable to prosecution if I have wilfully stated in it anything which I know to be false, or do not believe to be true.

Dated: ......27 November 2026...................

Signature: ......E. Fildes...................

Today I prepared a written record of the interview of Tegan Plant in this case that I conducted on 26 November 2026. I exhibit the written record as EF/4.

WITNESS STATEMENT

(Criminal Justice Act 1967, section 9; Criminal Procedure Rules, r. 16.2)

Statement of: ....Rosie Canter......................

Age of witness (if over 18, enter "over 18"): ....over 18.....................

This statement (consisting of two pages) is true to the best of my knowledge and belief and I make it knowing that, if it is tendered in evidence, I shall be liable to prosecution if I have wilfully stated in it anything which I know to be false, or do not believe to be true.

Dated: ......26 November 2026...................

Signature: ......R. Canter...................

I am Police Inspector Rosie Canter of Stockport Police Station, and I make this statement in relation to the VIPER identification procedure carried out on 26 November 2026.

On the above date, I was in charge of the Video Identification Parade (VIPER) at Stockport Police Station, which was conducted as part of the ongoing investigation into an allegation of attempted robbery at the New Dilhorne Bank on 19 November 2026.

Ms Isobel Ullger was brought in to take part in the procedure and see whether she could identify the person she saw enter the bank on 19 November 2026 and who threatened her.[4] I was in possession of a video image of the suspect Tegan Plant from our database and eight other video images of men of a similar description to that offered by the witness Isobel Ullger of the man who entered the bank.

Prior to the viewing of the video line-up of nine persons, I informed Ms Ullger of the following: "First I will show you all the images one after the other and then I will show them for a second time. Please watch the images in silence. I will then ask you whether you are able to make an identification of the person you saw enter the bank on 19 November 2026 and who threatened you. The person you saw may or may not be shown in these images".

The suspect, Tegan Plant, was positioned at position number 6 in the VIPER line-up. Ms Ullger was shown the video twice in accordance with the standard procedures. Afterwards, I said to her: "I am now going to ask you whether you are able to identify the man you saw enter the New Dilhorne Bank in Marple on 19 November

4 The procedure described here is an approximation of the correct procedure, not exact.

2026 and who came up to you and asked you to hand over money. Are you able to make any identification?" Ms Ullger replied, "Yes, number 6".

I said, "I will now run through the images again and pause the sequence at the man shown in image number six". I brought the image at position 6 onto the screen and asked Ms Ullger, "Is this the person you mean?" Ms Ullger said, "Yes". I said, "To be clear, is this the person you saw enter the New Dilhorne Bank on 19 November 2026 and who threatened you?" Ms Ullger replied, "Yes, one hundred percent. He has the same eyes and nose and face shape. I recognised him straightaway".

This brought the identification procedure to an end, and I escorted Ms Ullger out of the identification suite and back into the company of PC Ella Fildes.

I produced a copy of the video identification procedure recording as RC/01 and the written record as RC/02.[5]

5 These documents are not reproduced for the purposes of this case scenario.

IN THE CROWN COURT AT MANCHESTER

CROWN SQUARE

REX

V

TEGAN PLANT

EXHIBITS

RECORD OF INTERVIEW

Person interviewed: TEGAN PLANT

Place of interview: STOCKPORT POLICE STATION

Date of interview: 23 November 2026

Time commenced: 6.30 pm Time concluded: 6.42 pm Duration of interview: 12 minutes

Recording Reference No: 3575835 Exhibit Ref: EF/2

Interviewer: PC E FILDES

Other persons present: N/A

Counter Time	*Person Speaking*	*Text*
	Officer	The parties introduced themselves. The time and date were confirmed to be 6.30 pm on 23 November 2026. PC Fildes explained that Tegan Plant was entitled to be represented by the duty solicitor independent of the Police if he wished, but this was declined. OK, Tegan. You're here because you're under arrest on suspicion of attempting to rob the New Dilhorne Bank in Marple on 19 November and the purpose of this interview is to obtain information by questioning. Can I please remind you that you are still under caution. You do not have to say anything, but it may harm your defence if you do not mention when questioned something which you later rely on in court. Anything you do say may be given in evidence. Do you understand?
	Plant	Yeah, yeah. I know the score.
	Officer	Now, we've offered you the duty solicitor, but …
	Plant	Don't need a solicitor. Not done anything wrong, have I.
	Officer	Well, it is your right. It would be free advice and representation from a solicitor who is independent of the Police.
	Plant	Just get on with it, for God's sake.
	Officer	OK. Well, this is the thing, Tegan. Someone tried to rob the New Dilhorne Bank in Marple. It was a man. He walked in and approached the lady behind the counter and demanded that she hand over money. We think that was you, Tegan.
	Plant	No way! There's no way you can pin this on me. I have never tried to rob no bank ever!
	Officer	Hang on, Tegan. Let me tell you why we are saying this.
		(*Continued*)

Counter Time	*Person Speaking*	*Text*
	Plant	Oh yeah, I can't wait for this. Go on, then. Let's hear this.
	Officer	The man who went into the bank had an accomplice who waited in the car outside – the getaway driver. The man we think was you got out of the car and went into the bank and tried to rob it then came out empty-handed and got back in the car. Then the car drove off.
	Plant	Yeah, and? Doesn't sound like much to me.
	Officer	Wait, Tegan. Give me a chance to explain.
	Plant	Ok, yeah.
	Officer	We have an eyewitness who describes that car as a white Renault Clio the next day. It was just over the Derbyshire border in Charlesworth when we found it the next day. We found your DNA inside the car on the front passenger seat door handle.
	Plant	What!
	Officer	Yes, and the eyewitness at the bank saw the man get out of the car through the front passenger door. You see why we think it was you. Was it you?
	Plant	What car?
	Officer	The car we recovered was a Renault Clio. The registered number was CTH2 XCM.
	Plant	And my DNA was inside it? Oh, that's careless.
	Officer	Yes. The car seen outside the bank by the eyewitness was a light Renault Clio as well. The witness got the number plate down as XCM which is the same.
	Plant	Wait, what! They didn't get the full plate number?
	Officer	The witness noted down XCM, that's all he could remember.
	Plant	How do you know it's even the same car then if you don't even know the registration number!
	Officer	It was also a light-coloured Renault Clio, Tegan. Same car.
	Plant	Rubbish! You've got nothing on me!
	Officer	You have a limp, though, Tegan, don't you.
	Plant	What! What's that got to do with it?
	Officer	The lady working in the bank, the one who was threatened by the man who went in, she describes that the man had a limp.
	Plant	Oh, I see. Here we go again. You lot are always picking me up whenever someone with a limp is supposed to have done a job.
		(*Continued*)

Counter Time	*Person Speaking*	*Text*
	Officer	No, Tegan. It's the DNA in the car, the matching plate, the limp. It all adds up, doesn't it – you were the man who went in that bank, weren't you?
	Plant	No I wasn't. I can remember last Thursday, and I wasn't at any bank, I can tell you that for sure.
	Officer	OK. Where were you, then?
	Plant	I was at home with my mum. That's it. All day. The weather was bad, and her leg was bad.
	Officer	Her leg?
	Plant	Yeah, her leg. It's infected and last Thursday I had to stay with her and change the bandages. I was at home all day, morning, noon and night.
	Officer	How can you remember it was last Thursday?
	Plant	Come on it was only last week, wasn't it. Thursday and Friday, it was. I was at home both days, never left the house.
	Officer	You weren't, were you. You were out trying to rob that bank.
	Plant	No way! You have got nothing on me. It wasn't me. I've never even been in that car. It's not my DNA. Nothing more to say.
	Officer	Since you've got nothing else to say, I'll end the interview now. The time is 6.42 pm.
	Plant	Yeah.

RECORD OF INTERVIEW

Person interviewed: TEGAN PLANT

Place of interview: STOCKPORT POLICE STATION

Date of interview: 26 November 2026

Time commenced: 5.01 pm Time concluded: 5.07 pm Duration of interview: 6 minutes

Recording Reference No: 3578999 Exhibit Ref: EF/4

Interviewer: PC E FILDES

Other persons present: N/A

Counter Time	*Person Speaking*	*Text*
	Officer	OK, Tegan. You're here because you're under arrest on suspicion of attempting to rob the New Dilhorne Bank in Marple on 19 November and the purpose of this interview is to obtain information by questioning. Can I please remind you that you are still under caution. You do not have to say anything, but it may harm your defence if you do not mention when questioned something which you later rely on in court. Anything you do say may be given in evidence. Do you understand?
	Plant	So what is it now?
	Officer	Remember you have the right to see the duty solicitor free of charge.
	Plant	I know. Just carry on.
	Officer	You know that there was an identification procedure held today, Tegan. The lady from the New Dilhorne Bank who was the victim of an attempted robbery. You refused to attend the Police Station for it.
	Plant	Yeah, and?
	Officer	She identified you, Tegan.
	Plant	Oh bollocks.
	Officer	You were the man who tried to rob her, weren't you?

Counter Time	*Person Speaking*	*Text*
	Plant	No comment.
		Plant answered No comment to all subsequent questions

POLICE NATIONAL COMPUTER (PNC) – PREVIOUS CONVICTIONS RECORD

Subject Name: Tegan Plant

Date of Birth: 14 June 2002

Address: 15 St Jared's Close, Bredbury, Stockport

PNC ID: 123459876

PREVIOUS CONVICTIONS RECORD[6]

Date of Offence	*Date of Conviction*	*Court*	*Offence*	*Sentence*
12/03/2020	13/03/2021	Stockport Magistrates' Court	Theft from a shop (Shoplifting) Theft Act 1968, section 1 Convicted after trial	13/03/2021 Conditional Discharge, 6 months
15/06/2021	15/07/2021	Stockport Magistrates' Court	Driving with no insurance Road Traffic Act 1988, section 143 Guilty plea Breach of Conditional Discharge	15/07/2021 Fine £60, licence endorsed, 6 penalty points No separate penalty

(*Continued*)

6 Dates are given in British format, i.e. DD/MM/YYYY

Date of Offence	*Date of Conviction*	*Court*	*Offence*	*Sentence*
20/08/2021	15/03/2023	Manchester Crown Court	Blackmail Theft Act 1968, section 21 Convicted after trial Breach of Conditional Discharge	13/04/2023 Youth Rehabilitation Order 1 year No separate penalty
29/03/2024	22/04/2026	Manchester Crown Court	Assault occasioning actual bodily harm Offences Against the Person Act 1861, section 47 Convicted after trial	22/04/2026 Imprisonment 3 months

IN THE MANCHESTER CROWN COURT

CROWN SQUARE

REX

V

TEGAN PLANT

FORMAL ADMISSIONS

Pursuant to section 10 of the Criminal Justice Act 1967

The following facts for the purposes of criminal proceedings against TEGAN PLANT are admitted:

1. TEGAN PLANT has the following convictions recorded against him:

   a. On 13 March 2021, TEGAN PLANT was convicted of one offence of theft from a shop (shoplifting). The offence was committed on 12 March 2020;

   b. TEGAN PLANT had entered a Not Guilty plea, and a trial took place at Stockport Magistrates'" Court. During the trial TEGAN PLANT denied the allegation and gave evidence that he was not guilty. The magistrates convicted him;

   c. On 15 March 2023, TEGAN PLANT was convicted of one offence of blackmail. The offence was committed on 20 August 2021. The facts of the offence were that TEGAN PLANT came into possession of a valuable English Bulldog pet and then, acting alone, made an unwarranted demand of its owner for the payment of a £5,000 ransom for the return of the pet;

   d. TEGAN PLANT had entered a "Not Guilty" plea to the blackmail allegation, and a trial took place at Manchester Crown Court. During the trial TEGAN PLANT denied the allegation and gave evidence to the jury that he was not the person who had made the demand. The jury convicted him.

   e. On 22 April 2026, TEGAN PLANT was convicted of an offence of assault occasioning actual bodily harm. The offence was committed on 29 March 2024. The facts of the offence were that he approached a friend and demanded that the friend give him £1,000 to settle what Tegan Plant called a "business arrangement" that they had discussed earlier. The friend refused, saying that she had already made it clear she would not lend him money. As the friend tried to walk away, TEGAN PLANT grabbed her by the arm and pulled her to the ground, breaking her wrist.

   f. TEGAN PLANT entered a Not Guilty plea to the assault allegation, and a trial took place at Manchester Crown Court. During his trial, TEGAN PLANT denied the allegation and gave evidence to the jury that he had been acting in self-defence. The jury convicted him.

15.2 *Rex v Tegan Plant*, Defence Statement

DEFENCE STATEMENT

(Criminal Procedure and Investigations Act 1996, section 5 & 6; Criminal Procedure and Investigations Act 1996 (Defence Disclosure Time Limits) Regulations 2011; Criminal Procedure Rules 2025, rule 15.4)

Case details

Name of defendant: TEGAN PLANT

Court: MANCHESTER CROWN COURT (CROWN SQUARE)

Case reference number: T 2026/121962

Charge(s):

ALLOWING HIMSELF TO BE CARRIED IN A CONVEYANCE TAKEN WITHOUT AUTHORITY ATTEMPTED ROBBERY

When to use this form

If you are a defendant pleading not guilty:

(a) in a Crown Court case, you must give the information listed in Part 2 of this form;

(b) in a magistrates' court case, you may give that information but you do not have to do so.

The time limit for giving the information is:

14 days (in a magistrates' court case)

28 days (in a Crown Court case)

after initial prosecution disclosure (or notice from the prosecutor that there is no material to disclose).

How to use this form

1. Complete the case details box above, and Part 1 below;
2. Attach as many sheets as you need to give the information listed in Part 2;
3. Sign and date the completed form;
4. Send a copy of the completed form to:
   (a) the court; and
   (b) the prosecutor.

before the time limit expires.

If you need more time, you must apply to the court before the time limit expires. You should apply in writing, but no special form is needed.

DOI: 10.4324/9781003602019-16

Part 1: Plea

I confirm that I intend to plead not guilty to all the charges against me.

Part 2: Nature of the defence

I am pleading Not Guilty to the offence of attempted robbery alleged against me because I did not commit it. I take issue with the matters of fact alleged by the Prosecution that I was the man who entered the New Dilhorne Bank in Marple on 19 November 2026 and threatened Isobel Ullger with violence unless she handed over money.

The nature of my defence to this charge is alibi. At the time of the alleged attempt to rob the New Dilhorne Bank I was not at the New Dilhorne Bank. I was at the Swaggering Duck Public House on Newmarket Road in Bredbury with Thomas Ellington-Edge. I had arrived there about 2pm in the afternoon on 19 November and stayed there until about 10pm.

I intend to call the following witness of alibi:

Thomas Ellington-Edge
D.O.B. 1 July 2004
Usually resident at 15 Bernard's Road, Bredbury SK5 55R

I am pleading Not Guilty to the offence of allowing myself to be carried in a motor vehicle alleged against me because I did not commit it. I take issue with the matter of fact alleged by the Prosecution that I was at any stage in the motor vehicle.

The nature of my defence to this charge is alibi. If the vehicle whose door I had opened was used to take any robbers to the New Dilhorne Bank, I was not in the car or any car. I was at the Swaggering Duck Public House on Newmarket Road in Bredbury. I had arrived there about 2 pm in the afternoon on 19 November and stayed there until about 10pm.

I intend to call the following witness of alibi:

Thomas Ellington-Edge
D.O.B. 1 July 2004
Usually resident at 15 Bernard's Road, Bredbury SK5 55R.

I accept that the DNA recovered from the vehicle CTH2 XCM may be mine. I recall that a friend of mine was driving a green motor vehicle on the morning of the 19 November 2026 and he pulled up beside me in the street to ask what I thought of it. I looked inside the vehicle through the open passenger door, and I presume this is how my DNA ended up on the inside door handle. At no stage did I enter this vehicle or allow myself to be carried in it. I cannot now recall which friend it was.

Signed: ....T. Plant............................ defendant/defendant's solicitor

Date: ....31 January 2027............

WARNING: Under section 11 of the Criminal Procedure and Investigations Act 1996, *if you (a) do not disclose what the Act requires; (b) do not give a defence statement before the time limit expires; (c) at trial, rely on a defence, or facts, that you have not disclosed; or (d) at trial, call an alibi witness whom you have not identified in advance, then the court, the prosecutor or another defendant may comment on that, and the court may draw such inferences as it thinks proper in deciding whether you are guilty.*

15.3 *Rex v Tegan Plant*, Case Theories

Prosecution and Defence Case Theories

Introduction

Often cases will involve consideration of "rival" versions of events. In our case scenario of *Rex v Tegan Plant*, we can imagine that the prosecution version of events might be this:

> The defendant was the man who tried to rob the New Dilhorne Bank.

The defence version of events, on the other hand, might be this:

> The defendant was in the Swaggering Duck Public House at the time when the man tried to rob the bank and so he was not the man who tried to rob the bank.

Those two statements are, you may think, the bare minimum. They are pretty obvious. They are the end point, the destination that we want the Court to arrive at. To understand a case well enough to develop a prosecution case theory or a defence case theory, you must examine the evidence thoroughly – how it supports your version of events and how you will deal with evidence that appears to go against you. Being able to formulate a detailed account of events, from the perspective of whichever side you represent, is central to the idea of a case theory. This applies to every type of case, whether criminal, civil or otherwise.

Law students often find case theory difficult to grasp, but in practice barristers rely on it every day. You need a clear, detailed version of events that you want the court to accept, supported by an understanding of each piece of evidence individually and all the evidence collectively. In this chapter, we will develop both a prosecution and a defence case theory for the Plant case, assuming no prior experience in constructing case theories.

The idea of a case theory has always existed in the world of the advocate. In 1923, an English judge called Sir Edward Abbott Parry wrote a book called *The Seven Lamps of Advocacy*[1] in which he described the idea of case theory in this way:

1 I am grateful to Stuart Neale of Cobden House Chambers for pointing me in the direction of The Seven Lamps of Advocacy. Stuart is an expert on Judge Parry who in 1898 was shot (and survived) while sitting on a case at the Manchester County Court, the building now housing Cobden House Chambers (NB)

DOI: 10.4324/9781003602019-17

> The power of gathering up the scattered threads of facts and weaving them into a pattern surrounding and emphasising the central point of the case. In every case there is one commanding theory, to the proof of which all the facts must be skilfully marshalled.

That is pretty old-fashioned language! We prefer our way of describing a case theory as including reference to the evidence and explaining why the evidence points to the conclusion that you are asking the Court to come to. It is, though, exactly the same thing that Judge Parry was talking about more than a hundred years ago.

We pause here for a moment to emphasise that case theory is a method to deploy in preparing to conduct your advocacy. Remember, however, that you are not only representing the client in order to conduct advocacy. You are also there to advise. When we talk of a case theory we are only talking about that in terms of advocacy. Your overall approach to the case has to include advice to clients about settling or pleading.

In their opening speech to the jury in the *Plant* case, the prosecution are really saying to the jury: we will bring you evidence which, when you see and hear it, will make you sure that Tegan Plant was the front passenger in the Renault Clio car which pulled up outside the bank on 19 November 2026 and that he was the man who entered the bank and tried to rob it. They will explain what the evidence will be, and they will tell the jury *why* they say the evidence will make the jury sure and *why* the jury therefore should accept their version of events (that the defendant was the man who entered the bank and that he attempted to rob it). This is the prosecution case theory. You will often see it set out plainly in the prosecutor's opening speech.

The Defence rarely makes an opening speech, so they will target their approach to the witnesses with their closing speech in mind. They will cross-examine prosecution witnesses and call any evidence of their own which they wish to, so that in their closing speech they will be in a position to say to the jury: the Prosecution's evidence has not been strong enough to make you sure that their version of events is true, and the defence will say *why* the jury therefore should not accept it. Of course, a significant part of this will be about why the jury should accept their evidence that the defendant was at the Swaggering Duck Public House instead.[2] This is the defence case theory.

We can now look at the prosecution case theory and the defence case theory in a little more detail. In this document, we will be focusing mainly on the attempted robbery charge.

2 But remember that Tegan Plant does not have to prove he is innocent: he does not have to prove that he was at the Swaggering Duck Public House. Instead, the prosecution will have to make the jury sure that Plant was *not* at the Swaggering Duck Public House, rather than that he was at the New Dilhorne Bank attempting to rob Isobel Ullger.

Prosecution Case Theory

Because we are prosecuting, the *burden of proof* is on us to prove to the jury that Tegan Plant is guilty of the offences with which we have charged him. Often this will include proving to the jury that any defences that he is raising (e.g. self-defence, alibi, lack of dishonesty) are false. A defendant does not have to prove his innocence.

We will be successful in proving Tegan Plant's guilt if we make the jury sure that he is guilty; this is the *standard of proof*. This means that we must carefully consider what evidence we have available to us, and whether it will all be enough to drive the jury to the conclusion that they are sure he is guilty. If the defendant is raising any defences, we will need to make the jury sure that the defences are false. In other words, we need to analyse:

a. What do we need to prove legally in order to convict him (criminal lawyers call this proving the elements of the offence)?
b. What defence or defences are likely to be raised by the defendant to the charges?
c. What are the issues or areas of dispute between Prosecution and Defence that the jury will likely be focusing on when making their decision?
d. Is our evidence strong enough to persuade a jury so that they are sure of his guilt?

We are setting out to prove that the defendant is guilty of attempted robbery and allowing himself to be carried in a motor vehicle taken without the owner's consent. As always, we start by looking up the law on what we need to prove.

By section 8 of the Theft Act 1968 a person is guilty of robbery if he steals, and immediately before or at the time of doing so, and in order to do so, he uses force on any person or puts or seeks to put any person in fear of being then and there subjected to force.

Whenever we use the verb "to rob", that is really shorthand. What we mean when, as a criminal lawyer, we say "he robbed someone" is:

> he stole, and immediately before or at the time of doing so, and in order to do so, he used force on any person or put or sought to put any person in fear of being then and there subjected to force.

But of course, on the facts of Tegan Plant's case, what happened is alleged to be an attempt. This is because the man in the bank did not actually succeed in stealing from the bank. All allegations of attempting to commit a crime are charged under section 1 of the Criminal Attempts Act 1981: if, with intent to commit an offence, a person does an act which is more than merely preparatory to the commission of the offence [here, robbery], he is guilty of attempting to commit the offence.

We could order our thoughts on all of this in a Table:

	What must we prove for the offence of attempted robbery	On our reading of the case papers, is the defendant (D) likely to accept or dispute any of these facts?
1	The defendant ...	= Identification. In every case the Prosecution must prove that the person charged is the offender In his defence statement, D is disputing that he was the offender, and he raises the defence of alibi > Identification is therefore highly likely to be an issue at this trial > Prosecution must be alert to their obligation to make the jury sure the alibi is false
2	Attempted ...	= Did an act more than merely preparatory to committing robbery, and at the time he did it he intended to commit robbery (section 1 Criminal Attempts Act 1981) If Ullger's account is true, jury are likely to conclude that there was nothing more the man could have done in his plan to rob the bank, so it is likely the jury will be sure that what the man did was "more than merely preparatory" to robbing the bank > D's case appears to be that he was not present in the bank, so he is unlikely to challenge Ullger's account of "attempt", *but the Prosecution must still adduce evidence of this and prove this.*
3	To steal ...	= a legal ingredient of the offence of robbery. Theft is "the dishonest appropriation of property from another with the intention of depriving the other of it permanently" (section 1 Theft Act 1968) Ullger states: (a) "He shouted, 'Give me the money ...'"; and (b) "I heard him shout, 'I said, hand over the money.'" If this account is true, jury are likely to conclude that appropriating money with the intention of depriving Ullger of it was the man's objective. > Again: D's case appears to be that he was not present in the bank, so he is unlikely to challenge Ullger's account relating to stealing, *but the Prosecution must still adduce evidence of this and prove this.*
4	From Isobel Ullger ...	= alleged victim of the crime If Ullger's account is true, jury are likely to conclude that she was the person the man tried to rob > D's case appears to be that he was not present in the bank, so he is unlikely to challenge Ullger's account about this, *but the Prosecution must still adduce evidence of this and prove this.*

(*Continued*)

5	And immediately before or at the time of doing so, and in order to do so, he put Isobel Ullger in fear of being then and there subjected to force.	= a legal ingredient of the offence of robbery (section 8 Theft Act 1968) Ullger states: (a) "He shouted, 'Give me the money or I'll shoot you'". If Ullger's account is true, jury are likely to conclude that in order to carry out his intention to rob the bank, he was issuing Isobel Ullger with a threat of violence as to what would happen if she did not give him the money > D's case appears to be that he was not present in the bank, so he is unlikely to challenge Ullger's account about this, *but the Prosecution must still adduce evidence of this and prove this.*

This analysis shows us that we must plainly focus on identification as being the main issue in the case around which we must construct our case theory. But we must not forget that we still have to adduce evidence of all the other matters that we must prove, even though they may not be disputed.

The Prosecution case theory is a collection of common-sense conclusions that we draw from the evidence in the case. These conclusions lead to our statement (you might say, our "ultimate conclusion"): "This is why we say the defendant is guilty of the offence charged".

1. In a formal identification procedure conducted by the Police, Isobel Ullger, the sole witness to the attempt to rob the New Dilhorne Bank in Marple, identified Tegan Plant as the man who entered the bank, i.e. the would-be robber. She did this just a week after the incident at a formal police identification process held at Stockport Police Station. Ullger had been able to take a good look at the man during the robbery attempt. Although the would-be robber had entered the bank wearing a mask, he had slipped on the way in, and the fall had dislodged the mask. This meant that Ullger could see the man's eyes and his lower face from the nose down. She had him under observation for quite a few seconds in good light in circumstances where she was able to see a lot of his face. **The prosecution case is that Ullger's identification is reliable because the view she had of the robber was of good quality;**

2. When confronted in interview by the police with the fact that Ullger had identified him, Plant changed his approach. Up to that point, he had been confident and sure of himself, cocky, even. When told that he had been identified, he replied, "Oh bollocks" and thereafter replied No Comment. **The prosecution case is that Plant changed his approach because he realised he had been caught out;**

3. Ullger saw that the man in the bank walked with a limp. Tegan Plant, who she identified at the identification procedure at Stockport Police Station, also walked with a limp. The identification procedure took the form of facial

headshots only, and so Ullger did not know, and had no way of knowing, that the man she identified also had a limp. **The prosecution case is that it is not a coincidence that both the robber and Tegan Plant had a limp; Tegan Plant was the robber;**

4. An eyewitness (Hawkins) to the robber's arrival outside the bank saw that the person who entered the premises was a passenger in a light-coloured Renault Clio that pulled up outside. Tegan Plant's DNA was found on the inside front passenger door handle of this car. When he was told by the police in his interview that his DNA had been found in the car, his initial response was an acknowledgement of the truth: "my DNA was inside it? Oh, that's careless." Then he changed his account and said that the evidence of his DNA was wrong. Then in his subsequent defence statement he changed his account further, offering an explanation as to why his DNA would be there. **The prosecution case is**
   a. **The only sensible explanation for his DNA being on the inside front passenger door handle is that he was the passenger who Hawkins saw get out of the car and run into the Bank; and**
   b. **Plant is changing his account because he has realised he has been caught out;**

5. The changing stories. The defendant's latest account in his defence statement included the assertion that he had seen the car being driven by a friend, whose name he could not now recall, and that the defendant had touched the car when looking at it;
   a. These changes in his account indicate untruthfulness. **The prosecution case is that the truth never changes, and his accounts can be rejected because they are the lies of a man seeking to avoid responsibility for a crime he has committed;**
   b. It is not credible that he cannot remember the name of his friend. **The prosecution case is that there was in reality no friend; the whole story is a thin excuse to try and explain away his DNA;**
   c. In his defence statement, the defendant says he touched the car when he saw his friend in it during the morning of 19 November – but the assertion that this happened in the morning must be untrue since the car was not taken from its owner's driveway until 2 pm. **The prosecution case is that Plant has been directly caught out in a lie, given to try and avoid responsibility for a crime he has committed;**

   The only truth is that the defendant's DNA is in the car because the defendant was in the car when it arrived at the bank, and he was the man who got out of the car and tried to rob the bank;

6. Hawkins was able to get part of the car's registration number, the suffix XCM. A light-coloured Renault Clio car bearing the same suffix XCM had been taken from its owner's house in Mellor, just up the road from the New Dilhorne Bank, earlier the same day. Its owner (Barber) saw the car drive away from

her driveway at 2 pm. This was just short of four hours before the attempt was made to rob the Bank. Barber's car was found the next day in a nearby village called Charlesworth. Someone had set fire to the inside of the car in order to try and eliminate any traces of those who had been in the car since it had been taken – those who had tried to rob the New Dilhorne Bank. **The prosecution case is that it was Tegan Plant who set fire to the car to try and destroy any evidence that he had been in the car.** It was bad luck for Plant that this attempt did not eliminate the DNA that he had deposited when he touched the passenger door handle while he was being driven in the car;

7. Tegan Plant says he was not the man who tried to rob the bank. So where was he? He has changed his story about his alibi. In his police interview he said that he was at home with his mother all day when the car was taken from Barber's house and when the attempt to rob the bank took place. But in his subsequent defence statement, he now says that between 2 pm and 10 pm that day he was in the pub. **The prosecution case is that these changes in Plant's account about his alibi indicate untruthfulness. The only truth is that he was the man who tried to rob the bank and that he has been correctly identified by Ullger;**

8. It is no coincidence that Plant, the man picked out by Ullger at the identification procedure, was a man with previous convictions involving conduct whereby he had demanded money from other people. On 5 September 2025 he approached a friend and demanded that the friend give him £1,000 to settle an alleged "business arrangement" and when the friend refused, the defendant assaulted her. On 20 August 2021 the defendant came into possession of a valuable English Bulldog pet and then, acting alone, made an unwarranted demand of its owner for the payment of a £5,000 ransom for the return of the pet. The Prosecution say that the evidence of these previous convictions is relevant to an important matter in issue between the defendant and the prosecution, namely whether the defendant has a tendency to make unjustified demands of money from people. **The prosecution case is that Plant's convictions support the prosecution's assertion that he was the man who entered the bank and made an unjustified demand that Isobel Ullger hand over money.** [Relevant law: Criminal Justice Act 2003, section 101(1)(d), section 103(1)(a).]

Defence Case Theory

The defence case theory will be different from the prosecution case theory. Remember that the defendant in a criminal trial does not have to prove his innocence. Often a defence case theory does not lead the defence advocate to a realistic submission that the prosecution case is so poor that the whole prosecution should be dismissed. A lot of your defence case theory will be directed at showing why the prosecution evidence is not strong enough to support guilt.

The defence case theory is useful in helping you, the defence advocate, to crystallise your thoughts about where the prosecution weak points are and where the defence strong points are. Mostly, the strategy is to gain greater focus that helps plan the most effective cross-examination of prosecution witnesses.

A defence case theory often will not be able to "counter" every aspect of the prosecution case against the defendant. Here is our example of a defence case theory in the case of *Rex v Plant*:

1. When Isobel Ullger identified Tegan Plant as the robber at the identification procedure, she was simply mistaken. The incident must have been sudden and frightening. Whilst she says she had the man's face under observation for "a good few seconds and in good light", she is unable say what colour his eyes were. This indicates that her view and attention were (perhaps understandably) not as good as she thinks. Just a few seconds is in truth a very short period of time to observe facts of which the jury have to be sure;

2. The limp. Ullger says that the robber walked with a limp. The Prosecution case is that Ullger's identification of Plant as the robber is supported by the fact that, unknown to her, the man she identified also walks with a limp. But on the prosecution evidence, Ullger noticed the robber's limp after, not before, he had slipped and fallen on his way into the bank. The robber's limp, if he had one, is equally explicable by the accident of falling. The witness Hawkins notably uses the word "appeared" about the man's limp, which indicates he is less than sure, and he offers the weather conditions as a proviso, further indicating he is less than sure: "He appeared to be running with a limp, but the road and pavement were slippery with ice". Overall, the jury cannot be sure that the robber was permanently affected by a limp. The fact that Plant walks with a limp does not therefore support the Prosecution case that he is the robber;

3. The car. The evidence that Barber's car was the one that the robber used to rob the bank is poor. Barber's car is green in colour except for the two rear doors that are blue; Hawkins describes the robbers' car as white and says nothing about the two rear doors being a different colour. Barber's car has four doors; Hawkins describes the robbers' car as having two doors. Whilst Hawkins states that the registration number of the robbers' car ended with the letters

"XCM", the same as Barber's car, his observation is not reliable about that detail because he was observing the vehicle

a. From 30 metres away;
b. Through heavy snow;
c. On a dark night in winter;
d. In poor lighting because the streetlamp nearest the car was not lit.

Additionally, Hawkins was distracted when he was trying to watch events. Throughout, he was trying to locate his mobile phone amongst his clothing; then he dropped his phone in the snow and had to pick it up.

The accuracy of Hawkins's recollection was affected by his emotional view of the events (he uses the words "dramatic" and "shocked" in his witness statement);

4. Inconsistency between Ullger and Hawkins about the robber's appearance. Hawkins says the robber was in possession of a sack; Ullger makes no reference at all to the robber having anything with him. Hawkins says the man was wearing "a long sleeved black and white striped top; the stripes were horizontal", Ullger describes him wearing "dark trousers and a dark top ... pretty much all in black". These inconsistencies cast doubt on the accuracy overall of their descriptions of the robber. The prosecution submission that the identification of the defendant at the identification procedure is supported by other evidence is a weak submission;

5. Bad character. The case is weak and circumstantial, despite the witness Ullger identifying the defendant at an identification procedure as the man who entered the bank. In those circumstances, it would be unfair for the Prosecution to be permitted to tell the jury of the defendant's previous convictions. That evidence would have such an adverse effect on the fairness of the proceedings that the court ought not to admit it. [See Criminal Justice Act 2003, section 101(3); Police and Criminal Evidence Act 1984, section 78.]

15.4 *Rex v Tegan Plant*, Prosecution Opening Speech

Prosecution Opening Speech

Shortly before 5 pm on 19 November 2026, a masked man burst into the New Dilhorne Bank in Marple. He approached the member of staff working at the counter and shouted words to the effect of "Give me the money or I'll shoot you".

The Prosecution say that the masked would-be robber is this defendant, Tegan Plant. He has been identified by the member of bank staff working at the counter as the person who was responsible for the attempted robbery and has been linked to the stolen car that was used as the getaway car[1].

Let's look at that in a little more detail.

[Note to Self – Deal First with What Happened at the Bank][2]

The bank member of staff, Isobel Ullger, heard the door bang against the wall and saw the man, dressed pretty much all in black,[3] approaching her counter. He slipped and fell, but got back to his feet and demanded money, threatening, "Give me the money or I'll shoot you".

Ms Ullger noticed that the man walked with a limp and that his mask had ridden up, allowing her to see his facial features.

She was afraid that the man had a weapon – even though she did not see one – and so she ducked below the counter and pressed the emergency alarm. A loud siren sounded. When she eventually looked up, the man had gone.

1 The aim of this very simple introduction is to give the jury an immediate understanding of the case so that they will understand the greater detail that you will be dealing with in the remainder of your speech.

2 Headings are important – both to the jury, because they signify when you are changing topic; and to you, because they help you "translate" what you are reading with your eyes into what you are saying with your mouth. If somehow you lose your train of thought whilst you are on your feet, your headings will help you get back on track quickly. Decide: will you tell the jury each time you change topic, or will a longer pause be enough?

3 Here we use the witness's expression as she wrote it in her witness statement to the police, but without directly attributing it to her. In the Speeches chapter, we discuss the dangers of being explicit in an opening speech about what "the witness will say in evidence".

DOI: 10.4324/9781003602019-18

[Note to Self – Deal Next with Events Leading Up to the Robbery]

Earlier that day, at around 2 pm, Amy Barber's light green Renault Clio, registration CTH2 XCM, had been stolen from her driveway in Mellor, Stockport. The thief had hooked her keys through the letterbox. Ms Barber actually saw her car being driven away, but she did not see the driver.

Almost three hours later, at about 4.45 pm, William Hawkins was outside the New Dilhorne Bank in Marple. He saw a car travelling too fast for the conditions pull onto the pavement, and he saw a man wearing distinctive clothing and a mask jump out of the vehicle and run into the bank. He noted that the male walked with a limp. He also saw that the car registration contained the letters XCM, which he made a note of in his phone. The male who ran into the bank was wearing a stripy top and balaclava. The witness thought at the time that the car was a white-coloured car.

Both the eyewitnesses, Ms Ullger and Mr Hawkins, were under the stress of witnessing something that was both fast-moving and traumatic. You should consider that when looking at what they say and any differences that there may be in the evidence that they give.

[Note to Self – Deal Next with Evidence That Links the Defendant to the Crime]

It is the prosecution case that the robber fled the bank and made off in the waiting getaway car that was found the following day some distance away. The prosecution case is that the man seen by Mr Hawkins and the man inside the bank are the same person – this defendant. For sure he was not acting alone: an unknown accomplice was driving the getaway car.[4]

The getaway car was found the following day, some distance away. Someone had tried to set it on fire, but not successfully. A scene of crime officer swabbed the front passenger door handle and collected what appeared to be a flake of human skin.

Laboratory analysis linked[5] the DNA from that skin sample to the defendant, Tegan Plant.

When interviewed, the defendant denied the offence but admitted that he walks with a limp. He gave no explanation for why his DNA was found in the car.

A week later, on 26 November, Ms Ullger took part in a video identification procedure. She positively identified the defendant as the man who attempted to rob her. The defendant was interviewed by the police after the positive identification by Ms Ullger. When it was put to him that he had been identified he replied, "Oh bollocks".

4 On the facts of this case, it is completely irrelevant to Plant's criminal responsibility whether anyone else was also involved, and if they were, who it was. Decide: do you deal quickly with irrelevant topics to prevent the jury being distracted by them?

5 We say "linked" rather than "matched" because this is the safer way to deal with DNA evidence.

[Note to Self – Deal Next with the Two Charges Against the Defendant – Ask Jury to Look at the Copies of the Indictments in the Case]

The defendant faces two counts:

- Count 1 – Allowing himself to be carried in a vehicle that had been taken on the day of the attempted robbery – this is the car inside which his DNA was found;
- Count 2 – Attempted robbery at the bank.

You will hear the judge's full legal directions in due course, but for now all you need to hold in your mind is this:

- Robbery is when violence is threatened or used, at or before the time property is stolen, and in order to steal;
- Because no property was taken here, the charge is attempted robbery.

The key question for you will be whether the defendant was the person who attempted the robbery, and whether he allowed himself to be carried in that stolen vehicle knowing it had been taken without the consent of the owner.[6]

[Note to Self – Deal Next with Other Evidence in the Case and the Burden and Standard of Proof]

You will also hear some evidence about previous convictions of the defendant. This evidence has been agreed between the Prosecution and the Defence. At the end of the case, the judge will explain how you may use this evidence in your deliberations. For now, the prosecution says it shows a propensity for dishonesty and a propensity to approach people and make unjustified demands for money, but we stress that the judge will give you directions as to how to use those convictions at the end of the case.[7]

The judge will also direct you about the burden and standard of proof. It is the Prosecution that brings this case against Tegan Plant. You should consider separately each of the charges brought against Tegan Plant. The Prosecution say that it is a strong case on each charge against him. Each charge will only be proved if, at the end of the case, you have been satisfied so that you are sure of his guilt.

6 Summarise for the jury what they are being asked to decide – what the issues in the trial are.

7 Here you are making clear that it is the judge who is in charge. It's a sign of respect to the judge.

[Note to Self – Conclusions]

What I have said now by way of opening to you is not the evidence in the case – it is an overview of the key evidence that I expect you will hear. The prosecution say[8] that the identification by Ms Ullger, the DNA on the getaway car, the matching description of the limping man and the defendant's previous convictions all point to the same conclusions:

- The defendant was taken to the New Dilhorne Bank in Marple in a stolen vehicle;
- The defendant attempted to rob the bank.

We will now begin to hear the evidence.

8 Notice that this is a one-sentence summary of your four main points. Decide: will you count on your fingers for the jury as you make each of the four points? Coming at the end of your opening speech, a short summary such as this encapsulates your case neatly. It has a powerful effect if this is the last thing the jury hear you say in your speech.

16 *Rex v Gordon Heyworth*

Rex

v

Gordon Heyworth

[To give context, we imagine that the sentencing hearing for this case is scheduled to take place at Preston Crown Court on 24 April 2028]

DOI: 10.4324/9781003602019-19

INSTRUCTIONS TO COUNSEL:

Counsel is instructed that the client appeared at Preston Magistrates' Court where he indicated a Not Guilty plea to the single charge of dwelling house burglary and the matter was deemed too serious for summary trial and was sent to the Crown Court. At the plea and preparation hearing at the Crown Court, the defendant appeared over the videolink and pleaded guilty. The case was adjourned until today's date for sentence to allow for the preparation of a pre-sentence report.

CLIENT'S PROOF OF EVIDENCE:

I am very anxious to get off drugs. I use about one to two bags of heroin a day, which cost me £10 a time. So, I am using probably £100 worth of drugs per week. I now owe about £400 to a dealer. I started out owing this amount, but even when I pay some off it goes up again, due to "interest". I am totally trapped in this debt. The dealer keeps pressurising me to deal for him to help pay off the debt, but I don't want to do that; I want to be away from drugs, not surrounded by them.

I get £393 per month Universal Credit. I basically spend everything on drugs and more. I then do what I can to buy food and generally live. I have a Local Authority flat, but I am in rent arrears. I need to work with the council to sort this out.

I steal food to eat and to sell. The problem is that now most shops recognise me and don't let me in. That is why I burgled the house. And probably why I am so bad at it and did not wear gloves.

I am sorry that I upset the homeowners. I only shouted at him and threw the plant pot because I did not want to get caught. I thought they were on holiday because someone told me that they always were. Of course, I did not know that for sure. I sold the stuff I stole. I was going to take the car as well and hoped that the proceeds from the burglary would pay off my debts and keep me on drugs until I managed to get off them, and would mean that I would not have to steal anything for ages.

I panicked during the interview and then went on with that lie at the mags. But I have pleaded guilty; now I am before the Crown Court. I have never been here before.

Becky wants me to stop taking drugs, and that has given me a fresh impetus to get off them. I haven't felt like this for years. Her dad runs a garden business, and he is prepared to give me some casual work when he has a need for someone else. But I need to be off the drugs before he will. I want to work again and get my life back. I don't want to go to prison and lose my flat and Becky.

IN THE CROWN COURT AT PRESTON T 2028/638224

REX

v

GORDON HEYWORTH

INDICTMENT

Gordon Heyworth is charged as follows:

STATEMENT OF OFFENCE

BURGLARY OF A DWELLING, contrary to section 9(1)(b) of the Theft Act 1968.

PARTICULARS OF OFFENCE

GORDON HEYWORTH, on the 20th day of March 2028, having entered a dwelling, namely 10 Leytonstone Place, Goosnargh, as a trespasser, stole therein 500 Euros in money, an iPhone, a laptop and a set of electronic car keys.

WITNESS LIST

NAME	DATE OF STATEMENT
OLIVER HENSHAW	20/03/28
"	20/03/28
K FENTON	20/03/28
A SLATER	22/03/28

EXHIBIT LIST

Audio recording of police interview conducted on 22/03/28	AS/1
Written record of police interview conducted on 22/03/28	AS/2

WITNESS STATEMENT

(Criminal Justice Act 1967, s 9; Criminal Procedure Rules, r. 16.2)

Statement of: ....Oliver Henshaw......................

Age of witness (if over 18, enter "over 18"): ....over 18.....................

This statement (consisting of two pages) is true to the best of my knowledge and belief and I make it knowing that, if it is tendered in evidence, I shall be liable to prosecution if I have wilfully stated in it anything which I know to be false, or do not believe to be true.

Occupation: ......Magician..........

Dated: ......20 March 2028...............

Signature: ......O. Henshaw...............

On the evening of 20 March 2028, I was at home at 10 Leytonstone Place. This is in Goosnargh near Preston, where I live with my partner Emily Leong. We had gone to bed upstairs and were asleep.

At 2.50 am I was awoken by our dog barking. Alarmed by the noise, I got out of bed and rushed downstairs without stopping to put any clothes on. On reaching the hallway, I saw the burglar. I attempted to tackle him, but he side-stepped me and moved quickly back towards the kitchen. As he did so, he shouted, "Don't be a hero, or else I will do you".

I was not deterred and followed him into the kitchen. By the time I got there, he was already escaping through the rear patio door that leads out to the back garden. He pulled it shut behind him. When he turned back and saw me moving towards the door, he picked up a plant pot from the garden and threw it at the glass. It smashed the window, causing me to recoil. The man then ran off and escaped.

I looked round our house. The only point of entry was through the sliding section of the rear patio door that had been forced. All the kitchen drawers had been opened, and the contents were scattered across the worktops and the floor. He had obviously been in other downstairs rooms because drawers and sideboard doors were open in the living room and dining room. It was clear to me that a thorough search had been carried out. I immediately phoned the police then went and put some clothes on.

Afterwards, Emily and I checked the house and discovered that €500 had been taken from the kitchen drawer. In addition, an iPhone, a laptop and a set of electronic car keys for our £75,000 Jaguar were missing. Although the car keys had been stolen, the vehicle itself remained parked outside.

Due to fluctuating exchange rates, I cannot say precisely what the euros were worth. The iPhone had cost £700, the laptop £2,000 and the Jaguar electronic key required the vehicle to be reprogrammed, which cost £800. The damage to the sliding patio door, including the broken glass and locking mechanism, amounted to £2,000 in repairs.

WITNESS STATEMENT

(Criminal Justice Act 1967, s 9; Criminal Procedure Rules, r. 16.2)

Statement of: ....Oliver Henshaw......................

Age of witness (if over 18, enter "over 18"): ....over 18.....................

This statement (consisting of one page) is true to the best of my knowledge and belief and I make it knowing that, if it is tendered in evidence, I shall be liable to prosecution if I have wilfully stated in it anything which I know to be false, or do not believe to be true.

Dated: ......20 March 2028...............

Signature: ......O. Henshaw...............

I provide a victim personal statement because I want the Court to understand the impact this burglary has had on me and my family. We had only just moved into the property, and we had hoped it would be our home for at least the next five years. Since the incident, I feel very differently about the house. My partner and I no longer feel safe in our own home, and we have even talked about moving from the area because of how unsettled we now feel.

Securing the property afterwards, arranging repairs, and dealing with the Jaguar being re-programmed created a great deal of stress and took up a significant amount of time. I was particularly upset about losing the laptop, as it contained photographs of some of my children that I may never be able to replace. Fortunately, my children were not at home when the burglary happened. The whole experience has left us shaken and anxious in what should have been a place of safety.

WITNESS STATEMENT

(Criminal Justice Act 1967, s 9; Criminal Procedure Rules, r. 16.2)

Statement of: ....Ken Fenton......................

Age of witness (if over 18, enter "over 18"): ....over 18.....................

Occupation: Crime Scene Investigator with the Lancashire Constabulary

This statement (consisting of one page) is true to the best of my knowledge and belief and I make it knowing that, if it is tendered in evidence, I shall be liable to prosecution if I have wilfully stated in it anything which I know to be false, or do not believe to be true.

Dated: ......20 March 2028...............

Signature: ......K. Fenton...............

Today I attended the scene at 10 Leytonstone Place, Goosnargh, following the report of a burglary. During my examination of the premises, I recovered a significant number of fingerprints from various areas within the property. The volume was unusually high; in fact, I recovered more identifiable fingerprints from this scene than I have encountered at any other single crime scene during my service.

All recovered fingerprints were lifted and submitted for comparison. When the prints were checked against the police database, they produced a positive identification for an individual named Gordon Heyworth.[1]

WITNESS STATEMENT

(Criminal Justice Act 1967, s 9; Criminal Procedure Rules, r. 16.2)

Statement of: ....Alma Slater......................

Age of witness (if over 18, enter "over 18"): ....over 18.....................

Occupation: Police Officer

This statement (consisting of two pages) is true to the best of my knowledge and belief and I make it knowing that, if it is tendered in evidence, I shall be liable to prosecution if I have wilfully stated in it anything which I know to be false, or do not believe to be true.

Dated: ......22 March 2028...............

Signature: ......A. Slater..............

Today I attended 18 Bernard Crescent, Preston, and arrested a man I know to be called Gordon Heyworth on suspicion of burglary at 10 Leytonstone Place, Goosnargh. After cautioning and arresting him, Heyworth replied, "What burglary? What a load of rubbish".

I later interviewed Heyworth in connection with the burglary allegation. I exhibit the recording of the interview as AS/1 and the transcript that I prepared as AS/2. He denied the offence. He stated that he had visited the address to see the previous owner, a Mrs May, and that was why his fingerprints were there.

RECORD OF INTERVIEW

Person interviewed: GORDON HEYWORTH

Place of interview: PRESTON POLICE STATION

Date of interview: 22 March 2028

Time commenced: 1.30 pm Time concluded: 1.40 pm Duration of interview: 10 minutes

Recording Reference No: 8333261 Exhibit Ref: AS/2

Interviewer: PC A SLATER

Other persons present: Jim Regan, solicitor

Counter Time	Person Speaking	Text
	Officer	I would remind you that you are still under caution. You do not have to say anything, but it may harm your defence if you do not mention when questioned something which you later rely on in court. Anything you do say may be given in evidence. Now, what about this burglary at 10 Leytonstone Place in Goosnargh? You're under arrest for it. We found your fingerprints all over the inside of the premises.
	Heyworth	No idea what you're on about.
	Officer	Come on, Gordon.
	Heyworth	Oh wait, I know the address
	Officer	What?
	Heyworth	Yeah. I knew the woman who lived there before. Mrs May, she was called. I went round there loads. That's why you'll have found my prints. Right, that's it, I'm not saying no more to you rozzers.

Summary of Previous Convictions of Gordon Heyworth

Date of Birth: 14 September 1989

2008 – Affray – Fined £350

2010 – Drink Driving – Fined £500 and disqualified from driving for 18 months

2011 – Possession of Cannabis – Conditional Discharge 12 months

2015 – Theft, shoplifting – community order with 60 hours of unpaid work

2023 – Theft, shoplifting x 3, common assault and possession of heroin – community order 18 months with 100 hours unpaid work

2024 – Breach of community order – order continues and extended to 24 months

2025 – Theft, shoplifting – 2 months' imprisonment

2026 – Theft (stealing building materials from a building site) – 6 months' imprisonment

2027 – Theft, shoplifting – 2 months' imprisonment

PRE-SENTENCE REPORT (ADULT)

CONFIDENTIAL

Defendant: Gordon Heyworth

Date of Birth/Age: 14 September 1989, 38

Court: Preston Crown Court

Hearing Date: 24 April 2028

Offence(s): Burglary dwelling

Report Type (Fast/Standard Delivery): Standard Delivery

Report Author: M. Mort

Quality Assured By: D. Muscutt

Date Completed: 20 April 2028

1) Confidentiality and Purpose

This report is prepared solely for this court hearing to assist with the sentencing of the defendant. It is confidential and must not be used for other purposes without permission.

2) Sources of Information

Interview(s) with defendant; CPS documents; Previous convictions (PNC); Victim impact information; Assessment tools used.

3) Summary of the Offence

A dwelling house was burgled in the early hours of the morning in March 2028. The householder was disturbed by noise, and there was a confrontation with the offender.

4) Personal and Social Circumstances

Mr Heyworth is a 38-year-old man who grew up as one of four children and describes his childhood as unremarkable. He left school at 16 with few formal qualifications and was previously employed full-time as a warehouse team leader.

He has been married three times, and the breakdown of his third marriage five years ago marked a significant turning point, leading to escalating Class A drug use which he states began as a way to "numb the pain". Although he had experimented previously, this period marked his descent into addiction, which resulted in him losing his employment and subsequently engaging in acquisitive offending to fund both his usage and debts to drug suppliers.

He is currently accommodated in local authority housing, which he risks losing if it remains unoccupied for more than six months. He reports no other physical or mental health difficulties.

Mr Heyworth has recently formed a new relationship with his partner, Becky, who he says is supportive of his intention to stop using drugs, although he acknowledges he has not yet reduced his intake.

5) Previous Convictions and Pattern of Offending

Mr Heyworth has a number of previous convictions and reports that he had been in trouble for violence as a younger man. His current pattern of offending began following the breakdown of his third marriage, when his escalating use of Class A drugs led him to lose his employment and start committing acquisitive offences to fund his addiction. As his drug use increased, he also accrued debts to suppliers, which were enforced by threats of violence, causing his offending to escalate further in an effort to meet both his ongoing drug needs and his mounting debts.

No information was provided regarding his compliance with previous court orders or his response to past rehabilitative interventions.

6) Assessment

Mr Heyworth is assessed as being at high risk of reoffending, with this likelihood significantly heightened should he lose his accommodation.

His relevant dynamic needs centre primarily on his entrenched Class A drug use, which escalated following the breakdown of his third marriage and continues to drive his acquisitive offending in order to meet both his daily usage and debts to suppliers. Although he reports no other mental or physical health issues, his drug dependency represents the most prominent factor influencing his behaviour.

A potential protective factor is his recently formed relationship with his partner, Becky, who is supportive of his intention to stop using drugs, although he acknowledges he has not yet begun to reduce his intake. Access to stable accommodation, cessation of drug use, and re-engagement with employment are identified as factors that would reduce his risk of further offending.

He is assessed as being of low risk of causing serious harm to others.

7) Analysis and Sentencing Rationale

The recommended requirements are designed to address the core factors driving Mr Heyworth's offending, in particular his entrenched Class A drug use, which directly fuels both his acquisitive behaviour and the escalation caused by debts to suppliers.

A community-based intervention is considered proportionate to the seriousness of the offending and aligned to his identified dynamic needs, offering a structured opportunity to reduce his risk of reoffending through targeted drug treatment. The proposed period of supervision will also support work on victim awareness and reinforce accountability, while unpaid work provides a constructive punitive element.

These combined measures seek to balance public protection with rehabilitation, reflecting the link between reducing drug dependency, stabilising lifestyle factors, and lowering his overall likelihood of further offending.

8) Proposal for Sentence

The primary proposal is a community order incorporating 28 days of RAR-directed attendance and a drug rehabilitation requirement, during which Mr Heyworth would complete victim awareness work and structured sessions aimed at breaking his drug use.

He is assessed as suitable for a requirement of unpaid work, which would sit alongside supervision and group work as part of the order.

Should the court consider that the custody threshold is passed, an alternative option would be a suspended sentence order with the same rehabilitative and punitive requirements attached. If the court deems immediate imprisonment necessary, Mr Heyworth would undertake rehabilitative work in custody and then be subject to post-release supervision.

9) Victim Considerations

Mr Heyworth's victim describes feeling unsettled, shaken and anxious as a result of this offending.

10) Enforcement and Risk Management

Given Mr Heyworth's identified high risk of reoffending, effective enforcement and risk management will rely on sustained engagement with the proposed supervisory elements of a community order, particularly the RAR activities and the drug rehabilitation requirement programme, which is an onerous obligation.

His ongoing drug use and the instability that would arise if he were to lose his local authority accommodation are recognised as factors that would increase risk, and maintaining his tenancy is therefore an important part of managing that risk. During the period of supervision, compliance will be monitored through regular attendance at treatment groups and victim awareness work. Any failure to attend or to engage meaningfully would render Mr Heyworth liable to breach action through the court.

Should he be sentenced to immediate custody, risk management would continue through rehabilitative work in prison followed by post-release supervision.

Coordination between probation, drug treatment services and housing providers will be central to reducing his risk and stabilising his circumstances.

11) Defendant's Views

Mr Heyworth reports that he wants to get his life back on track. He recognises that the stabilising factors in his life are his relationship with his girlfriend Becky and his accommodation. His intention is to get back into work. If given the sentence outlined in this report, Mr Heyworth states he would comply with its terms.

12) Conclusion

The proposal is for a community order incorporating 28 days of RAR-directed attendance and a drug rehabilitation requirement.

13) Signatures

Report Author: D. Muscutt
Date: 19 April 2028
Quality Assurer: C. Mort
Date: 20 April 2028

17 Afterword, Reflections on Advocacy from the Authors

We have repeatedly made reference to the fact that advocacy is a deeply personal skill. Nigel and I are very different advocates to each other. We thought we would conclude the book with a few personal reflections on advocacy. As I was called a couple of years prior to Nigel, I have pulled rank and gone first.

Going to court and representing a side in a case is an honour and a privilege. It is also immensely enjoyable.

I say it is an honour and a privilege because you are often coming to the assistance of someone who is dealing with a traumatic low point in their life or dealing with some form of dispute that will have serious ramifications for them.

They are looking to you, their advocate, to combine a range of skills and knowledge that they do not possess themselves. They place their trust in you. Occasionally, they will place their liberty in your hands. Or their credibility. Other times, you will play a vital role in their business. You could have a massive part to play in whether they will ever see their children again.

With that in mind, you have no business being in court unless you work to be the very best that you can be. That must be your daily goal: to be better than you were the day before.

And so it is that we do not have the burden of just preparing the case that is before us. We have the burden to perform to the best of our abilities each and every time we walk into a courtroom. If you are not prepared to shoulder those two burdens, do not become an advocate.

If you do become an advocate you are going to have a wonderfully interesting career. You will see slices of life that you would never otherwise see. You will be involved in moments in court that are like scenes from the television. You will witness all that human nature has to offer. Often in a fifteen-minute period.

And you are going to suffer losses. Each loss should hurt you. But after each loss, you need to dust yourself off and get on with the next case. In the moment of a case going against you, it is right that you feel the disappointment because you should have put your all into that case, but none of us are guaranteed to win, and someone else needs your skills tomorrow.

The real key to losing is to do it beautifully. That is not to say that your aim is to lose, rather that your aim is to conduct each case with the same high level of skill, eloquence and craft so that both the wins and the losses share the same feature – you did the case beautifully well.

DOI: 10.4324/9781003602019-20

What makes for beautiful advocacy? It is not necessarily the voice of Geoffrey Cox KC and the language of William Shakespeare. Beautiful advocacy is thoughtful advocacy. It is advocacy conducted according to a plan. It is bespoke to the case. It is considered. It is efficient. It is where almost every word deployed has a reason for its existence in the case. It is advocacy performed by someone who cares for the precision and art of advocacy.

I thought I might take this opportunity to share a few of my bugbears of advocacy. My top six worst traits or habits of ugly advocacy.

I will begin with the template advocate. The defence barrister who has a portfolio of half a dozen closing speeches and three mitigations that he dusts off the shelf on a daily basis and changes the names and dates cannot do justice to their client's case in the particular circumstances of their case. Every template advocate I have ever heard sounds bored and is boring.

Then there is the lazy advocate. They have not read the papers. They telegraph to everyone that they do not believe their client. Their entire approach is that they want this whole thing to be over as soon as possible, a view often shared by juries and judges when the lazy advocate is before them.

Then there is the law school advocate. The advocate who is still doing everything the same way as they were taught on their professional vocational course. The advocate that has not tried something different since the day they first appeared in court.

Next is the timid advocate. The advocate who never stands their ground. The advocate who rolls over at the merest hint of opposition. The advocate who does not stand between their client and the angry judge, ready to absorb all the heat of the sun.

Now there is their close cousin: the "one setting" advocate. Where aggression and fight are permanently, inflexibly, substituted for guile and judgement. The advocate who thinks that any day when a witness has not cried is a bad day. An advocate who can even reduce their own witness to tears in examination-in-chief.

Finally, possibly the worst of all, the "sound of their own voice" advocate. The advocate who has to say something at every opportunity. The advocate who must ask a question of every witness – usually at least twenty questions of every witness. The advocate who must contribute something to every single discussion in the course of the case. The advocate who thinks the jury are going to want to listen to their closing speech for at least a day.

Be none of these advocates. Be the well-prepared advocate, the advocate who has written a speech based on the case and the evidence in it. Be the advocate who has exercised and displayed judgement over every aspect of the case. Be the advocate who cares about each case, each client. Be the advocate who wins, and loses, beautifully.

Jaime

I see the paradox in our writing a book about advocacy and then writing in our Introduction that you cannot learn advocacy from a book. You will be familiar with our mantra of "practise, practise, practise", and you will get lots of that in your formal vocational training. Afterwards, as you begin the job of advocacy, every piece of advocacy that you do will allow you to refine your skills. Our goal is that, with this book by your side from the beginning, you will be ready for it all. Now that you have reached the end of the book, I hope you agree.

In this Afterword I like Jaime's emphasis on the beauty of advocacy. I like it very much. It annoys me slightly that he thought of that way to express the thought, and I did not. He is dead right. Done beautifully, the simplest advocacy is a joy to observe, and it can be devastatingly effective in your cause. Learn to keep things simple and you will learn the skills of advocacy. The beauty will come, I promise you.

Back in September 2020, I started teaching on the University of Law's Bar Practice Course. From that point, the skills I had developed at Bar School in the early to mid-1990s, and which I had been deploying as an advocate for 25 years, became the subject matter of my workshops. Truth be told, I joined the University almost by accident. I had applied to be a visiting lecturer when the Covid pandemic hit. When the opportunity unexpectedly came to become a full-time lecturer instead, I thought I would take it to ride the pandemic out.

I am still here.

I am still here because I love the job. Showing our Bar students how to develop their advocacy skills in the few short months of the course leading to the assessments is a source of great pride for me, exceeded only when they receive their offers of pupillage and move on. I remember that period of my own life. If I could offer just one tip to help you learn advocacy, it would be this: when you take part in advocacy exercises, jump in with both feet. It is no use dipping a toe in gingerly. Do not hold back for fear of making mistakes. Mistakes are good; they are the key to progress. This is easier said than done, I appreciate. You will compare yourself with your workshop colleagues, perhaps unconsciously, and you will sometimes feel a lack of confidence. Realise that this is normal. You will have overcome many hurdles just to get into the position to start your vocational training. Do not lose sight of those achievements; instead, recognise them and build on them.

It is a great job to conduct advocacy for a living, and everyone can learn the skills. Enjoy the journey!

Nigel

Index

address *see* modes of address

being interrupted: during your speech 109; by the judge 93; *see also* interrupting

case theory: in advocacy assessments 163; in the coroner's court 107; in cross-examination 49, 58–9, 62; importance of 2; in *Plant* case scenario 16, 43–4, 47, 53, 58, 107, 200–8; in prosecution opening speech 102
civil cases: and closing speeches 113; and cross-examination 64; and examination-in-chief 29–30; and expert evidence 85; and opening speeches 103; and re-examination 72; and remote advocacy 135, 138; and submission advocacy 95; and vulnerable witnesses 128–9, 131; and written advocacy 145–6
closed questions 27–9, 65–6, 84
credibility of witnesses: challenging 51–2; in civil cases 72; in cross-examination 38–9; and expert evidence 82; generally 18–20, 105–6, 111–12; in pleas in mitigation 118; in re-examination 69–70, 73; in structure 64; undermining 48–9; vulnerable witnesses 132–3; *see also* credibility of you the advocate
credibility of you the advocate: with expert evidence 84–5; in pleas in mitigation 125; in speeches 112, 113; in submission advocacy 96; *see also* credibility of witnesses
cross-examination: advanced technique 64–8; build up 51–5; in civil cases 64; in criminal cases heard by judges 64; defensive nature 38–9; fundamentals 37–41, "golden rules" 59–63; how-to 41–64; lying witnesses 49–51; mistaken witnesses 51; previous inconsistent statements 55–9; undermining witnesses 48–9

etiquette: bowing to the judge 6; entering or leaving the courtroom 6; with litigants in person 7; shaking hands 9; *see also* interrupting and being interrupted
examination in chief: advanced technique 30–6; in civil cases 29–30; fundamentals 12–16; how-to 16–29
expert evidence: advanced technique in cross-examination 85; advanced technique in examination-in-chief 82; in civil cases 85; fundamentals 74–9; how to cross-examine 82–5; how-to examine-in-chief 79–82

hostile witnesses 14–15

interrupting: expert witnesses 82; judge 9; in remote hearings 138; witnesses 26–7; *see also* being interrupted

leading questions: in cross-examination 41–8, 63; in evidence-in-chief 15–27; and expert evidence 81; of hostile witnesses 14–15; in re-examination 69–70

memory-refreshing 14, 15; in remote cases 138
modes of address: in civil courts 8; with clients 5–6; with judges 94–5

open questions: in coroners' courts 157; in cross-examination 67; in examination-in-chief 28; in expert evidence 81

pace: in advocacy assessments 161; in cross-examination 63–4, 67–8; in examination-in-chief 26–7; in expert evidence 81–2; in re-examination 73; in

speeches 104–6, 114; with vulnerable witnesses 130
previous inconsistent statements *see* cross-examination

re-examination: advanced technique 73; in civil cases 72; fundamentals 69; how-to 69–72

signposting: in closing speeches 110–11, 115; in expert evidence 80; in opening speeches 104–5; in pleas in mitigation 122; in remote advocacy 138; in submission advocacy 94; with vulnerable witnesses 131–2; in written advocacy 142

structure: in advocacy assessments 162; of closing speeches to a jury 110–11; of cross-examination generally 55, 63; of cross-examination of experts 84–6; of examination-in-chief 31–2, 34–6; of examination-in-chief of experts 79–81; of pleas in mitigations 119–22; of submissions in civil cases 95; of submissions to a judge 10–11, 89–93; of tag questions 46–7

tag questions: in cross examination 42–8; with vulnerable witnesses 131

wellbeing 10

For Product Safety Concerns and Information please contact our EU representative GPSR@taylorandfrancis.com Taylor & Francis Verlag GmbH, Kaufingerstraße 24, 80331 München, Germany